CONTEMPORARY ISSUES IN LANGUAGE AND DISCOURSE PROCESSES

Edited by

Donald G. Ellis
University of Hartford

William A. Donohue
Michigan State University

LEA

LAWRENCE ERLBAUM ASSOCIATES, PUBLISHERS

1986   Hillsdale, New Jersey   London

Lawrence Erlbaum Associates, Inc., Publishers
365 Broadway
Hillsdale, New Jersey 07642

Library of Congress Cataloging-in-Publication Data
Main entry under title:

Contemporary issues in language and discourse processes.

   Bibliography: p.
   Includes indexes.
   1. Discourse analysis—Addresses, essays, lectures.
2. Psycholinguistics—Addresses, essays, lectures.
3. Communication—Psychological aspects—Addresses,
essays, lectures. I. Ellis, Donald G. II. Donohue,
William A., 1947-
P302.C622 1986   401'.41   85-27476
ISBN 0-89859-788-9

Printed in the United States of America
10 9 8 7 6 5 4 3 2 1

Contents

Contributors

Pam Benoit • University of Missouri, College of Arts and Science, 115 Switzler Hall, Columbia, Missouri 65211

Julie A. Burke • University of Iowa, Department of Communication and Theatre Arts, 239 Jessup Hall, Iowa City, Iowa 52242

Brandt Burleson • Purdue University, Department of Communication, Heavilon Hall, West Lafayette, Indiana 47907

Robert T. Craig • Temple University, Department of Speech, Philadelphia, Pennsylvania 19122

Mary E. Diez • Alverno College, Department of Professional Communication, Milwaukee, Wisconsin 53215

William A. Donohue • Michigan State University, Department of Communication, East Lansing, Michigan 48824

Donald G. Ellis • University of Hartford, Department of Communication, West Hartford, Connecticut 06117

Vince Follert*

Beth Haslett • University of Delaware, Department of Communications, Newark, Delaware 19711

---

* deceased

Robert Hopper • University of Texas, Department of Speech Communication, Austin, Texas 78712

Sally Jackson • University of Oklahoma, Department of Communication, Norman, Oklahoma 73019

Scott Jacobs • University of Oklahoma, Department of Communication, Norman, Oklahoma 73019

Susan Koch • Bell Communications Research, 435 South Street, Morristown, New Jersey 07960-1961

Jennifer Mandelbaum • University of Texas, Department of Speech Communication, Austin, Texas 78712

Margaret L. McLaughlin • University of Southern California, Speech Science and Technology, University Park, Los Angeles, California 90007

Sally Planalp • University of Illinois, Department of Communication, Urbana-Champaign, Illinois 61801

Victor Raskin • Purdue University, Department of English, West Lafayette, Indiana 47907

John Searle • University of California, Department of Philosophy, Berkeley, California 94720

Introduction:
Language, Communication,
and Discourse Processes

A few weeks ago while strolling along the pier of a favored vacation spot lined with expensive yachts, we noticed a rather interesting proclamation embossed on the front of a young woman's shirt. It read, "THE ONE WHO DIES WITH THE MOST TOYS WINS." This insight stimulated a discussion of our most favored toys and the ways in which we use them to improve our quality of life. However, after this brief accounting, we concluded that language, and not our possessions of upward mobility, was the toy we relied on most frequently to alter our states of consciousness.

Quite simply, manipulating language is extremely entertaining. Its extraordinary flexibility in accomplishing an infinite number of human objectives has stimulated a variety of academic pursuits for centuries. As communication scholars we are keenly interested in the ways in which language constrains the process of communicating. For example, we want to expose the structural properties of language, identify the conventional forces that provide criteria for language choices, develop an understanding of the cognitive mechanisms responsible for producing and making sense of language, and learn better methodologies for revealing these discoveries.

The challenge in pursuing this interest is gaining access to these structural properties, conventional forces, and cognitive mechanisms. For an increasing number of scholars, the study of discourse, or the sequential use of language to pursue pragmatic goals, provides this access. Understanding discourse teaches us how communicators use language to propose social distance, manage conflict, make requests, appear polite, organize talk, repair social activities, create organizational rituals, and so on. The research literature in communication, linguistics, sociology, social psychology and other fields contains a rich display of work dealing with these specific features of discourse.

Perhaps it is time to pull back somewhat from these specific interests and pursue some of the more general issues underlying the study of discourse. Approaching these more general issues provides an opportunity to better critique our work, and achieve greater progress in organizing our efforts. The purpose of this book falls in line with this rationale. Our goal in editing this volume is to provide various perspectives on three key issues facing scholars interested in how language is used communicatively in discourse. At this point it is probably

1

appropriate to describe these issues as a means of explaining the overall concept of this book. This description of the issues is followed by a summary of the chapters. This introduction concludes by proposing how these chapters can extend our understanding of discourse and potentially solve some of the problems circling above this area of inquiry.

THE CONCEPTUAL FRAMEWORK

The first issue this volume addresses has generated considerable interest among discourse scholars. How does knowledge guide the organization of discourse? More specifically, how do we use cognitive scripts and schemes to interpret strings of communicative acts and then formulate coherent attachments to these strings? Each of the chapters is written from the perspective that cognitive theories of discourse must address both the interpretation and production problems as a means of accounting for the sequential nature of interaction.

The second issue addresses the problem of research methodology. How scholars ought to structure their accounts of communicative sequences and provide evidence for their claims has received very little attention as an independent subject of inquiry. One explanation for this lack of attention may be traced to the inherent interdependence of phenomena and observer characterizing qualitative areas of research in the social sciences. With this kind of relationship it is difficult to identify generalizable rules of inquiry. Nevertheless, accounts of discourse continue to use data to support claims. The chapters in this volume offer general guidelines suggesting how, and what kind of data might best accomplish this task.

The third issue presented considers the viability of focusing on interactants' goals as the primary organizing feature of discourse sequencing and production. The chapters in this section argue that although other theoretical accounts of sequencing are available, they must include an analysis of individuals goals in the interaction. Each chapter identifies a critical problem in studying interaction goals, and then proposes several conceptual means of solving these problems.

Because these three issues are central to the study of discourse, and because each of the chapters moves in different, but complementary directions to address these issues, we felt it was necessary to extend and critique the chapters in each section. We asked three scholars familiar with these issues to comment on the contributions of the chapters and to pull together the key arguments proposed by the authors. But more importantly, we asked the critics to go beyond these arguments and to give us their own perspective on these issues.

Our reason for providing this criticism is based on a value we share for increasing the quantity and quality of criticism in this area. Criticism serves well to identify strengths and weaknesses in an area, particularly when that area is in its formative stages. We hope that the critiques offered in this volume will help scholars focus on those ideas that appear most useful for their research problems.

Finally, a volume that proposes to sort among some of the key issues underlying an area of inquiry probably ought to be introduced by one of the founders and most influential contributors to that area. John Searle consented to comment on the appropriateness of using Speech Act theory as a means of accounting for discourse sequencing. Searle's introductory essay is his first attempt to extend speech acts beyond the technical problem of specifying the features of illocutionary acts to considering what speech acts tell us about communication.

Searle begins his chapter by critiquing speech act theory, Grice's maxims, and Sacks, Schegloff, and Jefferson's sequential rules perspective as a means of explaining the process of sequencing talk. Searle contends that we should abandon these perspectives as communicative scholars, and focus instead on "shared intentionality," and the conversationalists "background" understandings. These arguments are consistent with those arguing that goals are a primary organizing feature for communicators.

Because we have introduced the first chapter in the volume, it is probably appropriate to summarize the remaining chapters as a more indepth means of indicating how the arguments surrounding each of the three issues tie together.

Chapter Summaries

Cognitive Processes.   Raskin begins this section by proposing a script-based semantic theory. Raskin argues that his theory can account for how meaning is generated for all usages of language. Structurally, meaning is generated by a script-based lexicon that each individual sustains in any given conversation. The significant contribution of Raskin's theory is that it specifies the combinatory rules linking scripts. This theoretical move provides for the sequential nature of interaction.

The second chapter in this section is provided by Burleson. Like Raskin, Burleson is interested in scripts, but from a different perspective. Burleson uses scripts to understand the structure of "motive-seeking" conversations as a means of making attribution theory more functional for communication researchers. After reviewing various attribution models, Burleson uses Weiner's attributional perspective to argue that motive-seeking conversations creates several attribution schemes that serve to sequentially organize the conversation. Burleson provides a number of conversational segments to illustrate how these attributional schemes serve as an organizing tool for the interactants.

The third contribution to this section by Haslett extends van Dijk's schema theories to account for children's developing knowledge of narrative superstructure, or the form of the narrative. In a study examining children's abilities to create narratives, Haslett found that the use of particular narrative structures is a function of age with the older children using significantly more evaluative structures than the younger children. She uses van Dijk's schema model to identify the specific age differences in narrative development.

Planalp provides the commentary on this section of papers. Not only does she carefully critique each chapter, but Planalp moves beyond this objective to interrelate each of the perspectives represented in the papers. She argues that the main problem in learning how world knowledge guides the organization of discourse is specifying the content and structure of that knowledge in addition to the processes by which the knowledge is acquired, stored, accessed, and restructured. Planalp concludes that these chapters represent significant progress in working toward these goals, but that much more research is needed.

Research Methods.   Jackson deals with the difficult methodological problem of how to structure evidence in building a claim about discourse processes in the lead chapter in this section. She contends that the practice of analytic induction is best served in research by generating a clear empirical claim about what was found in the research, and by ruling out opposite or theoretical alternatives to the claim. In focusing on the use of examples as the customary means of supporting empirical claims about discourse, Jackson argues that contrastive examples must also be used. Without contrastive examples it is difficult to specify the parameters of the claim.

In the second chapter of the section, Jacobs focuses more directly on the issue of how examples ought to be used in formulating claims about language and discourse processes. Jacobs begins by arguing that the demonstrative power of examples lies in their intuitive emergence. From this intuitive stance, the researcher uses examples to support claims about the structural possibilities and coherent configurations generated by the discourse system. Jacobs then describes the kinds of examples used to justify discourse claims, and then provides a study of "confrontation" to illustrate how the various forms of examples can be used most effectively.

While Jacobs and Jackson address the conceptual issues associated with using various forms of evidence to support discourse claims, Hopper, Koch, and Mandelbaum focus on the technical problems of recording, transcribing, analyzing and reporting results in the third chapter in this section. Their recommendations for accomplishing these tasks are most useful for researchers using conversation analysis (qualitative descriptions of speech events and sequences) as opposed to discourse analysis (quantitative accounts of coded discourse functions). Their technical guidelines could be very useful for communication scholars in developing standards for preparing and analyzing transcripts of natural talk.

McLaughlin's commentary on the methodology section distills several of the issues raised by the authors in this section. By presenting a study about bragging behavior, McLaughlin argues that it is important to establish clear boundaries for identifying units of behavior, incorporate content considerations into coding schemes, note actors' adjustments during interaction, and take into account deviations from the discourse model. She concludes that these methodological considerations are critical to making more advanced claims about discourse.

Interaction Goals. In this first chapter addressing the issue of interaction goals, Burke begins by critiquing Speech Act theory. She contends that this perspective presupposes knowledge of speakers' communicative intentions. In addition, Burke rejects cognitive science as a means of accounting for discourse sequencing because it too excludes interactant goals. Burke argues that researchers should focus on factors influencing speakers' plans and goals, and illustrates how such an inquiry might unfold by conducting a study of the discourse produced by subjects assembling a water pump.

Diez continues this focus on goals in the second chapter in this section by analyzing how individuals use goal knowledge in the negotiation context to organize discourse. She defines three types of discourse work negotiators use in achieving their goals: (a) coherence, or making connections between utterances; (b) distance, or the ongoing definition of relational control; and (c) structuring, or managing the organizational features of the interaction. Each of these types of discourse work is discussed as a set of production and comprehension rules.

In the concluding chapter in this final section of the volume Benoit and Follert seek to integrate this goals-based approach to discourse sequencing into script theory. They begin by pointing out that scripts are the cognitive schemes that contain identifyers (information for recognizing a script), appositions (socially shared conventions for act-intention relationships), and schematizers (the conventional structures organizing the situation into a coherent whole). Benoit and Follert contend that these appositions are necessary for individuals to coordinate their intentions so they can produce and interpret discourse.

In responding to these chapters Craig attempts to differentiate among types of goals identified in these chapters. He differentiates first between functional and intentional goals with the former dealing with the action the speaker performs by making a certain utterance, and the latter serving as a cognitive representation of the state of the work that would result from a sequence of actions known as a plan. The second distinction is between positive and dialectical goals. The former are goals involved directly in the causal process of producing behavior whereas the later refer to retrospectively "discovered" goals. The third distinction is between formal and strategic goals with the former involved in producing official purposes of events and the latter referring to the pursuit of individual goals. After discussing how each of the articles dealing with goals can be organized around these distinctions, Craig explores the problem of drawing inferences about goals on the basis of indirect evidence.

Extensions

As indicated previously, our goal in presenting these chapters is to assess current directions in the area of language and discourse, by providing some perspectives on key issues that will help to expand the significance, influence, and utility of the area. Hopefully, such expansions will address some of the key theoretical problems currently faced by researchers in this area. For example, the chapters dealing with scripts provide several conceptual mechanisms for integrating scripts and moving toward understanding the sequential nature of communication. The methodology essays identify some important limits and requirements for using examples to warrant claims about discourse. The chapters dealing with communicator goals identifies ways of conceptualizing goals that makes them more accessible to researchers.

In addition to these theoretical advances, these chapters could open up some popular communication contexts to more refined levels of analysis. For example, understanding the development of initial interaction contexts might now be accomplished in greater detail using script theory because the means for moving between scripts is more clearly identified. Sorting out communication tactics in conflict situations might also be facilitated by looking at how language is used to negotiate individual goals.

We hope that these chapters will also stimulate other attempts to pull away from specific empirical interests and identify other key issues that will allow researchers interested in language, communication, and discourse to continue expanding and strengthening this area. The organization of issues in this volume, including extensive summary, critique, and theoretical development, provides one model for structuring such future projects.

Donald G. Ellis
William A. Donohue

1 Introductory Essay: Notes on Conversation

John R. Searle
University of California

This chapter discusses various issues in the theory of speech acts. They hang together to some extent, but it will not be clear how they do until this chapter is completed.

There is a real difficulty with traditional, orthodox speech act theory that has to do with the restricted nature of its subject matter. The speech act scenario is simple. It is enacted by the two great heroes of speech act theory, "S" and "H." The speech act works as follows: S goes up to H and cuts loose with an acoustic blast; if all goes well, if all the felicity conditions are satisfied, if S's noise is infused with intentionality, and if all kinds of rules come into play, then the speech act is successful and nondefective. After that, there is silence; nothing else happens. The speech act is concluded and S and H go their separate ways. Traditional speech act theory thus is largely confined to single speech acts. But the trouble is that in real life speech acts are often not like that at all. In real life, speech characteristically consists of longer sequences of speech acts, either on the part of one speaker, where there is a continuous discourse; or it consists, more interestingly, of sequences of exchange speech acts where there is a conversation.

Now the question naturally arises: Could we get an account of conversations parallel to our account of speech acts? Could we, for example, get an account that gave us constitutive rules for conversations in a way that we have constitutive rules of speech acts? My answer to that question is going to be "No." But we can say some things about conversations; we can get some interesting insights into the structure of conversations. So, before we conclude that we cannot get an analysis of conversations parallel to our analysis of speech acts, let us see what sorts of regularities and systematic principles we can find in the structure of conversations.

The first principle to recognize (and it's an obvious one) is that in a dialogue or a conversation, each speech act creates a space of possibilities of appropriate response speech acts. Just as a move in a game creates a space of possible and appropriate countermoves, so in a conversation, each speech act creates a space of possible and appropriate response speech acts. The beginnings of a theory of the conversational game might be a systematic attempt to account for how particular moves, particular illocutionary acts, constrain the scope of possible appropriate responses. But when we see how far we can get with this approach, we see that we really do not get very far. To show this, first consider the most promising cases, so it can be seen how special and unusual they are. Let us consider the cases where we do get systematic relationshps between a speech act and the appropriate response speech act. The best cases are those that are misleadingly called *adjacency pairs*. The favorite cases are question and answer sequences. In such cases there are very tight sets of constraints on what constitutes an appropriate answer given a particular question. Indeed, the constraints are so tight that the form of the question determines and matches the form of an appropriate answer. So, if I ask you a yes/no question, then your answer, if it's an answer to the question, has to count either as an affirmation or a denial of the propositional content of the original question. If I ask you a wh-question, I give you a propositional function and your appropriate response has to be to fill in the value of the free variable. For example, the question, "How many people were at the meeting?" is equivalent to "I request you: you tell me the value of X in 'X number of people were at the meeting.' " That is, every question, in my taxonomy at least, is a request; it is a directive, and it is always a request for the performance of a speech act.

However, there are a couple of interesting qualifications to be made to these points about questions. One is this: I have said in *Speech Acts* (Searle, 1969) that every question was a request for information, but that is obviously wrong if you think about it. It was brought home to me very forcefully when the book was in press, and one Friday afternoon a small boy said to me "Do you promise to take us skiing this weekend?" In this case, he was asking for a promise, not a piece of factual information. He was requesting me either to promise or refuse to promise, and of course, those are speech acts different from assertions.

A second qualification is this: I said that the structure of questions determines and matches the structure of answers. But an apparent counterexample can be found in the exasperating English modal auxiliary verbs. There are cases where the structure of the interrogative does not match that of the appropriate response. If I say to you "Shall I vote for the Republicans?" or "Shall I marry Sally?", the appropriate answer is not "Yes, you shall," or "No, you shall not." Nor even "Yes, you will," or "No, you won't." The appropriate answer is, oddly enough, imperative—"Yes, do" or "No, don't." That is, "Shall I?" doesn't invite a response using a modal auxiliary verb, rather it seems to be a request for advice. (Now, how that got lexicalized in the meaning of "shall," I do not know.) So the appropriate answer if I say "Shall I vote for the Republicans?" is imperative— it is either "Yes, do" or "No, don't." Shall-questions, then, form a class of exceptions to the general rule.[1]

There are other classes of speech acts in addition to questions that serve to determine appropriate responses. An obvious case is direct requests to perform speech acts. So, if I say to you "Say something in Portuguese" or "Tell me about last summer in Brazil," then those are straightforward, direct requests to perform speech acts, and they constrain the form of a possible appropriate reply, if you are complying with the request.

The previous are obviously two classes where the diologic sequence of initial utterance and response is internally related in the sense that the semantic value of the first speech act is only effectively realized given a certain kind of constrained appropriate response. How far can we get in discovering other such classes?

Well, a third and rather large class, are those cases where the speaker performs a speech act that requires acceptance or rejection on the part of the hearer. For example, an offer, a proposal, a bet, or an invitation are all incomplete speech acts in an important sense: their illocutionary point only takes effect if the speech act is accepted by the hearer; unlike, for example, assertions, they cannot stand alone, and the hearer is constrained by the structure of the speech act to accept it or reject it. Let us consider, for example, offers. An offer differs from a promise in that an offer is a kind of conditional promise, but the form of the conditional is always conditional on the acceptance by the hearer. So, I am only obligated by my offer to you if you accept the offer. The offer, then, invites acceptance or rejection and the illocutionary point of the offer is only fully achieved if you accept it. Offers are commissives, but they are conditional commissives, and it is a very special kind of condition, namely, conditional on acceptance by the hearer. Similarly with bets, if I say to you "I bet you $5 that the Republicans will win the next election," that is not yet a bet. It only becomes a bet if you accept it. The bet has only been effectively made if you say "OK, you're on" or "I accept your bet" or whatever. If we consider cases like these, that is, offers, bets, invitations, it looks as if we are at last getting a class of speech acts where we can extend the analysis beyond a single speech act, where we can discuss sequences. But it seems that this is a very restricted class. If we consider assertions, there are no such constraints. There are indeed general conversational constraints of the Gricean sort and other kinds. For example, if I say to you "I think the Republicans will win the next election" and you say to me "I think the Brazilian government has devalued the Cruzeiro again," at least on the surface your remark is violating a certain principle of relevance. But

---

[1] I am indebted to Julian Boyd for discussion of this point.

notice, unlike the case of offers and invitations, the illocutionary point of my speech act was nonetheless achieved. I did make an assertion, and my success in achieving that illocutionary point doesn't depend on your making an appropriate response. In this case, you are just being rude, or changing the subject, or are being difficult to get on with if you change the subject in that way. But it is hard to see how you are violating a constitutive rule of a certain kind of speech act, if you just change the subject.

Now, there are certain kinds of formal or institutional speech act sequences where there are rules that constrain the sequencing. Here one thinks of courtrooms, formal debates, parliamentary procedures, and the like. But, in all of those cases, there are a set of extralinguistic rules that impose a series of ceremonial or institutional constraints on the sequencing of utterances. Everybody knows exactly what to say and in what order, because the discourse is highly ritualized. The bailiff says "Everybody rise!", and then everybody rises. And then the bailiff says "The Superior Court of the state of California, County of Alameda, is now in session." The Honorable J. B. Smitherby presiding," And then J. B. Smitherby comes and sits down. The bailiff says, "Be seated and come to order," and then we can all sit down. The judge then starts conducting the proceedings in a highly ritualized fashion. Any incorrect move is subject to an "objection" that the judge is required to rule on. But that is hardly a good sample of natural discourse. On the contrary, if you sit through a court hearing you are struck by its unnatural, highly structured and ceremonial character. Nonetheless there is something to be learned about the nature of conversation in general from this example and that is that conversation only can proceed given a structure of expectations and presuppositions. This point is discussed later.

So far it appears that traditional speech act theory will not go very far in giving us sequencing rules for discourse. So let us thrash around and see if we can find some other basis for a theoretical account. What I am going to conclude is that we will be able to get a theoretical account, but it won't be anything like our account of the constitutive rules of speech acts. I want to turn to two efforts or two approaches to giving a theoretical account, and show in what ways I think they are inadequate. They both have advantages, but they also have certain inadequacies. First, the Gricean approach with Grice's principles of conversation, and then some work in a subject that used to be called "ethnomethodology" but might better be described as a form of socio-linguistics.

Let us start with Grice (1975). Grice has four maxims of quantity, quality, manner, and relation. Quantity has to do with such things as that you shouldn't say too much or too little; manner has to do with the fact that you should be clear; quality has to do with your utterances being true, and relation has to do with the fact that your utterances should be relevant to the conversation at hand. I want to say that although I think these are very valuable contributions to the analysis of language, they really are not very helpful in explaining the formal structure of conversation. Why not? To begin with, the four are not on a par. For example, the requirement of truthfulness is indeed an internal constitutive rule of the notion of a statement. It is a constitutive rule of statement making that the statement commits the speaker to the truth of the proposition expressed. There is no way to explain what a statement is without explaining what a true statement is, and without explaining that anybody who makes a statement is committed, other things being equal, to the truth of the proposition that he expressed in making the statement. It is the condition of satisfaction of a statement that it should be true, and it is an internal defect of a statement if it is false. But the other Gricean features are not like that. The standards of relevance, brevity, clarity, and so on, unlike truth, are not in that way internal to the notion of the speech act. They are all external constraints on the speech act, external constraints coming from general principles of rationality and cooperation. It is not a constitutive rule of statement making that a statement should be relevant to the surrounding discourse. You can make a perfectly satisfactory statement, qua statement, and still change the subject of the conversation altogether.

Well, one might say "So much the better for Grice." After all, what we are trying to explain is how speech act *sequences* can satisfy conditions of being *de facto* internally related, in the way discussed earlier, without there being necessarily any internal requirement of that relation, that is, without there being any *de jure* requirement of the sort that we had for pairs involving offers, invitations, and bets. One might say: what we want are not constitutive rules but precisely maxims of the Gricean sort. But the trouble is that in the way we have a reasonably clear, intuitive, and theoretical notions of truth or of evidence, we don't in that way have any such clear notion of, for example, relevance. In general, utterances in a coherent conversation do meet standards of relevance, but what exactly is relevance? If we are going to be able to give a theoretical account of relevance, we would have to give an account of it that was independent of any concept of a conversation. Otherwise our account would be circular. I don't think we can give that kind of analysis of relevance. Relevance, although it is certainly a fact about discourse and it is crucial in understanding discourse, has rather little explanatory power in characterizing the structure of a conversation because of the form of relevance in question seems to require a prior understanding of precisely such talk exchanges as conversations in order to have any application. You can't explain what a conversation is in terms of relevance, because you have to know what kind of relevance is involved already before you can characterize it correctly as conversation and not just as a sequence of disordered utterances. Similarly, it seems to me, the other two maxims have rather limited power for explaining the structure of conversation. They both have to do with efficiency in communication, and so they don't provide a very powerful apparatus for getting at the details of conversational structure. Efficiency is only one among many constraints on talk sequences of the sort we have in dialogues.

Although I think that the Gricean maxims are very useful in their own realm, they won't give us, for conversation, anything like what the rules of speech acts give us for individual speech acts.

Let us now turn then to the efforts of some sociolinguists who have been studying the structure of conversation, as they would say, "empirically." One such effort at explaining the phenomenon of turn-taking for conversations is provided in an article by Sacks, Shegloff, and Jefferson (1974). They think that they have a set of rules, indeed, "recursive rules," for turn-taking in conversations. They say:

> The following seems to be a basic set of rules governing turn construction providing for the allocation of a next turn to one party and coordinating transfer so as to minimize gap and overlap. (1) For any turn at the initial transition relevance place of an initial turn construction unit: (a) If the turn so far is so constructed as to involve the use of a current speaker's select-next technique, then the party so selected has the right, and is obliged to take next turn to speak, no others have such rights or obligations and transfer occurs at that place. (b) If the turn so far is so constructed as not to involve the use of a current speaker's select-next technique, then self-selection for next speakership may, but need not be instituted. First speaker acquires rights to a turn and transfer occurs at that place. (c) If the turn so far is constructed as not to involve the use of a current speaker's select-next technique, then the current speaker may but need not continue unless another self-selects. (2) If at the initial transition relevance place of an initial turn constructional unit neither 1a nor 1b is operated, and following the provision of 1c current speaker has continued, then the rule set a-c reapplies at the next transition relevant place, and recursively at each next transition relevant place until transfer is effected. (pp. 702–703)

That is the rule for conversational turn-taking. Now, I have puzzled over this for a while, and my conclusion (though I am prepared to be corrected) is that that couldn't possibly be a rule for conversational turn-taking simply because nobody does or could follow it. The notion of a rule is, after all, rather closely connected with the notion of following a rule. And I want to argue that nobody does or could follow the turn-taking rule. Now what exactly does the rule say when it is stated in plain English? It seems to me they are saying the following: In a conversation a speaker can select who is going to be the next speaker, for example, by asking him or her a question. Or the speaker can just shut up and let somebody else talk. Or he or she can keep on talking. Furthermore, if the speaker decides to keep on talking, then next time there is a pause in the conversation (that's called a "transition place"), the same three options apply. And that makes the rule recursive, because once you have the possibility of continuing to talk, that means the rule can apply over and over.

Now, as a description of what actually happens in a normal conversation, that is, a conversation where not everybody talks at once, the rule could hardly fail to describe what goes on. But that is like saying that this is a rule for walking: If you go for a walk, you can keep walking in the same direction, or you can change directions, or you can sit down and stop walking altogether. Now notice that the walking rule is recursive, because if you keep on walking, then the next time you wonder what to do, the same three options apply—you can keep on walking in the same direction, you can change directions, or you can sit down and quit walking altogether. As a *description* of what happens when people go for a walk, that could hardly be false, but that doesn't make it a recursive *rule* for walking. The walking rule is like the Sacks, Schegloff, and Jefferson (1974) rule in that it is almost tautological. It is not completely tautological because there are always other possibilities. When walking, you could start jumping up and down or do cartwheels. In talking, everybody might shut up and not say anything or they might break into song or they might all talk at once. But the real objection to the rule is not that it is nearly tautological, because lots of rules are tautological and none the worse for that. For example, systems of constitutive rules define tautologically the activity of which the rules are constitutive. So, for example, the rules of chess or football tautologically define chess or football; and the rules of speech acts say, for example, tautologically that if you make a promise you undertake an obligation. That is not my real objection. The objection to this kind of "rule" is that it is not really a rule and therefore has no explanatory power, because the notion of a rule is logically connected to the notion of following a rule, and the notion of following a rule is connected to the notion of making one's behavior conform to the content of a rule because it is a rule. So for example, when I drive in England, I follow the rule: Drive on the left-hand side of the road. Now that seems to me a genuine rule. Why is it a rule? Because the content of the rule plays a causal role in the production of my behavior. If another driver is coming directly toward me the other way, I swerve to the left, i.e., I make my behavior conform to the content of the rule. In a theory of intentionality, we would say that the intentional content of the rule plays a causal role in bringing about the conditions of satisfaction. The rule has the world-to-rule direction of fit, that is, the point of the rule is to get the world, i.e., my behavior, to match the content of the rule. And it has the rule-to-world direction of causation, i.e., the rule achieves the fit by causing the appropriate behavior. (For a further explanation of these notions, see Searle, 1983.) This is just a fancy way of saying that the purpose of the rule is to influence people's behavior in a certain way so that the behavior matches the content of the rule, and the rule functions as part of the cause of bringing that match about. I don't just as a matter of *chance* drive on the left-hand side of the road in England. I do it because that is the rule of the road.

Notice now a crucial fact for the discussion of the conversational turn-taking rule. There can be extensionally equivalent descriptions of behavior that do not all state the rules that I am following. Take the rule: Drive on the left-hand side of the road. We might describe my behavior either by saying that I drive on the left, or, given the structure of English cars, by saying that I drive in such a way that while staying in one lane I keep the steering wheel near the centerline and I keep the passenger side nearer to the curb. Now that actually happens in British cars when I drive on the left-hand side of the road. But that is not the rule that I am following. Both rules provide true descriptions of my behavior, but only the first rule—the oned about driving on the left—actually states a rule of my behavior, because it is the only one whose content plays a causal role in the production of the behavior. The second, like the Sacks, Schegloff, and Jefferson (1974) rule, describes a consequence of following the rule, given that the steering wheel is located on the right, but it doesn't state a rule. The so-called rule for conversational turn-taking, like much similar research I have seen in this area, is like the second rule statement and not like the first. That is, it describes the phenomenon of turn-taking as if it were a rule, but it couldn't be a rule because no one actually follows that rule. The surface phenomenon of turn-taking is partly explicable in terms of deeper speech act sequencing rules having to do with internally related speech acts of the sort that we talked about before; but sometimes the phenomenon of turn-taking isn't a matter of rules at all.

Let us go through the cases. Case A: "Current speaker selects-next speaker." Well, speakers hardly ever directly select a subsequent speaker. People don't normally say in conversation "I select you to speak next," or "You talk next." Sometimes they do. If a master of ceremonies gets up and introduces you as the next speaker, then you are selected to talk next. He has certainly selected you to talk. But such cases are very unusual. Those are cases where the speaker literally selects somebody. But it is not very common. What normally happens, rather, is that the speaker asks somebody a question, or makes him an offer. The rules that determine that the second person is to speak aren't rules of "speaker selects-next technique," but they are rules of asking questions or making offers. The surface phenomenon of speaker selection is not the explanation; the explanation is in terms of the rules for performing the speech acts in question, the internally related speech act pairs. The "speaker selects-next" rule is not a rule; it is an extensionally equivalent description of a pattern of behavior that is also described, and more importantly explained, by a set of speech act rules. Now consider the second case. Case B: Next speaker self-selects. That means that there is a pause and somebody else starts talking. That rule says that when there is a break in the conversation anybody can start talking, and whoever starts talking gets to keep on talking. This doesn't even have the appearance of being a rule because it doesn't specify the relevant sort of intentional content that plays a causal role in the production of the behavior. Case C is: current speaker continues. Again, that is not a rule, and for the same reason. No one is following it. It just says that when you are talking, you can keep on talking. But you don't need a rule to do that.

Well then, if such rules are no help to us, let us go back to the beginning of our discussion. I said that it would be nice if we could get a theory of conversation that matches our theory of speech acts. I am not optimistic. I have examined two directions of investigation, but I think that they do not give us the sorts of results we wanted. That is not to say, however, that we cannot give theoretical accounts of the structure of conversation and that we cannot say important, insightful things about the structure of conversation. What sort of apparatus would we use to do that? Here I want to mention a couple of features that I think are crucial for understanding conversation, and indeed, for understanding discourse generally.

One of the things we need to recognize about conversations is that they involve shared intentionality. Conversations are a paradigm of collective behavior. And the shared intentionality in conversation is not to be confused with the kind of iterated intentionality that you get in discussions like those of Schiffer and David Lewis, where you get what they call "mutual knowledge." In the case of mutual knowledge, I know that you know that I know that you know . . . that p. And you know that I know that you know that I know . . . that p. They try to reduce the shared aspect to an iterated sequence, indeed, an infinite sequence of iterated cognitive states about the other partner. I think that their analysis distorts the facts. Shared intentionality isn't just a case of a conjunction of individual intentionality about the other person's intentionality. To illustrate this point I give a rather crude example of shared intentionality. Suppose you and I are pushing a car. When we are pushing a car together, it isn't just the case that I am pushing the car and you are pushing the car. No, I am pushing the car as part of *our* pushing the car. So, if it turns out that you weren't pushing all along, you were just going along for a free ride and I was doing all the pushing, then I am not just mistaken about what you were doing, but I am also mistaken about what I was doing, because I thought not just that I was pushing (I was right about that), but that I was pushing as part of *our* pushing. And that doesn't reduce to a series of iterated claims about my propositional attitudes towards your belief about my belief about your belief.

The phenomenon of shared collective behavior is a genuine social phenomenon, and it underlies a lot of social behavior. We are blinded to this fact by the traditional analytic devices that treat all intentionality as strictly a matter of the individual subject. I believe that a recognition of shared intentionality and its implications is one of the basic things we will have to have in understanding conversation. The idea that shared intentionality can be entirely reduced to complex beliefs leads to those incorrect accounts of meaning where it turns out you have to have a very large number of intentions in order to perform such simple speech acts as saying goodbye, or asking for another beer, or saying "Hi" to someone when you meet him or her in the street. You have to have some intentionality, but you don't have to keep piling it on and on in the way that you find in some authors. Shared intentionality is one device needed for analyzing conversation.

Now, there is another device I think we need for understanding conversation, and indeed, for understanding of language generally, and that is the notion of what I call the "background." Now, let me work up to that briefly. Take any sentence, and ask yourself what you have to know in order to understand that sentence. Take the sentence: George Bush intends to run for the presidency. In order fully to understand that sentence, and consequently, in order to understand a speech act performed in the utterance of that sentence, it just isn't enough that you should have a lot of semantic contents that you glue together. Even if you make them into big semantic contents, it isn't going to be enough. What you have to know in order to understand that sentence are such things as that the United States is a republic, they have an election every 4 years, in these elections there are candidates of the two major parties, the person who gets the majority of the electoral votes becomes president. That list is indefinite, and you can't even say that all the members of the list are absolutely essential to understanding the sentence; because, for example, you could understand that sentence perfectly well even if you didn't understand about the electoral college. But there is no way to put all of this information into the meaning of the word *president*. The word *president* means the same in "George Bush wants to run for president" and in "Mitterand is the president of France." It isn't that there is some lexical ambiguity over the word *president,* it is just that the kind of knowledge you have to have to understand those two utterances doesn't coincide. All of that network of knowledge or belief or opinion or presupposition I want to give a name to; I call it the "network". If you try to follow out the threads of the network, if you think of what you would have to know in order to understand the sentence "George Bush wants to run for president," you eventually reach a whole lot of stuff that looks really weird if you try to say that they are part of your knowledge or belief. For example, you will get to things like: people generally vote when conscious, or there are human beings, or elections are generally held at or near the surface of the earth. These propositions are not like the genuine belief I have to the effect that larger states get more electoral votes than smaller states. In the way that I have a genuine belief about the number of electoral votes that goes to the state of Michigan, I don't in that way have a belief that elections go on at or near the surface of the earth. If I was writing a book about American electoral practices, I just wouldn't put that proposition in. Why not? Well in a way, it is too fundamental to count as a belief. It functions rather as part of the background stance that I take toward the world. There are sets of skills, ways of dealing with things, ways of behaving, cultural practices. The fact that part of my background is that elections are held at or near the surface of the earth manifests itself in the fact that I walk to the nearest polling place and don't try and get aboard a rocket ship or something like that. The fact that the table in front of me is a solid object is not manifested in any belief as such, but rather in the fact that I'm willing to put things on it, or that I pound on it, or I rest my books on it, or I lean on it. Those, I want to say, are stances, practices, way of behaving. This then for our present purposes is the thesis of the background: all semantic interpretation, and indeed all intentionality, rests on a background that does not consist in a set of propositional contents, but rather, consists in presuppositions that are, so to speak, preintentional or prepropositional.

In order to illustrate the operation of the background in the production and comprehension of conversation, I consider an example from real life. The following conversation took place on British television immediately after the conservative party victory that brought Mrs. Thatcher to power as Prime Minister for the first time.[2]

First Speaker: I think you know the question I'm going to ask you. What's the answer?

Second Speaker: We'll have to wait and see.

FS: Would you like to?

SS: It all depends.

Two things are clear from this brief snatch of conversation. First, the amount of information contained in the lexical meanings, that is, in the semantic contents of the words and sentences uttered, is very minimal. Literally speaking, neither party says much of anything. Secondly, it is clear that the two participants understand each other perfectly well, and that a great deal is being conveyed. Now what is it that the two speakers have to know in order to understand each other so well on the basis of such minimal semantic content? And, what would we have to understand as spectators in order to understand what was being communicated in this conversation? Well, we might begin by listing the propositional contents that were known by British television viewers as well as by the two participants and that enabled them to understand the conversation. The list might begin as follows: The first speaker is Robin Day, a famous British television news broadcaster. The second speaker is Edward Heath, the former Conservative Prime Minister. It is well known that Mr. Heath hates Mrs. Thatcher and Mrs. Thatcher hates Mr. Heath. Now, the question on everyone's mind at the time of this conversation was, "Would Heath serve as a minister in a Thatcher cabinet?" It is obvious that the conversation construed simply as a set of utterances carrying literal semantic content is unintelligible. The natural temptation is to assume that it is made intelligible by the fact that these additional semantic contents are present in the minds of the speaker, the hearer, and the audience. What I am suggesting here is that they are still not enough. Or rather, that they are only enough because they themselves rest on a set of capacities that are not themselves semantic contents. Our ability to represent rests on a set of capacites that do not themselves consist in representations.

In order to see how this works, let us imagine that we actually plugged in the semantic contents that we think would fix the interpretation of the conversation. Suppose we imagine the participants actually saying,

---

[2]My attention was called to this conversation by Philip Johnson-Laird.

FS: I am Robin Day, the famous British television news broadcaster.
SS: I am Edward Heath, the former British Conservative Prime Minister, and I hate Mrs. Thatcher, the present British Conservative Prime Minister.

Now, if we plug in such semantic contents as these, it looks as if we have converted the conversation from something that is almost totally mysterious on the face to something that is completely intelligible on the face. But if you think about it for a moment, I think you will see that we haven't made any real, in principle, advance over the original conversation. The original conversation was intelligible only because the participants and the viewers had a lot of information that wasn't explicit in the conversation. But now this new conversation is similarly intelligible only because the participants and the observers still have a lot of information that is not explicit in the conversation. They understand the conversation as revised only because they understand what sorts of things are involved in being a Prime Minister, in hating other people, in winning elections, in serving in cabinets, and so on. Well, suppose we plugged all that information into the conversation. Suppose we imagine Heath actually stating a theory of the British government, and Day actually stating a theory of human hostilities and their role in personal relationships. So now we imagine the conversation enriched in something like the following fashion:

FS: Hatred normally involves a reluctance to engage in close association with or appear to be accepting favors from the hated person.
SS: The authority of the Prime Minister in the British constitution has altered considerably since the days when the PM was considered *primus inter pares,* prior to the time of Walpole. The Prime Minister now has an authority that enables him or her to appoint and dismiss cabinet ministers almost at will, an authority tempered only by the independent popularity and political standing of other members of the party in the country at large.

Now that is the sort of thing people have to know in order to understand this conversation properly. But even if we plugged all of these propositions into the conversation, even if we filled in all of the information that we think would fix the right interpretation of the original utterances, it would still not be enough. We would still be left in our original position where the understanding of the conversation requires prior intellectual capacities, capacities that are still not represented in the conversation.

The picture we have is this. We think that because the original semantic contents encoded in the literal meaning of the sentences uttered are not at all sufficient to enable communication to take place, then communication takes place because of prior collateral information which speaker, hearer, and observer possess. This is true as far as it goes, but the problem still remains. The prior collateral is no more self-interpreting than the original conversation. So it looks like we are on the start of a regress, possible infinite. The solution to our puzzle is this. Both the original utterances and the prior collateral information only function, that is, they only determine their conditions of satisfaction, against a background of capacities, stances, attitudes, presuppositions, way of behaving, modes of sensibility, and so on, that are not themselves representational. All interpretation, understanding, and meaning, as well as intentionality in general, functions against a background of mental capacities that are not themselves interpretations, meanings, understandings, or intentional states. The solution to our puzzle, in short, is to see that all meaning and understanding goes on against a background that is not itself meant or understood, but that forms the boundary conditions on meaning and understanding, whether in conversations or in isolated utterances.

REFERENCES

Grice, H. P. (1975). Logic and conversation. In P. Cole & J. L. Morgan (Eds.), *Syntax and semantics*, Vol. 3, speech acts. New York: Academic Press.

Sacks, H., Schegloff, E. A., & Jefferson, G. (1974). A simplest systematics for the organization of turn-taking for conversation. *Language, 50*, 696–735.

Searle, J. R. (1969). *Speech acts: An essay in the philosophy of language*. Cambridge: Cambridge University Press.

Searle, J. R. (1983). *Intentionality: An essay in the philosophy of mind*. Cambridge: Cambridge University Press.

SCRIPTS, PLANS, AND COGNITIVE PROCESSES

2

Script-Based Semantic Theory

Victor Raskin
Purdue University

This chapter briefly outlines an original script-based semantic theory. After providing some background information on the goals and format of the proposed theory in the first section, the chapter introduces some necessary elements of contextual semantics, describes the accepted format of semantic theory, and then focuses on the notions of script and script-based lexicon that are essential for the theory. Combinatorial rules that link the scripts together to calculate the semantic interpretation of the sentence are also described, as are the important issues of the justification and evaluation of the theory.

GOALS OF SEMANTIC THEORY

The primary goal of any semantic theory is to model the semantic competence of the native speaker in its relevant manifestations—just as the goal of any linguistic theory is to model linguistic competence as a whole. Semantic theory is a formal object that provides semantic entities with descriptions that are supposed to match the speaker's intuitive judgments about the same entities. If the entities in question are sentences, which is most often the case, semantic theory provides them with semantic interpretations that should approximate the best they can, the meanings of the same sentences as perceived intuitively by the speaker.

Practically, however, the output of a formal linguistic theory can only match the speaker's competence with respect to a particular pre-selected feature or (more rarely) features. The theory assigns the feature to some entities and withholds it from others; the speaker is capable of passing an intuitive judgment about the same entities and may characterize them as having the same feature in some cases and lacking it in others. If the set of entities to which the feature was assigned by the theory coincides with the set of entities that the speaker characterizes as having the feature, the theory is corroborated by the speaker and can be said to model his or her competence well.

Just as Chomsky based his linguistic theory on the feature of grammaticality, Katz and Fodor (1963) based their semantic theory, the first formal semantic theory in the defined sense of linguistic theory, on the features of ambiguity, semantic normalcy, and paraphrase relations between sentences. According to these authors, semantic theory should model at least these semantic abilities of the native speaker (1):

(1)   (i)   to determine the number of readings (meanings) of each sentence
        (ii)   to determine the content of each reading
        (iii) to detect semantic anomalies, i.e., to distinguish normal sentences, i.e., sentences that are well-formed semantically, from semantically deviant sentences
        (iv)   to perceive paraphrase relations between sentences, i.e., given some two sentences, to determine whether they mean the same or not as well as, given one sentence, to come up with another sentence that means the same

Thus, their semantic theory was supposed to detect the (three-way) ambiguity of (2i) and the (two-way) ambiguity of (2ii) and to determine the content of all the involved readings (bird-related, money-related and legal, for the former sentence, and tolerance-related and birth-related, for the latter). It was also supposed to realize that the word *paid* disambiguated (2iii). The theory was to detect the semantic deviance of (2iv-v) and to perceive the paraphrase relation between (2vi) and (2vii).

(2)   (i)   The bill is large.
        (ii)   She cannot bear children.
        (iii) The bill is large but need not be paid.
        (iv)   He painted the walls with silent paint.
        (v)   Colorless green ideas sleep furiously.
        (vi)   The dog bit the man.
        (vii) The man was bitten by the dog.

Although Katz and Fodor's interpretive semantics has been under attack since shortly after its inception (see Katz, 1967, 1971, 1972; Lakoff, 1971a; McCawley, 1976; Weinreich, 1966) nobody has really expressed any concern or doubt about (1), not even at the time of the heaviest onslaught on Katz by the generative semanticists (see Bar-Hillel and Raskin, 1975; Fodor, 1977; Kempson, 1977;

Lyons, 1977, Maclay, 1971; Raskin, 1972, 1975, 1980, for further discussion of the interpretive-generative conflict of the late 1960s and early 1970s). It was the scope of the abilities in (1) that the generative semantics saw differently, including in them, especially in (1ii), more and more of what became known as pragmatics and what was essentially contextual information both of a linguistic and extralinguistic nature.

Interpretive semantics was unambiguously anti-contextual. In fact, Katz and Fodor argued that no semantic theory could possibly account for the meaning of every sentence in every possible setting. A hypothetical theory that could achieve that could be thought of as a function, taking as its arguments the sentence itself, its grammatical description, and its semantic interpretation (including, of course, the set of its possible readings and an abstract characteristic of the setting, i.e., context), and having as its value one or more or no readings out of the possible set of readings for the sentence, depending on the situation in which the sentence is uttered. Thus, the setting (3i) would disambiguate (4) as (5i), whereas the setting (3ii) would disambiguate the same ambiguous sentence of (4) as (5ii):

(3)   (i)   The hunters did some shooting and nobody else did.
        (ii)   Somebody was shooting at the hunters.
(4)   The shooting of the hunters was terrible.
(5)   (i)   The hunters were shooting very poorly.
        (ii)   Somebody shot the hunters and that was terrible.

The setting of (6) will render (7) odd and thus deprive it of all the readings it might possibly have:

(6)   It is day time.
(7)   This is the happiest night of my life.

The setting of (8) will not disambiguate (9) entirely but will reduce the number of its possible readings from 3 to 2 eliminating (10i):

(8)   An intellectual conversation is taking place.
(9)   He follows Marx.
(10)   (i)   He dogs the footsteps of Karl.
        (ii)   He is a disciple of Karl's.
        (iii) He postdates Karl.

According to Katz and Fodor, in order to construct such a semantic theory a complete theory of settings will be necessary, and the latter will require a structured and formalized description of all the knowledge the speakers have about the world. The sentences of (11–15) are listed by Katz and Fodor to illustrate their claim that the knowledge which is internalized by the native speaker and used to understand very similar sentences very differently is of an extremely specific and varied nature—it can be listed informally as (16).

(11) (i)   Our store sells horseshoes.
      (ii)   Our store sells alligator shoes.
(12) (i)   Should we take the junior back to the zoo?
      (ii)   Should we take the lion back to the zoo?
      (iii) Should we take the bus back to the zoo?
(13) (i)   Can I put the wallpaper on?
      (ii)   Can I put the coat on?
(14) (i)   Joe jumped higher than the Empire State Building.
      (ii)   Joe jumped higher than you.
(15) (i)   Black cats are unlucky.
      (ii)   People who break mirrors are unlucky.
(16) (i)   Horses wear shoes.
      (ii)   Shoes are made of alligator skin.
      (iii) Children are frequently taken to look at the animals in the zoo.
      (iv)   Lions are kept in the zoo.
      (v)   Buses may include the zoo in their itinerary.
      (vi)   Wallpaper is glued onto the wall.
      (vii) Coats are worn by people on their persons.
      (viii) The Empire State Building is a building and cannot jump.
      (ix)   You can jump.
      (x)   Black cats are believed to bring ill luck.
      (xi)   Breaking mirrors is believed to bring ill luck.

It seems obvious to Katz and Fodor that such a theory of settings, no matter how conceived, is unattainable, and therefore a semantic theory that includes it is inachievable. As a result, the scope of their semantic theory is limited to the meaning of the sentence in isolation, beyond and independently of any context.

It is firmly maintained here that such a semantic theory is devoid of any interest because it fails to explain what a particular sentence means. The most important reason a theory like Katz and Fodor's is vacuous is because there are no sentences in isolation. I demonstrate later that a more powerful lexicon easily relates the polysemous phrases in (11–15) that are responsible for the potentially different readings, to the corresponding items in (16), thus minimizing the need in extralinguistic information of the kind Katz and Fodor consider unattainable.

The native speaker, or any user of a language, cannot possibly be interested in the meaning of a sentence in isolation because they never encounter a sentence in isolation. In discourse, every sentence usually comes surrounded by other sentences preceding and/or following the sentence in question. Even if it is not the case, the speaker and hearer find themselves in a particular situation and are jointly aware of its many features. This linguistic and extralinguistic contextual information is taken into account when the sentence is uttered and comprehended and it becomes part of the intended meaning. Even when the speaker is exposed to a single sentence without any context, e.g., in a linguistic experiment such as the grammaticality test, he or she immediately visualizes a situation of which the sentence in question may be part and the speaker's comprehension of the sentence depends heavily on this imaginary context. Perhaps only a linguist is capable of abstracting a sentence from any potential context and discussing the meaning it might have in this artificially construed situation—because linguists are trained to do that. However, the usefulness of the notion of isolated meaning is highly dubious because it is completely divorced from the user's meaning of the same sentence. One striking and important difference between the two conceptions of meaning is that according to the meaning-in-isolation point of view, practically every sentence is ambiguous whereas in real discourse it would be easily and unnoticeably disambiguated by the context—think, for instance, of (2i–ii), (4) or (9).

In other words, every sentence is perceived by the hearer already in some context. If the context is not given explicitly, by the adjacent discourse or extralinguistic situation, the hearer supplies it from his or her previous experience. If the hearer is unable to do that, he or she is very unlikely to comprehend the sentence at all or at least fully.

When a potentially ambiguous sentence is uttered by the speaker, usually only one reading of it occurs to him or her and the sentence is intended in this one meaning. The reason for that is, of course, that only one context in which the sentence can be used is obvious to the speaker: it is either the real context in which the sentence occurs or the imaginary context that comes to the speaker's mind most easily. Usually only one reading of a potentially ambiguous sentence is perceived by the hearer—for exactly the same reasons. Normally, the speaker's obvious context coincides with the hearer's obvious context, but this is not necessarily the case, and misunderstandings occur in the cases of non-coincidence. The obvious context of a sentence can vary with the same speaker and hearer from occasion to occasion and from situation to situation.

It is the existence of the obvious context and its psychological validity for the speaker and hearer that explains the well-known phenomenon that many linguists and especially psycholinguists are seriously bothered by. Exposed to sentences like (17), native speakers typically fail to perceive its two-way ambiguity. At the same time, some in the subject group will come up with the meaning paraphrased as (18i) and others with (18ii). In other words, native speakers are potentially aware of the ambiguity but are typically unable to realize both of the meanings at the same time. What happens is that one of the contexts presents itself to them as the obvious context and squeezes the other one out. Which of the two becomes the obvious context depends on a number of factors concerning the speakers' personal background and experience, their idiolect, and their most recent encounters with the objects or events referred to in the sentence. On a different occasion the other context might easily prevail but the crucial thing is that it is only one at any time and not both.

(17)   Flying planes can be dangerous.
(18)   (i)   Flying planes are dangerous.
        (ii)   Flying planes is dangerous.

Grice's (1975) semantic theory places a heavy emphasis on a notion that is in fact very similar to the obvious context. His earlier (1957) analysis of meaning, the "non-natural" meaning, which is dependent only on the speaker's intention and the hearer's recognition of it, practically excludes the literal, or in his terms, conventional (1975, p. 44), meaning of the sentence from consideration. Although his account may be demonstrated to be largely self-contradictory for this very reason (see Raskin, 1977, 1979b, for further discussion), what is more important here is that his insightful and seminal notion of *implicature* is heavily dependent on the notion of the obvious context, thus validating it even further.

The issue of the obvious context as well as that of the setting theory, which Katz and Fodor considered impossible, raise the important problem of the boundary between the knowledge of language and the knowledge of the world, or in other terms, between *linguistic knowledge* and *encyclopedic knowledge*. Linguistics has always been held responsible for the former but not for the latter. In semantic terms, it presumably means that any semantic theory should account for what the speaker understands by virtue of his or her knowing the language, while all kinds of inferences related to what he or she knows about the world fall beyond the scope of the theory.

The existence and importance of this boundary was repeatedly brought up by Bar-Hillel in the 1950s in the entirely different context of automatic translation. Arguing that high quality translation by the computer was not feasible, after years of his own pioneering research in the field, he named as the main obstacle the impossibility to supply the translation machine not only "with a dictionary but also with a universal encyclopedia" (1960, p. 176). Without such an encyclopedia, however, Bar-Hillel pointed out, the computer would be unable to assign the correct meaning to the word *pen* in (19):

(19)   Little John was looking for his toy box. Finally he found it. The box was in the *pen*.

The problem that is involved here is indeed not "one that concerns translation proper . . . but a preliminary stage of this process, viz., the determination of the specific meaning in context of a word which, in isolation, is semantically ambiguous" (Bar-Hillel, 1960, p. 175), and we might add, the impossibility to supply the encyclopedia to the machine means simply that we are unable to come up with a formal, i.e., explicit, description of the necessary semantic information. In the case of (19) the necessary information includes, of course, the relative measurements of *box, pen*₁ ("an implement for writing"), and *pen*₂ ("a small enclosure for animals and children"). In other cases, naturally, the necessary information varies a great deal and can, in principle, include virtually all there is in the world (and some of what there is not). This additional information about the world, which one needs to possess in order to calculate the correct meaning of a word in a context, is obviously just as necessary to calculate the correct meaning of the sentence that contains the word.

Most recently, the problem of the boundary between our knowledge of language and our knowledge of the world has assumed still another guise. The former kind of knowledge is assigned to the proper domain of *semantics* whereas the latter is delegated to *pragmatics*. In a somewhat half-hearted follow-up to Katz's struggle against the attacks by the generative semantics, the struggle that gave way, after generative semantics disintegrated, to the in-house fight between him as a rigourous interpretivist adhering to the Standard Theory of Chomsky (1965) and Katz and Postal (1964), on the one hand, and Chomsky (1971, 1972, 1975, 1977) and Jackendoff (1981) as revisionist interpretivists who have adopted first the Extended Standard Theory and then the Revised Extended Standard Theory, Katz is the proponent of *autonomous semantics* and his adversaries of *non-autonomous semantics*.

Autonomous semantics presupposes a clear-cut distinction between semantic competence and semantic performance. Semantic competence includes meaning proper and should be studied by semantics. Semantic performance goes beyond semantics and actually belongs in pragmatics. Semantic competence is the knowledge of linguistic meaning. Semantic performance is the knowledge of extra-linguistic meaning. For various methodological reasons Katz wishes to exclude the latter from consideration entirely (see, for instance, Katz, 1980), thus being perfectly consistent with Katz and Fodor (1963) in his preference for a neat even if vacuous theory.

Non-autonomous semantics "claims that no clean point of separation exists where logical or semantic inference leaves off and pragmatic or knowledge-based inference begins; rather, the two kinds of inference are interdependent, or based on the same principles, or both" (Jackendoff, 1981, p. 425). According to Chomsky, only a very small part of meaning, the one he refers to somewhat misleadingly as "logical form," belongs to his sentence grammar. The rest of it, "meaning proper," incorporates information from the speakers' knowledge of the world.

The fight between the two sides reveals a surprising lack of difference with regard to the feasibility of semantic research. Katz wants to discard most of semantics and study the uninteresting remainder. Chomsky and Jackendoff strive to broaden the scope of semantic phenomena by claiming that more and more information should be included in semantics and that this information is basically of a pragmatic nature. In doing this, they exclude every single semantic phenomenon from Chomsky's sentence grammar and therefore from linguistics in general, for Chomsky does not have any non-sentence grammar to offer. (Support for their position came recently from unexpected quarters—Nida, 1979, declared recently that he no longer believed in the existence of the boundary between the linguistic and the extralinguistic.)

If Katz's position is vacuous, Chomsky and Jackendoff's is outright defeatist and not really distinct from the spirit of Bloomfield's notorious anti-semantical statement in which he claimed that "in order to give a scientifically accurate definition of meaning for every form of a language, we should have to have a scientifically accurate knowledge of everything in the speakers' world. The actual extent of human knowledge is very small, compared to that," concluding, accordingly, that we cannot know the meaning of any word with the exception of technical and scientific terms that are members of well-defined nomenclatures (Bloomfield, 1933, p. 139). Similarly, Chomsky and Jackendoff declare every semantic phenomenon and issue to be dependent on pragmatic factors related to "the speakers' belief systems" (Jackendoff, 1981, p. 425) and, therefore, also inaccessible, even if they do not say so explicitly.

The goal of the semantic theory proposed here is to account for the meaning of every sentence in every context it occurs. The theory does not incorporate our entire knowledge of the world and does not claim that it is possible to do so. It subscribes to the view shared by most if not all sciences that the ultimate impossibility or infinity of the problem should not prevent us from trying to get as far in our knowledge as possible. The theory recognizes the existence of the boundary between our knowledge of language and our knowledge of the world and, being a linguistic theory, does not account for what is on the other side of the boundary. However, it pushes the boundary much further out than any other available formal semantic theory. The feasibility and practicality of the approach are discussed later.

ELEMENTS OF CONTEXTUAL SEMANTICS

The format of Katz and Fodor's semantic theory includes the lexicon and the projection rules. The function of the lexicon is to model the native speaker's knowledge of the meanings of the words. The function of the projection rules is to model the native speaker's ability to combine the meanings of the words that make up the sentence into the meaning of the whole sentence. No semantic theory proposed before or after interpretive semantics has ever objected to this format in principle though there has been a great deal of controversy about the semantic material that should go into these two basic components. It is obvious, however, from the discussion in the previous section that in order to account for the meaning of a given sentence in a given context the semantic theory should be able to go beyond the meanings of separate words. Thus, in order to calculate the semantic interpretation of (2iii) correctly the theory must be able somehow to relate a certain meaning of *bill* and a certain meaning of *paid* and reject all the other meanings of these two words as incompatible. In order to calculate correctly the semantic interpretations of (3–15) the theory should be able to relate the semantic material of each of these sentences, i.e., the meanings of the words and of their combinations to some semantic material outside the sentence. To be able to perform both of these and similar operations, semantic theory should resort to the kind of information that is distinct from the meanings of separate words and from the rules that combine those meanings—at least as they are presented in interpretive semantics and its rivals: the now defunct generative semantics, Extended Standard Theory or Revised Extended Standard Theory (see the previous section and references there).

It appears that extralexical information, i.e., those semantic properties evoked by the words that are not usually accommodated in lexicons of any kind is quite essential for the comprehension of numerous ordinary sentences of natural language, e.g., (20):

(20)   (i)   John was a dime short and had to do without milk.
        (ii)   Mary saw a black cat and immediately turned home.
        (iii) Mary came into the room and all the men were charmed by her even before they sat down again.

(20i) cannot be fully comprehended if the hearer does not possess the knowledge of the basic commodity–money–commodity formula, and no entry for milk in any dictionary or lexicon is likely to mention money. (20ii) is based on the availability of the piece of information about black cats being "unlucky." (20iii) evokes the now obsolete rule of etiquette according to which men stood up when a woman came into view, and the sentence is utterly incomprehensible to those who are not familiar with the rule. That extralexical knowledge is important can be further demonstrated by a set of related examples (21) for which no such information exists and that are therefore perceived as odd:

(21)   (i)   John was a dime short and had to do without family.
        (ii)   Mary saw a black cat and immediately bought a stamp.
        (iii) Mary came into the room and all the men were charmed by her even before they sneezed.

In the last decade and a half, there has emerged a number of works from which it can also be deduced that some semantic information that is not stored in the lexicon, is involved in the process of calculating the meaning of such a compound linguistic entity as the sentence. I continue to call this kind of semantic information *extralexical* in spite of the fact that the lexicon I propose later incorporates this information.

One of the early proposals introducing extralexical information into semantic theory came from Staal (1967) and Bar-Hillel (1967) in their responses to interpretive semantics. The former proposed to expand their lexicon by accommodating in it such conversive semantic relations as those between *follow* and *precede* or *buy* and *sell*. The latter also saw the inability to accommodate relations like these as a major deficiency of the theory but went further in his criticism claiming that the format of the theory could not accommodate this kind of semantic information in principle. According to Bar-Hillel, conversives and similar relations are, in fact, meaning rules, distinct both from the lexicon and projection rules, and as such, along with other meaning rules, e.g., Carnap's (1955) meaning postulates, cannot, and should not, be squeezed into a dictionary format of any kind. Because the native speaker is clearly aware of these rules or relations, it follows that an adequate semantic theory should store this information beyond the lexicon whose format cannot accommodate it.

Next came presupposition. The notion of presupposition was introduced into linguistic theory to denote one of those statements that should be true or describe a state of affairs that should have taken place prior to the utterance of a certain sentence. Defined in logical terms by Frege (1892) and Strawson (1950), the presupposition of a sentence should be true in order for the sentence itself to be either true or false, e.g., for (22i) or its negation, (22ii), to be either true or false, their common presupposition, (23), must be true. In general, as immediately follows from the logical definition of presupposition, a sentence and its negation share the same presupposition(s).

(22)   (i)   I meant to insult him.
       (ii) I did not mean to insult him.
(23)   I insulted him.

Negation can, therefore, be used as a diagnostic test for (logical) presupposition: take a sentence, negate it; if something remains from the content in spite of the negation it is a good candidate for presupposition.

This logical notion of presupposition was used by Kiparsky and Kiparsky (1971), somewhat redundantly, to further illustrate the difference between such "factive" verbs as *regret, comprehend, ignore, resent,* etc., and such "non-factive" verbs as *assert, suppose, maintain, claim,* etc. The factives, e.g., (24i), presuppose their complement (24iii) whereas the non-factives do not, e.g., (24iii):

(24)   (i)   I regretted being late.
       (ii) I claimed being late.
       (iii) I was late.

A broader notion of presupposition was proposed by G. Lakoff (1971b). His pragmatic notion of presupposition includes various conditions that should be satisfied in order for the sentence to be "appropriate," including such individual factors as subjective assumptions and personal beliefs of the speakers. Thus, according to him, the well-formedness (or, for that matter, the truth, the appropriateness, or the aptness) of any sentence in (25) depends on whether the speaker believes that the corresponding condition for each of them in (26) is satisfied:

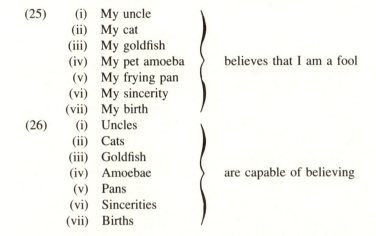

(25)	(i)	My uncle	
	(ii)	My cat	
	(iii)	My goldfish	
	(iv)	My pet amoeba	believes that I am a fool
	(v)	My frying pan	
	(vi)	My sincerity	
	(vii)	My birth	
(26)	(i)	Uncles	
	(ii)	Cats	
	(iii)	Goldfish	
	(iv)	Amoebae	are capable of believing
	(v)	Pans	
	(vi)	Sincerities	
	(vii)	Births	

The notion of presupposition used in this chapter and elsewhere (see Raskin, 1978a, for further discussion) differs both from logical and pragmatical presupposition (see Keenan, 1971) and from Cooper's (1974) conceptual presupposition. It cannot pass the negation test just as pragmatical presupposition but it is not as individual-dependent. In fact, it is as objective as logical presupposition. It can be defined as a set of conditions that should obtain in order for a sentence to be comprehended fully. The extralexical nature of presupposition in any version must be obvious by now.

The notion of semantic recursion developed by this writer in the mid-1960s provides a somewhat different perspective of the conditions that have to be met for the sentence to be understood correctly. It relates these conditions to certain elements of the sentence, presents a taxonomy of those elements and constructs a near-algorythm for discovering those conditions (see Raskin, 1968, 1978a, for a more detailed account of semantic recursion).

According to this view, the meaning of each sentence is considered to be a function of at least two factors (27), besides its own constituents and the way they are combined together.

(27)	(i)	the degree of understanding of the previous discourse (if any)
	(ii)	the quantity of pertinent information the hearer possesses

It is assumed that the greater (27i–ii) are purely quantitatively the fuller the sentence is comprehended. It is also assumed that there is a whole spectrum of partial comprehension for most ordinary sentences. Most sentences require one or more operations of semantic recursion to obtain the additional semantic information that is necessary for its complete comprehension and that is not contained in the sentence itself. The operations of semantic recursion that may be performed, in various combinations, with respect to a given sentence may be represented as (28):

(28) (i)   distinguishing all the non-self-sufficient elements of the sentence, viz., words that refer to something outside the sentence
(ii)   relating the sentence to the previous sentence in the discourse, which has already been interpreted in the sense of (27i–ii)
(iii)   relating the sentence to the pertinent information not contained in the previous discourse

The elements of the sentence mentioned in (28i) are called the *semantic recursion triggers* of the sentence. (28ii) is, of course, the principle that renders the approach recursive in the mathematical sense: first, the first sentence of the discourse is interpreted in terms of outside information; then, the next sentence is interpreted in the same way but this time the complete information obtained on the previous cycle, with regard to the first sentence, is taken into account as well, and so on. The pertinent information mentioned in (28iii) will include various elements of the hearer's experience and knowledge of the world such as common sense, logical models, evaluative scales, accepted patterns of humor, and so on (see Script-Based Lexicon section).

In terms of semantic recursion, sentences form a continuous scale with two poles. On the one pole of the scale, there are those sentences that contain no recursion triggers whatsoever—their meaning follows immediately from that of the lexical items it consists of and of the ways in which they are combined. Such sentences are quite special and rare, and they are termed *non-indexical* (Bar-Hillel, 1954, p. 259), *eternal* (Quine, 1960, p. 191ff) or *non-circumstantial* (see Raskin, 1979a). Most sentences require some semantic recursion, but on the other pole of the scale there are sentences that cannot be comprehended correctly at all by anybody who is not familiar with the previous discourse and/ or does not share the previous experience with the speaker/writer. Those sentences are likely to contain factual or literary allusions, non-universal associations and conventions, "coded messages," taboos, etc. The examples of (29) illustrate the two poles and a case in between. (29i) is a classical example of a non-indexical, non-recursive sentence. (29ii) is a maximally recursive sentence from a Russian novel. The sentence will not be comprehended by those unfamiliar with the preceding part of the novel where the peculiar expression was used in a context that determined its highly idiosyncratic, euphemistic meaning, namely "to make love." The reader not in the know will see that the heroes are spending a night in a house, not at all on a train, and will therefore fail to interpret (29iii), perfectly meaningful to him or her otherwise, in a context that rules out any meaning [cf. (6)–(7)]. (29ii) is a typical recursive sentence that can be understood partially without any semantic recursion and fully with semantic recursion.

(29)   (i)   Ice floats on water.
        (ii)   Watch your speed—we are.
        (iii) That night they jumped off the train again.

Brushing aside the somewhat dubious grammaticality of the popular Indiana road sign in (29ii), we can analyze it from the point of view of semantic recursion. At least four out of the five words are semantic recursion triggers:

(30)   (i)   *watch*: watching here means making sure from time to time that you are not exceeding a certain speed—it does not mean looking at the speedometer all the time
        (ii)   *your*: the message is addressed to automobile and motorcycle drivers, not to pedestrians, joggers, cows, car passengers, helicopter pilots, UFO's, etc.
        (iii) *speed*: there is a Federal speed limit and any violation of that law is, in theory, punishable
        (iv)   *we*: the law is enforced by the police, and *we* must stand for some representatives of this body detailed to a certain sector of the assigned area at a certain time

It is clear that a representative of a different civilization who happens to understand English but not to be familiar with (30), will grasp only the semi-empty meaning of (29ii) loosely paraphrased here as (31):

(31)   Somebody is urged to become engaged in visual inspection of a certain feature of a motion though some other people are saying that they are doing it already themselves.

Semantic recursion triggers may be of a simpler or more complex nature. The most elementary recursion triggers are grammatical. The grammatical triggers signify semantic recursion by virtue of their membership in a certain grammatical category, and they do it whenever and wherever they occur in a simple and prescribed way. Pronouns and the definite article are the simplest semantic recursion triggers in English—their typical use is exemplified in (32), with the elicited semantic information from previous discourse also underlined:

(32)   (i)   *John* came up to Mary. *He* was smiling.
        (ii)   I saw *a Porsche* on the street. *The* car was red.

Much more complex semantic recursion triggers are lexical. The lexical triggers elicit additional semantic information by virtue of their individual lexical meaning, e.g., *and so on, and so forth* (how?), *similarly* (to what?), *above-mentioned* (what? where?) as well as *good* (by what standards?), *proper, adequate, bad,* etc. (The questions in parentheses illustrate the kinds of semantic information elicited by each example because, of course, every question is exactly this—an elicitation of certain information.) Depending on the nature of a specific trigger, different rules of semantic recursion are applied to the sentence. As a result, the notion of semantic recursion seems to have an edge over that of presupposition both in terms of detalization and in terms of linguistic constructiveness—no rules have been proposed for discovering the presupposition(s) of any given sentence. Semantic recursion also makes the extralexical nature of the phenomenon truly explicit.

Another interesting extralexical concept was proposed in linguistics and in the philosophy of language at approximately the same time though not entirely independently. Gordon and Lakoff's (1975) conversational postulates, later interestingly reviewed by Morgan (1977), were essentially an attempt to transpose Grice's (1975) implicature into formal linguistics, whereas Searle's (1975) indirect speech acts have a great deal in common with both conversational postulates and implicature (see Raskin, 1977, 1979b, for further discussion). All the three notions can be exemplified by (33):

(33)   (i)   Can you pass me the salt?
        (ii)   Pass me the salt.

(33i) is an example of Grice's implicature because it is not used in its conventional, i.e., literal meaning—the latter is a question whereas, in fact, the sentence is a request. Gordon and Lakoff postulated the existence of a special kind of linguistic rules, conversational postulates, which are internalized by the native speaker. One such conversational postulate, (34i) in their simple predicate-calculus formalism, "translated" here into plain English as (34ii), transforms (33i) into (33ii).

(34)   (i)   ASK(a,b,CAN(b,Q))*→REQUEST(a,b,Q)
        (ii)   When *a* (the speaker) asks *b* (the hearer) whether *b* can do *Q* (in this particular case, to pass the salt) and does not happen to mean it literally (hence the asterisk), what he actually means is that he requests the hearer to do it

An essentially similar analysis, though in an entirely different and less formal framework, is proposed by Searle (1975) who can be interpreted as treating (33i) as a direct but unintended speech act of question used as an indirect but intended speech act of request (cf. Searle, 1969).

Obviously, conversational postulates have to be postulated for all cases of implicature, and whether it is feasible or not, they clearly constitute a legitimate kind of extralexical information available to the native speaker who will, indeed, interpret (33i) as (33ii) unless some very strong clues to the contrary are present in the discourse.

The notion of possible worlds was borrowed by linguistics and the philosophy of language from mathematical logic where a possible world functions as a domain at which propositions are defined (see, for instance, Hughes and Cresswell, 1968). Informally, it can be described as a set of all possible states of affairs or, even more simply, a set of all possible situations. In this sense, it is similar to Carnap's (1956) notion of state-description (pp. 9ff). The comprehension of a sentence and the judgment of its appropriateness clearly depend on the world the sentence is perceived in. Human history can be perceived discretely as a sequence of different worlds: thus, (35) would not evoke any possible situation to an American colonial settler (though he or she would perhaps understand all the words) but would to a modern New Yorker:

(35)   I have only three subway tokens left.

On the other hand, (36) can only be comprehended fully and considered appropriate in a world that is possible but distinct from the one we know:

(36)   I have only three subway tokens, two gym tokens, and one love
            token left.

An interesting philosophical, logical, and linguistical problem concerns reference and similarity across possible worlds. Is, for instance, Shakespeare of his own time identical to whom and what we mean by Shakespeare now? Do such abstract words as *good, love, truth, God,* etc., or for that matter, such specific words as *car, missile, tank,* etc. mean the same or similar things in the worlds of different epochs and possible worlds—obviously, a word like *tank,* for instance, did not mean 'an armored, self-propelled combat vehicle, armed with cannon and machine guns and moving on a caterpillar tread' until the said thing was invented, but even after that, do we mean the same when we use the word now as what people meant when they used the word 70 years ago or as what a science-fiction writer may mean? (See Kripke, 1972; Lewis, 1973; van Dijk, 1977, for further discussion.)

Presupposition, semantic recursion, conversational postulates, implicatures, and indirect speech acts are not the only repositories of extralexical information that the speaker is aware of and has to internalize in order to be successful in communication. Inference rules, entailments, conjectures, clichés, allusions, and so on, should perhaps be added to the list of what the competent speaker should be able to operate with. Even engaged in a bitter controversy and coming from very different backgrounds, an orthodox and formal grammarian of the sentence and a typical philosopher of language seem to express similar views on the importance of extralexical information: whereas Chomsky (1975) emphasizes the importance of the speaker's "unspecified assumptions, beliefs, attitudes, and conventions" (p. 30) for the comprehension of a sentence, Searle (1975) puts forward the similar notion of "mutually shared background information of the speaker and the hearer, together with an ability on the part of the hearer to make inferences" (p. 61).

Although these recently developed concepts dealing with various aspects of extralexical information have been extremely useful for semantic theory in general, none of them has been incorporated in any form into any existing formal semantic theory. Nobody has proposed to incorporate any form of extralexical information in the lexicon (thus rendering it lexical). On the other hand, no attempt, with a possible exception of Weinreich's (1966) ill-defined *semantic generator*, has been made to define a separate format for extralexical information within any formal (or, for that matter, informal) semantic theory outside of its lexicon, either. In fact, as briefly indicated in the Goals of Semantic Theory section, the recognition of the existence and importance of extralexical information on Chomsky's and some others' part seems to signify for them the impossibility of a complete and formal semantic theory. A format for a semantic theory that does incorporate extralexical information is proposed in the next section.

FORMAT OF SEMANTIC THEORY

The proposed format for a semantic theory incorporating extralexical information consists of two components that are similar in principle to the dictionary component and projection-rule component of interpretive grammar. The first component, the lexicon, contains lexical information that approximates the speaker's knowledge of the meanings of the words. The other component, the combinatorial rules, combines the meanings of the words into the semantic interpretation of the whole sentence to which the words belong. This second component approximates the ability of the speaker to derive the meaning of the sentence out of the meanings of the words that make up the sentence.

From the time the first semantic theories emerged in the context of modern linguistic theory, it has been more or less taken for granted that one of the components of any such theory is a set of characterizations of the individual meanings of separate words, e.g., a lexicon with lexical entries for each word of the language and each meaning of the word. Katz and Fodor (1963) made this assumption rather obvious by saying, "What has always been unclear about a semantic theory is what component(s) it contains *besides a dictionary* (the emphasis is mine—V.R.)" (p. 492). Their opponents have never really doubted the necessity of the lexicon either (see, however, Bar-Hillel, 1967)—even when the generative semanticists objected against the postulation by Standard Theory of a lexicon in syntax and a dictionary in semantics, they always considered one of them necessary—it was the duplication of effort they objected to.

However, the inclusion of a dictionary in a semantic theory is based on a strong assumption, namely that the individual word has a meaning. Although seemingly obvious, this assumption has been the center of a recurring controversy for centuries. Does the word have an inherent meaning or does it acquire it only when used in a sentence? In the former case, a dictionary is required. In the latter case, no dictionary can accommodate all the shifting meanings acquired by words in infinitely different situations of their use and the dictionary should be replaced by a system of rules assigning meaning to words on the basis of conditions of use, probably along the lines of the setting theory mentioned in the first section.

Since the ancient Indian theory (in the fourth group, the *nirukta*, of the third canonical collection, the *vedanga* of Vedic documents; see Zvegincev, 1964, p. 9) which claimed that the word *cuckoo* only means what it seems to mean because it can be used in some sentence, various scholars have maintained this view in different forms. Both traditional semantics (Bréal, 1897; Darmesteter, 1887; Paul, 1886) and classical semantics (Ogden & Richards, 1923; Stern, 1931; Ullmann, 1951) took it for granted that meaning was an inherent property of the word—to the practical exclusion of other meaningful linguistic entities (morphemes, phrases, sentences, texts) from consideration. However, toward the middle of this century, Wittgenstein founded an extremely influential school of thought in the philosophy of language according to which language is use and no abstract entity called *meaning* can be assigned to any word outside the use of this word: "the word 'meaning' is being used illicitly if it is used to signify the thing that 'corresponds' to the word. That is to confound the meaning of a name with the bearer of the name. For a *large* class of cases—though not for all—in which we employ the word 'meaning' it can be defined thus: the meaning of a word is its use in the language." (Wittgenstein, 1953, p. 80.) In linguistic semantics, this idea was most closely reflected in Firth's (1957) "meaning by collocation" (p. 198). According to Firth, the meaning of *dark* contains the ability of this word to be combined in a phrase with *night,* and conversely, the meaning of *night* contains its ability to be combined with *dark.* Numerous other linguists from various schools and trends also related the meaning of the word to its use explicitly and implicitly (see, for instance, Benveniste, 1962; Buck, 1949; Harris, 1954; Hill, 1958; Sørensen, 1970).

Behaviorists and neo-behaviorists in semantics have defined *meaning* in terms of the situation of use—both negatively (i.e., with the intent to take meaning out of the domain of linguistic research) and positively (i.e., in an earnest attempt to shed light on this elusive concept). The most notable example of the former was, of course, Bloomfield (1933) who defined the meaning of a linguistic form as "the situation in which the speaker utters it and the response it calls forth in the hearer" (p. 139). Realizing the extreme crudity of this definition Bloomfield (1933) added that "we must discriminate between the non-distinctive features of the situation . . . and the distinctive, or linguistic, meaning (the semantic features) which are common to all situations that call forth the utterance of the linguistic form" (p. 141). For Bloomfield, all this meant that meaning was to be taken out of consideration (see also the Elements of Contextual Semantics section). However, if this definition is to be taken seriously and positively, as it was, and I believe, still is, done by some followers of Bloomfield (see, for instance, Fries, 1954), then one should expect certain features to be present in any situation in which a certain word is used, and those features would then constitute the meaning of the word. Thus, a certain cluster of features associated by the native speaker with the word *shirt* should be present in all the situations evoked by (37):

(37) (i) Bring me my shirt.
  (ii) This shirt is frayed.
  (iii) I need a new shirt.
  (iv) Shirts were rarely worn before the 14th century.
  (v) What a lovely shirt!
  (vi) Do you wear a size 15 shirt? (Alston, 1964, p.26)

It is clear that the situations evoked by the examples hardly overlap on any features though the same word is present in all of them. It is also clear that any native speaker will recognize the word *shirt* in all of them as being used in its ordinary and familiar meaning. If the meaning is clearly there and the common features are not, the behaviorist account is counter-intuitive and therefore deficient.

In general, the concept of the word and its inherent meaning is psychologically real to the native speaker. People talk about the meaning of words, they look them up in dictionaries, they learn the words from foreign language. It can, of course, be argued that even a minimal amount of schooling will bias the native speaker of virtually any language in favor of words because education depends on the notion and freely uses the term. In spite of all these reservations one cannot help agreeing with Benveniste (1962) who says, "Please permit me, for the sake of convenience, to keep this decried—and irreplaceable—term" (p. 123).

The question, "Does the word possess meaning in isolation or does it acquire meaning only in the sentence?" addressed also by Gardiner (1932, 28ff), is actually similar to the issue of the meaning of the sentence in isolation as discussed in the first section. The sentence means something concrete and specific only in a certain setting but it does have an inherent meaning. Similarly, the meaning of the word may vary considerably in actual use but it does characterize the word inherently. An adequate linguistic theory must, therefore, accommodate both of these non-contradictory properties of the sentence and of the word, and its ability to do so is one of the tests of its adequacy.

In fact, there is no contradiction between meaning as an inherent property of the word and meaning as use. The meaning of every word can be successfully and non-circularly defined as a set of elementary units of meaning each of which is the ability of the word to be used in a different phrase of the language. Developed by Zvegincev (1960, 1968; see also Raskin, 1979c), the theory of elementary units of meaning, *monosemes*, was revised and formalized by this author and practically applied to automatic natural-language processing (Raskin, 1971). The proposed script-based semantic theory is a direct descendant of that approach.

The script-based semantic theory recognizes the meaning of the word and accounts for it in the lexicon. However, it is done in a way that is rather different from the usual lexicons associated with formal semantic theories. In fact, the treatment of the word meaning by the script-based theory is especially compatible with the view that meaning is use (see the Script-Based Lexicon section).

The second component of the script-based semantic theory is the combinatorial rules. Their basic function is to combine the meanings of the words that make up the sentence and that are characterized in the lexicon into the semantic interpretation, or simply meaning, of the whole sentence. As described in the first section, the meaning of the sentence calculated in this way should coincide with the meaning assigned to it intuitively by the native speaker. This means that in view of (1), the combinatorial rules should produce two or more different interpretations for an ambiguous sentence, no interpretation for an anomalous sentence, and identical interpretations for paraphrases. The script-based semantic theory takes these requirements for an absolute minimum and adds a few more to them (38):

(38) (i) to detect and mark the source(s) of ambiguity, if any, much more explicitly than in interpretive semantics or other semantic theories

(ii) to disambiguate a potentially ambiguous sentence in a non-ambiguous linguistic or extralinguistic context

(iii) to detect and mark the source(s) of anomaly, if any, much more explicitly than in other semantic theories

(iv) to produce semantic interpretations of deviant sentences approximating those perceived by native speakers (cf. Katz, 1964; Ziff, 1964)

(v) to produce associations along the lines of those which are evoked by the sentence in the speakers' minds

(vi) to ask questions soliciting more information if the sentence raises them and to answer them if the information is recursively available

(vii) to produce implicatures where present and potential implicatures wherever possible

(viii) to discover the presuppositions of the sentence, if any

(ix)   to characterize the world in which the situation described by the sentence takes place, in the aspects pertinent to the sentence

Naturally, the combinatorial rules depend heavily on what it is they are combining, and it is the script-based lexical entries from the lexicon associated with the theory that enable it to achieve (38). However, the combinatorial rules should be both powerful and subtle in handling, shaping, and rubricising the semantic information provided by the lexicon. The operations of (38) will not, for the most part, be performed by the theory separately, one after the other. Rather, it will aim to produce a formal account of the context of the sentence in a broad but delimitable sense, and the result of each operation from (38) must be easily identified as a certain part of this context.

The lexicon of the script-based semantic theory and the combinatorial rules are described in the next two sections.

SCRIPT-BASED LEXICON

The lexicon of the proposed semantic theory is based on the notion of *script* (see also Raskin, 1981). The script is a large chunk of semantic information surrounding the word or evoked by it. The script is a cognitive structure internalized by the native speaker and it represents the native speaker's knowledge of a small part of the world. Every speaker has internalized rather a large repertoire of scripts of "common sense" that represent his or her knowledge of certain routines, standard procedures, basic situations, and so on, for instance, the knowledge of what people do in certain situations, how they do it, in what order, etc. Beyond the scripts of common sense every native speaker may, and usually does, have individual scripts determined by his or her individual background and subjective experience and restricted scripts that the speaker shares with a certain group (e.g., family, neighbors, colleagues, etc.) but not with the whole speech community of native speakers of the same language.

What is labelled here *script* has been called *schema, frame, daemon*, etc. On the other hand, the term *script* has been reserved sometimes for a temporal sequence of frames. The notion has been used extensively in a number of adjacent fields such as psychology, sociology, anthropology, artificial intelligence, education (see, for instance, Bartlett, 1932; Bateson, 1972; Chafe, 1977; Charniak, 1972, 1975; Freedle, 1977, 1979; Goffman, 1974; Minsky, 1975; Schank, 1975a, 1975b; Schank & Abelson, 1977; Schank & Colby, 1973; Tannen, 1979). I will not elaborate here on the terminological differences between the use of the term *script* here and the use of the same or similar terms elsewhere. However, in the Justification and Evaluation of Semantic Theory section I discuss one important aspect in which the scripts as used here differ from the ones used elsewhere in principle even if not in format or design.

Formally or technically, every script is a graph with lexical nodes and semantic links between the nodes. In fact, all the scripts of the language make up a single continuous graph, and the lexical entry of a word is a domain within this graph around the word in question as the central node of the domain. Somewhat tentatively and simplistically, (39) represents a domain of the continuous graph that (partially) contains two lexical entries—for *color* and *artifact*.

(39)

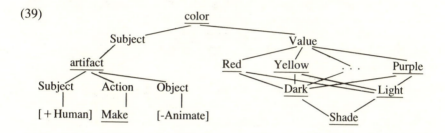

As shown in (39), the links characterize the relations between the nodes, often but not necessarily in terms of the roles assigned to one node with regard to the other. Two important features of the scripts not shown in (39) are the distance and the emphasis. The first feature involves the relative length of the links between the nodes. Thus, the link between *color* and *artifact* is, in fact, much longer than those between *artifact* and the three nodes under it, which reflects the fact that the idea of color is much less related to the meaning of *artifact* than the situation of a human producing something inanimate. The second feature emphasizes certain nodes with respect to others. Thus, in the domain of the graph that is the lexical entry for *artifact,* the node [− Animate] should be emphasized to reflect the fact that it is this node that is actually the central part of the meaning in question.

The fact that the constituents of the sentence evoke pieces of semantic information that go beyond the usual lexical entries for these constituents in the existing ordinary dictionaries or in the lexicons of the existing formal semantic theories has already been illustrated by the examples of (20), especially when compared to (21). Similarly, the native speaker will understand (40i) and (40ii) differently—the former will not raise any question as to the reason for John's failure, whereas the latter will (in other words, (40ii) will be recursive where (40i) will not):

(40) (i)   John tried to eat his hamburger with a spoon but did not succeed.
      (ii) John tried to eat his hamburger with a fork and knife but did
            not succeed.

The semantic difference between the two sentences cannot be accounted for
in terms of an ordinary lexicon, whether formalized or not. Thus, a typical
dictionary such as *Webster's New Collegiate Dictionary* (1976) would describe
the appropriate meanings of the key words as (41):

(41) (i)   EAT vt: 1. To take in through the mouth as food: ingest, chew
             and swallow in turn
      (ii)   HAMBURGER n: 2. A sandwich consisting of a patty of ham-
             burger [ground beef] in a split bun
      (iii) SPOON n: 1. An eating or cooking implement consisting of a
             small shallow bowl with a handle

Neither these lexical items nor the ones in terms of which they are described
(e.g., *sandwich, beef, bun*) contain any information about the fact that ham-
burgers do not belong to the class of liquid or dry substances that can be eaten
with a spoon. However, it is exactly this piece of semantic information that
makes the speaker's perception of (40i) different from that of (40ii). Because
this semantic information is obviously available to the native speaker its source
is a script that includes a small domain like (42i). The full script for *spoon* will
also include additional links and nodes such as (42ii–iv):

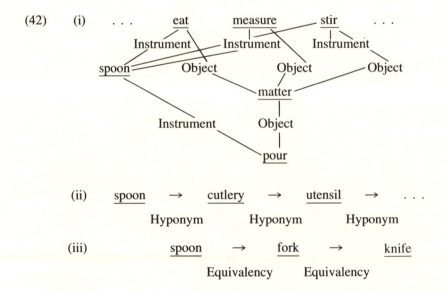

(42) (i)   . . .   eat   measure   stir   . . .

(iv)

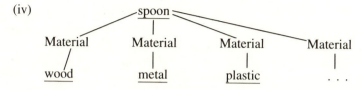

The names assigned to the links both in (39) and (42): 'object', 'subject', 'action', 'instrument', 'material', 'hyponym', 'equivalency' [membership in the same category], 'value' can be treated simply as convenience terms for the purposes of this chapter. Generally, the theory resorts to two alternative ways to accommodate this type of information: (a) postulating a number of standard semantic relations along these lines and trying to keep them at a limited number and at roughly the same level of abstractness in order to avoid the arbitrariness and unwieldiness of Mel'čuk's (1974, 1979) "sense↔text" model, or (b) postulating abstract, non-lexical nodes corresponding each to one type or subtype of link and having all the pertinent lexical nodes connected with those non-lexical nodes by the same unnamed link. According to the latter alternative, each verb, for instance, will be connected by an unnamed link to one of the non-lexical nodes marked 'Subject' which will contain exactly the kind of subject the verb takes, e.g., [+Animate] for *sleep*. Both alternatives are interestingly compatible with, though clearly distinct from, Fillmore's (1968) early idea of deep cases. Both alternatives presuppose a multidimensional graph and, given the complexity and heterogeneity of semantic information involved, it is naive to expect anything simpler than that.

Every word of the sentence is characterized by a limited domain of the continuous semantic graph. Every word evokes this domain, and obviously, the most adjacent nodes, i.e., the nodes connected to the word-itself node by the shortest links, are evoked more strongly than the less adjacent nodes. In principle, because the graph is continuous and all-inclusive, every word evokes everything that is there in the graph, and this seems to be a good approximation of the native speaker's semantic performance. In practice, however, the limits of the evocation process are determined by the purposes of the semantic analysis, and the rest of the potentially evocable information is disregarded. For the purposes of this chapter, the evoked domain can be limited to the word-itself node and to one "circle" of surrounding nodes connected with the word by a limited number of such essential links as 'subject', 'object', 'activity', etc. (43i–ii) are representative examples of a greatly simplified, streamlined and discretized format of script.

(43)   (i)   DOCTOR
              Subject: [+Human] [+Adult]
              Activity: > Study medicine

                        = Receive patients: patient comes or doctor visits
                                    doctor listens to complaints
                                    doctor examines patient
                        = Cure disease: doctor diagnoses disease
                                    doctor prescribes treatment
                        = (Take patient's money)
            Place: > Medical School
                        = Hospital or doctor's office
            Time: > Many years
                        = Every day
                        = Immediately
            Condition: Physical contact

(ii)   LOVER
        Subject: [+Human] [+Adult] [+Sex: x]
        Activity: Make love
        Object: [+Human] [+Adult] [+Sex: x̄]
        Place: Secluded
        Time: > Once
                    = Regularly
        Condition: If subject or object married, spouse(s) should not
        know
        (Note: '>' means 'past,' '=' means 'present')

The scripts of (43) are not very elementary in the sense that they themselves utilize the material of other scripts, which is usually the case with scripts. It is important to understand that in the full-fledged script-based semantic theory, the scripts are constructed from the elementary level up in order to avoid the typical lexicographic circularity.

COMBINATORIAL RULES

Every word of the sentence evokes a script or scripts with which it is associated. Obviously, the node for an ambiguous word will be the center of two or more domains of the continuous graph, and, in principle, each of these domains will be evoked when the word is uttered. The main function of the combinatorial rules in the script-based semantic theory is to combine the scripts evoked by the words of the sentence into one or more compatible combinations. An unambiguous sentence will be associated with just one compatible combination of evoked scripts, an n-way ambiguous sentence with n compatible combinations. The semantic interpretation of the sentence does not coincide with the compatible combination(s) of evoked scripts but is determined by it/them. (44i) is a blend of two hackneyed examples from semantic works of the last 2 decades, the word *bachelor* and the sentence *the man hit the colorful ball,* first discussed by Katz and Fodor (1963) and then by their friends and foes alike. With another potentially ambiguous word, *paralyzed,* thrown in, (44i) is a representative example of the ambiguous sentence treated in terms of the evoked scripts by the combinatorial rules. In (44ii), the evoked scripts are assigned tentative and almost arbitrary but self-explanatory names for the sake of this discussion. (44iii) lists all the potentially compatible combinations of the evoked scripts (with the scripts for *the,* DEFINITE, UNIQUE, and GENERIC - cf. (48)—omitted for the sake of simplicity):

(44) (i)   The paralyzed bachelor hit the colorful ball
      (ii) 1. DISEASE 1. MARRIAGE 1. COLLISION 1. COLOR   1. ARTIFACT
            2. MORAL   2. ACADEME 2. DISCOVERY 2. EVALUA- 2. ASSEMBLY
                                                   TION

            3. KNIGHT
            4. SEAL

      (iii) 11111, 11112, 11212, 11222, 12111, 12112, 12212, 12222,
            13111, 13112, 13212, 13222, 14111, 21111, 21112, 21212,
            21222, 22111, 22112, 22212, 22222, 23111, 23112, 23212,
            23222

The 12 scripts listed in (44ii) can be theoretically combined in 64 ways. The combinatorial rules will reduce this number to the 25 potentially compatible combinations listed in the obvious way in (44iii). Thus, 11212, for instance, is a combination of Script 1 for *paralyzed,* Script 1 for *bachelor,* Script 2 for *hit,* Script 1 for *colorful* and Script 2 for *ball,* and it is paraphrased below as (45i). 14111 and 23222 are paraphrased as (45ii) and (45iii), respectively:

(45) (i)   A never-married man who cannot move (some of) his limbs discovered (found himself at) a large dancing party abundant with bright colors.
      (ii) A fur seal which cannot move (some of) its limbs pushed (with its nose?) a spheric object painted in bright colors.
      (iii) A young knight who serves under the standard of another knight and who finds that he is unable to act (a pacifist?) discovered (found himself at) a large and picturesque dancing party.

Although it does follow from (44) that (44i) is potentially 25-ways ambiguous, for most native speakers it would be hard to discover all these ambiguities without their being prompted by the appropriate obvious contexts (see the first section). Whenever (if ever) (44i) is actually used, the actual linguistic and extralinguistic context will disambiguate it for any native speaker, and the combinatorial rules should be able to do the same, otherwise the theory will lose its adequacy. This requirement on the combinatorial rules is just one of the many listed between (1) and (38), and (46) is an example on which the functioning of the combinatorial rules will be non-technically illustrated:

(46)   I got up in the morning, took a shower and made myself some breakfast.
            Then I went out and started the car.
(47)   Then I went out and started the car.

(46) is a short discourse, and the combinatorial rules will be applied to its second sentence, repeated as (47) for a convenient reference, and demonstrated to handle all the required items in (1) and especially (38). First, let us list the scripts evoked by the words of (47)—for the sake of simplicity again, they are not really given but rather alluded to in an informal and self-explanatory way:

(48)   (i)   THEN adv: 1. At that time
                            2. Next in order of time
                            3. In that case
        (ii)   I pron: 1. Speaker or writer
        (iii) GO OUT v: 1. Leave shelter
                            2. Entertain oneself outside one's home
        (iv)   AND conj: 1. [Connection or addition]
        (v)   START vt: 1. Cause to move
                            2. Bring into being
                            3. Begin the use
        (vi)   THE det: 1. [Definite]
                            2. [Unique]
                            3. [Generic]
        (vii) CAR n: 1. Horse carriage
                            2. Automobile
                            3. Railway carriage
                            4. Cage of an elevator

At Stage Zero of the process of semantic interpretation of (47), the scripts evoked by its words will include a few more scripts unlisted in (48), e.g., the adjective script for *then* as in *the then secretary of state* or the intransitive script(s) for *start* as in *he started when he heard the shot*. The combinatorial rules filter these syntactically inappropriate scripts on the basis of the syntactic structure associated with (47):

(49)

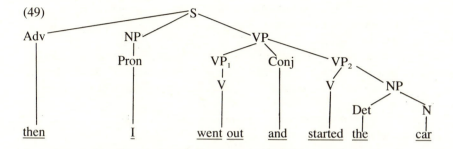

The part of the scripts that is most related to the syntactic information of (49) is the set of named links or, alternatively, non-lexical nodes discussed in connection with (42) in the Script-Based Lexicon section. Combining this information from the scripts with (49), the combinatorial rules get rid of those scripts evoked by the words in (47) which are syntactically incompatible with (49).

At Stage One, the combinatorial rules have to determine which mode of communication (47) is uttered in. If there are no clues to the contrary or, most often, no explicit clues at all, the combinatorial rules introduce the *bona-fide communication mode* (cf. Grice, 1975; Searle, 1969; Raskin, 1979d, p. 328), viz. the "ordinary," information-conveying mode (no lying, acting, joking, etc.). In this mode, unlike Katz and Fodor's projection rules, the combinatorial rules are geared not to come with all the potential ambiguities, as was done in (44), but on the contrary, to disambiguate a(–n always) potentially ambiguous sentence to exactly one, most probable meaning. For this purpose, all the scripts evoked by a word are divided into two parts. The first part contains exactly one unmarked script (for instance, the most frequent one); the second part contains all the other, marked, scripts—the marking there can be hierarchical, from the least marked to the most marked. Unless some clues to the contrary are present in the context, the combinatorial rules will always push the unmarked script for the word forward. If it turns out to be impossible, the combinatorial rules change the marking of the scripts for the word temporarily, for the purposes of the processed discourse, and declare another script unmarked. It is assumed here that the scripts with underlined numbers are treated as unmarked in (48). The combinatorial rules can then be expected to come up with a semantic interpretation for (47) that can be loosely paraphrased as (50):

(50)   After having done something else, the speaker left a shelter and brought (the engine of) some definite car to move.

After having used the unmarked scripts for the words of the sentence, the combinatorial rules have to check whether those scripts involve any conditions on their use and if so, whether these conditions are satisfied. Thus, in the case of *then* there should be a mention of a previous action in the discourse, and (46) satisfies this condition. However, in the case of *the*, the script DEFINITE can only be used if the discourse contains a previous reference to an object of the class denoted by the noun following *the*. This condition is not satisfied, and the combinatorial rules switch to the other script of *the* concluding that the car in question is unique for the speaker, i.e., the only car the speaker has at his or her disposal.

The combinatorial rules will do some remarking of the scripts on their own—if, for instance, the text is about railways, then at the beginning of its processing some clue will indicate that the intended script for *car* is, in fact, Script 3 of (48), and then the combinatorial rules will declare that script unmarked for the current discourse. The marking of the scripts for a word also change in the course of history—thus, some 200 years ago, the unmarked script for *car* was apparently Script 1 of (48).

On the basis of other features of the involved scripts, the combinatorial rules will generate the statements of (51) as the presuppositions of (47) and the statements of (52) as the probable presuppositions of (47).

(51) (i) The speaker is human.
      (ii) The speaker is able-bodied.
      (iii) The speaker is past infancy.
      (iv) The speaker knows something about cars.
(52) (i) The shelter is the speaker's home.
      (ii) The car is very near the shelter.
      (iii) The speaker started cars before.

The combinatorial rules will also generate the inferences of (53) as well as the probable inferences of (54):

(53) (i) The speaker has the use of the car and the (ignition) key to it.
      (ii) The car was not inside the shelter.
(54) (i) The speaker intended to go somewhere by car.
      (ii) The speaker probably did not come back in.

The combinatorial rules will also generate the question of (55). They will fail to answer it on the basis of the previous discourse and will attempt to answer it on the basis of the information about the world accumulated in the process of semantic information of the previous discourse, if any, or semantic information postulated in advance, if any. If no answer is available to (55), the combinatorial rules will record (55) as unanswered and will attempt to answer it every time new information is obtained in or around the discourse.

(55)   Who is the speaker?

The combinatorial rules will list every lexical node which is contained within the selected scripts for the sentence, collect the scripts for those words and put them in a special storage marked ASSOCIATIONS. In the case of (47), this will probably involve the scripts for such words as *you, he, she*, etc., *time, shelter, move, in, bring, vehicle, engine.*

-The combinatorial rules will also add the obtained semantic interpretation for (47) to another special storage marked WORLD INFORMATION. The latter operation involves comparison of the information contained in the semantic information for (47) with the information already stored in WORLD INFOR-MATION. The main goal of the comparison is to use the information in this storage to disambiguate the sentence if the combinatorial rules have failed to do it so far. This will not be necessary perhaps for (47) in bona fide communication but it will be necessary for a syntactically ambiguous sentence such as (56 = 17) because the instruction to use the unmarked scripts in the process of its semantic interpretation will still preserve the potential ambiguity as either (57i) or (57ii).

(56)   Flying planes can be dangerous
(57)   (i)   It happens that flying planes is dangerous.
       (ii)   It happens that flying planes are dangerous.

In the case of (56), if WORLD INFORMATION contains some statement to the effect that planes are the subject of discourse, the combinatorial rules will disambiguate (56) as (57i). If, on the contrary, the discourse is on flying as an activity, they will disambiguate the sentence as (57ii).

On the other hand, WORLD INFORMATION may already contain any of the statements in (58), which, of course, will contradict (47). Then the com-binatorial rules will have to opt for one of the alternatives in (59).

(58)   (i)   The speaker does not have a car at his/her disposal.
       (ii)   The speaker is outside.
      (iii)   The car is already started.
       (iv)   The car is a railway car.
(59)   (i)   Declare the sentence anomalous and list a conflict with one of
              the statements in (58) as the reason
       (ii)   Change the mode of communication to non-*bona fide*
      (iii)   Determine the scripts shared by (47) and the conflicting state-
              ment in (58) and check whether the conflict can be resolved by
              switching to another script of the same word

The last two options in (59) would involve going back to Stage One previously mentioned and starting the process of semantic interpretation from there.

Option (59ii) would mean considerable changes in the described procedure, the most important of which is the different goal with regard to disambiguation: the combinatorial rules would no longer be instructed to disambiguate each sentence to just one meaning by using the unmarked scripts. The marking may be kept, but the instruction will be to obtain all the compatible combinations of scripts and thus all the potential meanings of the sentence.

In various forms of non-bona fide communication, the combinatorial rules are instructed not to discard syntactically or semantically deviant sentences but rather to introduce minor changes in the scripts causing the deviance and calculate the semantic interpretations conditional on these changes. This will often lead to metaphors, implicatures and language innovations. In other words, in the non-bona fide modes, the combinatorial rules will slightly modify their format with regard to the operations described above and also assume some additional responsibilities.

JUSTIFICATION AND EVALUATION OF SEMANTIC THEORY

The ultimate goal of any linguistic theory is to describe the mental mechanisms underlying language. Much more realistically, as stated briefly in the first section, linguistic theory tries to model the native speaker's performance in some one significant aspect. In other words, when the output of the theory (sentences, descriptions, semantic interpretations, etc.) is compared with that of the native speaker, an ideal match should be obtained between certain subclasses of objects within the two outputs, and the subclasses are distinguished according to a certain important feature assigned to those objects both by the theory and by the native speaker. Thus, if the assigned feature is grammaticality—as it almost invariably is within transformational grammar—then what the theory characterizes as a grammatical sentence should be also perceived intuitively as such by the native speaker. If a theory passes this test, then according to Chomsky (1965), it reaches the level of descriptive adequacy.

It has been argued elsewhere that a good linguistic theory cannot be based on any single feature, especially not on grammaticality (see Raskin, 1976; cf. McCawley, 1976). A good semantic theory must, in fact, be based on a number of semantic abilities of the speaker that manifest themselves by the speaker's intuitive judgments of the sentence. Besides the feature of grammaticality, revised to include meaningfulness and elements of pragmatics (see the first section) and manifested in the grammaticality-awareness of the native speaker, other semantic abilities can be shown to include truth-value-awareness, presupposition-awareness, coherency-awareness, context-awareness, and appropriateness-awareness (see Raskin, 1978b, 1979e). The output of such a theory should match that of the speaker in all of these different though related aspects, and the level of descriptive adequacy is only achieved if all of the featured mentioned both in (1) and in

(38) are the same for every single sentence the theory interprets semantically. The script-based semantic theory is certainly designed to meet this requirement. However, this is not good enough.

A descriptively adequate theory may be too crude or too superficial, for instance, if the assigned feature it is based on is too crude, superficial or, worse, irrelevant. A descriptively adequate theory can be none of the above but still inferior to some other descriptively adequate theory. In this case, the one that achieves the level of explanatory adequacy is preferred over the other. Explanatory adequacy is only achieved when the theory is based on entities and relations which are close to the ones which determine the speaker's performance. If this happens, the theory actually matches the speaker's intuition better than some other theory.

No other semantic theory is available for comparison with the script-based semantic theory since the level of descriptive adequacy postulated for the latter between (1) and (38) is significantly higher than that achieved by its predecessors. However, the concern for explanatory adequacy is very important for this research. It is firmly believed here that if an earnest attempt is not made to demonstrate that the postulated theoretical concepts get as close as possible to the linguistic reality the theory is trying to match, the theory will fail in the long run, e.g., in attempts to extrapolate it to other data, even if it seems "to do the job" on the data it is being applied to in this particular case—in other words, a linguistic theory that is not justified in this sense is going to be ad hoc and, therefore, not even a theory as this term is used here.

The script-based semantic theory should be justified with regard to both of its components, the scripts and the combinatorial rules. For the purposes of this chapter, it will certainly suffice to justify the combinatorial rules in terms of their end product: if the obtained semantic interpretation(s) matches (match) the meaning(s) of the sentence, then the combinatorial rules are adequate. The justification of any combinatorial rule consists mainly of the application of this criterion, anyway, but it also includes the step-by-step matching of the intermediate applications of the rules to the scripts with the speakers' intuitions about those intermediate results, and we do not need to go into these complicated procedures here.

The most important part of the justification procedure for the theory is, however, the justification of the format and content of the scripts. The best way to do this seems to be by using the most popular justification device used by linguists both consciously and unconsciously, namely by showing that a deviant sentence results if something is not taken into account. Thus, given a certain script presented in a certain format, for instance, (43i), one can come up with any number of sentences such as (60), each of which violates the script by contradicting a certain element of semantic information contained there:

(60)   (i)   This kestrel is our village doctor.
        (ii) This baby is our village doctor.

(iii)   Our village doctor has never treated a patient in his life.
(iv)   A deaf doctor is the best doctor.
(v)   Our doctor never examines his patients.
(vi)   Our doctor never knows what is wrong with you.
(vii)   I am not going to cure you—I am a doctor.
(viii) After elementary school, I took a three-week crash course and became a doctor.
(ix)   As your doctor, I would like very much to meet you finally after 40 years of active correspondence.

According to Grice's (1975) co-operative principle, the hearer of every such sentence will make an effort to treat them as non-deviant if he or she possibly can. However, if no clues are contained in the discourse to indicate that the sentences in (60) are not meant literally—and in bona fide communication, clues to this effect are unlikely to be forthcoming—the hearer will conclude that each of the sentences is odd, deviant, anomalous. To the extent that this is the case, each of these sentences justifies the inclusion of a certain semantic element in an appropriate rubric of the script.

(60i–ii) are the simplest because they violate a feature of the subject, [+ Human] and [+ Adult], respectively. Such violations should even be detected and filtered out by the strict subcategorization and selection restriction rules, operating on the lexicon of the Standard Theory (Chomsky, 1965). The deviance of the other examples cannot be formally accounted for by any non-script-based semantic theory.

(60iii) violates an important element listed under activity, which requires of a doctor to see and treat patients—whoever does not, hardly qualifies for the degree and/or position. Similarly, (60iv) renders another element of activity difficult or impossible to carry out, namely, for the doctor to listen to the patient's complains. (60v–vii) also involve various elements listed under activity, and they are self-explanatory. (60viii) involves a time restriction that refers to the past and requires that a few years be spent on studying medicine. Finally, (60ix) violates the crucial condition of a face-to-face contact for the interaction between a doctor and a patient to become possible.

It is obvious that not all of the sentences in (60) are equally deviant. Everyone of them can be interpreted as metaphorical, facetious and/or involving an implicature. On their literal meaning, however, some of them are quite difficult to interpret though an elaborate construction can save them in marginal cases, e.g., a very competent doctor who lost his or her hearing very recently, after many years of successful practice, can perhaps continue his or her activities with the patients he or she knows so well that the doctor can diagnose their diseases without talking to them. However, the very need of a special situation and an elaborate explanation underscores the (partial) semantical abnormality of (60).

The inclusion of an element of semantic information in a script is considered justified if there exists a sentence such that it contradicts this element of the script and is deviant for this reason alone. Conversely, if a semantically deviant sentence involving a script does not contradict any element of it, the semantic information contained in the script is not complete and should be supplemented with the element in question.

As was mentioned in the Script-Based Lexicon section, the concept of script has been widely used recently in a variety of language-related fields. One important difference between its use there and here is that, outside of the script-based semantic theory, no systematic effort has been made to justify the format or content of the postulated scripts. Scripts are postulated "to do a job," and if the job seems to be done, if "the system works," the scripts are considered to be the right ones. Not only does that mean that another "job," even of a similar kind, may be impossible to do with the help of the conceptual equipment, scripts, rules, etc., developed for the previous "job" because, of course, such an approach is ad hoc on principle, but even more crucially, one can never be certain that the job is indeed done or, more precisely, that the job which is done is the job one wanted done.

On the surface of it, when the system is taught to behave like a restaurant patron and the appropriate scripts have been introduced into it (see, for instance, Schank, 1975a), it seems to be easy to check whether it does behave as one or not. In fact, however, unless the degree to which the system understands the situation is carefully controlled, it may successfully simulate human linguistic performance in a limited number of situations by generating the right sentences without really understanding them, and the researcher or, more likely, the users of the system can be fooled. As a result, the system will be unable to handle an ever so slightly unusual situation which a restaurant patron may also find him or herself in.

One of the most dramatic examples of a clever ad hoc system was provided by Weizenbaum (1966). His "Eliza" simulated very successfully a dialogue between a patient and a psychoanalyst of a particular persuasion. Eliza, the system, was the shrink, and the human operator was the patient. The patient could type in any kind of statement, e.g., (61i), and Eliza was programmed to respond appropriately, e.g., (61ii):

(61)   (i)   I miss my mother so . . .
        (ii)   Tell me more about your family.

However, in processing (61i), Eliza did not, nor tried to, achieve any degree of understanding. In fact, (61ii) was one of a few alternative responses triggered by the word *mother*. Eliza cleverly created an illusion of a reasonably intelligent dialogue but was not actually engaged in one—as a result, it could be easily tricked. When a few years ago, playing with Eliza, as many computer users have enjoyed doing for almost 2 decades, I typed in (62i), knowing, of course, how Eliza would process it, Eliza promptly generated the same response of (61ii).

(62)   I don't miss my mother and I hate talking about my family.

Naturally, Eliza could not understand the inappropriateness of her response. In most cases, however, with a few clever hedging, stalling and repeating devices, it performed very well—in other words, "did the job." When almost a decade later, the psychoanalysts started talking about Eliza and its therapeutic value, Weizenbaum panicked and tried to explain, out of intellectual honesty, that the system was not based on understanding. As a result, he found himself in a peculiar position in which he attacked his own system and others defended it against him (see Weizenbaum, 1977). That was a clear case when many people, including experts in the field in which Eliza pretended to perform, could not distinguish between her "doing the job" and not "doing the job."

Controlling the degree of understanding of a computer system using scripts is, in fact, hardly distinguishable from the problem of script justification as it has been dealt with here. If, for the smooth functioning of the system, it should approximate the degree of understanding exhibited by the native speaker, the scripts should better approximate the cognitive structures internalized by the native speaker. The serious problem that arises in this connection is that of the feasibility of the approach.

The problem of feasibility can be shown to have at least two distinct facets: the resolution problem, i.e., the possibility to distinguish scripts from non-scripts, and the finiteness problem, i.e., whether it is reasonable at all to think of a semantic theory and its lexicon as associated with a finite but more or less complete and consistent body of scripts. The former problem has been largely taken care of in our previous discussion of script justification. We conclude this section and the chapter with a brief discussion of the finiteness problem.

It should be noted that linguistics in general has not so far been overspoilt with concern for either of the two facets or for that matter, with concern for feasibility of any form. I know of no systematic attempts on the part of linguists to justify the proposed conceptual apparata, either in their entirety or in terms of their undefined primitives, otherwise than comparing them to other, equally unjustified, concepts of apparata. The general tendency in linguistics recently has been to postulate a certain conceptual apparatus and to demonstrate that it helps solve a certain problem. This has been backed with claims (see Chomsky, 1965) that no rigorous procedure can be proposed for what we might call "linguistic heuristics."

As far as scripts are concerned, however, a certain negative assumption has prevailed for many years, hindering considerably the development of linguistic theory in this direction, namely that it is impossible to structure and use in linguistics our entire knowledge of the world, and therefore, that no script-based theory is possible (cf. the first section). The first half of this assumption may well be true; the second part, however, is, one would hope, false and, in any case, not entailed by the first. It is obvious that our entire civilization is a large number of scripts, that the more scripts one has internalized the deeper one's comprehension, which could be amply illustrated by jokes, literary allusions, and other texts inaccessible to the non-initiated. It is equally clear that to try and formulate a theory incorporating all the existing scripts would not perhaps be practical. However, this is not at all necessary for the construction of a successful script-based semantic theory. A theory can be feasible without meeting this unreasonable demand of universality which cannot be met by any recognized theory or technique in linguistics.

Three aspects of feasibility can be briefly outlined with regard to the proposed semantic theory.

First, as in the case of almost all of the current theories and approaches, a number of scripts can be simply postulated and demonstrated to provide a solution for a linguistic problem which cannot be solved (at all or at least as easily) without them. One example of such a problem is the treatment of (19–21) or, for that matter, (40). Another example of a problem to which scripts must be applied is the problem of the theoretical ambiguity of a sentence in isolation and its disambiguation in discourse (see Goals of Semantic Theory and Combinatorial Rules sections).

Secondly, it is quite revealing to study a restricted sublanguage of a natural language in its entirety, together with the world associated with this sublanguage, in the framework of script-oriented semantics. Both the inventory of scripts is more limited in a sublanguage and the problem of Emeneau's patterning of reality seems to be much more manageable in the limited world served by the sublanguage, e.g., football reports, weather forecasts or texts in a very limited field of science or technology (see Emeneau, 1950; for a detailed discussion of sublanguages see Raskin, 1971). In a sublanguage, it is possible to study all the scripts in their hierarchy—from the most elementary, "commonsensical" ones to the most sophisticated and complex scripts.

Thirdly, and more interestingly, a heuristic procedure of script discovery can be outlined in terms of comparing the semantic interpretation of a sentence obtainable on the basis of an "ordinary" lexicon and the semantic/pragmatic meaning actually perceived by the speaker—the way it was outlined with regard to (40). The discrepancy between the two interpretations is to be filled with an appropriate script or set of scripts which is discovered in this way.

ACKNOWLEDGMENT

The paper is based on a chapter from Raskin (1984—copyright 1985 by D. Reidel Publishing Co., Dordrecht, Holland), which was slightly abridged, revised, and updated for this volume. It is printed here with the kind permission of the publisher.

REFERENCES

Alston, W. P. (1964). *Philosophy of language*. Englewood Cliffs, NJ: Prentice-Hall.

Bar-Hillel, Y. (1954). Indexical expressions. *Mind, 63*, 359–379.

Bar-Hillel, Y. (1960). A demonstration of the non-feasibility of fully automatic high quality translation. In F. L. Alt (Ed.), *Advances in computers. Vol. 1. The present status of automatic translation of languages* (Appendix III, pp. 158–163). New York: Academic Press. Reprinted in his *Language and Information*, Reading, MA - Jerusalem: Addison-Wesley - Jerusalem Academic Press, 1964, pp. 174–79.

Bar-Hillel, Y. (1967). Dictionaries and meaning rules. *Foundations of Language, 3*, pp. 409–414. Reprinted in his *Aspects of Language*, Jerusalem: Magnes, 1970, pp. 347–353.

Bar-Hillel, Y., & Raskin, V. (1975). Is this semantic theory? *Semiotica, 14*, 81–91.

Bartlett, C. (1932). *Remembering*. Cambridge: Cambridge University Press.

Bateson, G. (1972). *Steps to an ecology of mind*. New York: Ballantine.

Benveniste, E. (1962). Les niveaux de l'analyse linguistique. In *Proceedings of the 9th International Congress of Linguists*, Cambridge, MA: no pub., pp. 491–98. Reprinted in his *Problèmes de linguistique générale*, 1966, pp. 119–131. Paris: Gallimard.

Bloomfield, L. (1933). *Language*. New York: Holt.

Bréal, M. (1897). *Essai de sémantique*. Paris: Hachette.

Buck, C. D. (1949). *A dictionary of selected synonyms in the principal Indo-European languages: A contribution to the history of ideas*. Chicago: University of Chicago Press.

Carnap, R. (1955). Meaning and synonymy in natural language. *Philosophical Studies, 6*, 33–47.

Carnap, R. (1956). *Meaning and necessity*. Chicago: University of Chicago Press.

Chafe, W. L. (1977). Creativity in verbalization and its implications for the nature of stored knowledge. In R. O. Freedle (Ed.), *Discourse production and comprehension* (pp. 41–56). Norwood, NJ: Ablex.

Charniak, E. (1972). Towards a model of children's story comprehension, AI TR-266, M.I.T.

Charniak, E. (1975). Organization and inference in a frame-like system of common knowledge. In R. C. Schank & B. L. Nash–Weber (Eds.), *Theoretical issues in natural language processing* (pp. 42–51). Cambridge, MA: Bolt, Beranek & Newman.

Chomsky, N. (1965). *Aspects of the theory of syntax*. Cambridge, MA: M.I.T. Press.

Chomsky, N. (1971). Deep structure, surface structure, and semantic interpretation. In D. D. Steinberg & L. A. Jakobovits (Eds.), *Semantics* (pp. 183–216). Cambridge: Cambridge University Press.

Chomsky, N. (1972). *Studies on semantics in generative grammar*. The Hague - Paris: Mouton.

Chomsky, N. (1975). *Reflections on language*. New York: Pantheon.

Chomsky, N. (1977). *Essays on form and interpretation*. New York: North-Holland.

Cole, P., & Morgan, J. L. (Eds.). (1975). *Syntax and semantics. Vol. 3. Speech acts*. New York: Academic Press.

Cooper, D. E. (1974). *Presupposition*. The Hague - Paris: Mouton.

Darmesteter, A. (1887). *La vie des mots étudiée dans leur significations*. Paris: Delagrave.

Davidson, D., & Harman, G. (Eds.). (1972). *Semantics of natural language*. Dordrecht - Boston: Reidel.

Emeneau, M. B. (1950). Language and non-linguistic patterns. *Language, 26(2)*, 199–209.

Fillmore, C. J. (1968). The case for case. In E. Bach & T. A. Harms (Eds.), *Universals in linguistic theory* (pp. 1–88). New York: Holt, Rinehart, & Winston.

Firth, J. R. (1951). Modes of meaning. *Essays and studies of the English association*, New Series, 4, pp. 118–49. Reprinted in his *Papers in Linguistics 1934–51*, New York - London: Oxford University Press, 1957, pp. 190–215.

Fodor, J. D. (1977). *Semantics: Theories of meaning in generative grammar*. Massox, Sussex: Harvester.

Fodor, J. A., & Katz, J. J. (Eds.). (1964). *The structure of language: Readings in the philosophy of language*. Englewood Cliffs, NJ: Prentice-Hall.

Freedle, R. O. (Ed.). (1977). *Discourse production and comprehension*. Norwood, NJ: Ablex.

Freedle, R. O. (Ed.). (1979). *New directions in discourse processing*. Norwood, NJ: Ablex.

Frege, G. (1892). Uber Sinn und Bedeutung. *Zeitschrift für Philosophie und philosophische Kritik, 100*, 25–50. English translation: P. T. Geach and M. Black (Eds.), *Translations from the Philosophical Writings of Gottlob Frege*, 1966, 2nd ed. reprinted, pp. 56–78. Oxford: Blackwell.

Fries, C. C. (1954). Meaning and linguistic analysis. *Language, 30*, 1, 57–68.

Gardiner, H. (1932). *The theory of speech and language*. Oxford: Clarendon.

Goffman, E. (1974). *Frame analysis*. New York: Harper & Row.

Gordon, D., & Lakoff, G. (1975). Conversational postulates. In P. Cole & J. L. Morgan (Eds.), *Syntax and semantics. Vol. 3. Speech acts* (pp. 83–106). New York: Academic Press.

Grice, H. P. (1957). Meaning. *Philosophical Review, LXVI*, 377–88.

Grice, H. P. (1975). Logic and conversation. In P. Cole & J. L. Morgan (Eds.), *Syntax and Semantics, Vol. 3, Speech acts* (pp. 41–58). New York: Academic Press.

Harris, Z. (1954). Distributional structure. *Word, 10* (2–3), 146–62.

Hill, A. A. (1958). *Introduction to linguistic structures: From sound to sentence in English*. New York: Harcourt, Brace.

Hughes, G. E., & Cresswell, M. J. (1968). *An introduction to modal logic*. London: Methuen.

Jackendoff, R. (1981). On Katz's autonomous semantics. *Language, 57*(2), 425–435.

Katz, J. J. (1964). Semi-sentences. In J. A. Fodor & J. J. Katz (Eds.), (pp. 400–416).

Katz, J. J. (1967). Recent issues in semantic theory. *Foundations of Language, 3*, 124–94.

Katz, J. J. (1970). Interpretive semantics *vs.* generative semantics. *Foundations of Language, 6*, 220–259.

Katz, J. J. (1971). Generative semantics is interpretive semantics. *Linguistic Inquiry, 2*, 313–331.

Katz, J. J. (1972). *Semantic theory*. New York: Harper & Row.

Katz, J. J. (1980). Chomsky on meaning. *Language, 56*(1), 11–41.

Katz, J. J., & Fodor, J. A. (1963). The structure of a semantic theory. *Language, 39*(1), 170–210. Reprinted in: Fodor & Katz, 1964, pp. 479–518.

Katz, J. J., & Postal, P. M. (1964). *An integrated theory of linguistic descriptions*. Cambridge, MA: MIT Press.

Keenan, E. L. (1971). Two kinds of presupposition in natural language. In C. J. Fillmore & D. T. Langendoen (Eds.), *Studies in linguistic semantics* (pp. 45–54). New York: Holt, Rinehart, & Winston.

Kempson, R. M. (1977). *Semantic theory*. Cambridge: Cambridge University Press.

Kiparsky, P., & Kiparsky, C. (1971). Fact. In D. D. Steinberg & L. A. Jakobovits (Eds.), (pp. 345–369).

Kripke, S. (1972). Naming and necessity. In D. Davidson & G. Harman (pp. 253–355).

Lakoff, G. (1971a). On generative semantics. In D. D. Steinberg & L. A. Jakobovits (pp. 232–296).

Lakoff, G. (1971b). Presupposition and relative well-formedness. In D. D. Steinberg & L. A. Jakobovits (pp. 329–340).

Lewis, D. (1973). *Counterfactuals*. Oxford: Blackwell.

Lyons, J. (1977). *Semantics, 1 and 2*. Cambridge: Cambridge University Press.

McCawley, J. D. (1976). Some ideas not to live by. *Die Neuren Sprachen, 75*, 151–165.

Maclay, H. (1971). Overview. In D. D. Steinberg & L. A. Jakobovits (pp. 157–182).

Mel'čuk, I. A. (1974). *Opyt teorii lingvisticeskix modelej "Smyls—Tekst"/An Essay on a Theory of Linguistic Models "Sense-Test"*. Moscow: Nauka.

Mel'čuk, I. A. (1979). *Studies in dependency syntax*. Ann Arbor, MI: Karoma.

Minsky, M. (1975). A framework for representing knowledge. In P. H. Winston (Ed.), *The psychology of computer vision* (pp. 211–277). New York: McGraw Hill.

Morgan, J. L. (1977). Conversational postulates revisited. *Language, 53,* 277–284.

Nida, E. (1979). *Languages are for communicating.* Plenary address to the American Association of Applied Linguists, Los Angeles.

Ogden, C. K., & Richards, I. A. (1923). *Meaning of meaning.* London: Kegan Paul, Trench, Trubner.

Paul, H. (1886). *Prinzipien der Sprachgeschichte,* Halle a. S.: Niemeyer.

Popper, K. R. (1972). *Objective knowledge: An evolutionary approach.* Oxford: Clarendon.

Quine, W. V. O. (1960). *Word and object.* Cambridge, MA: MIT Press.

Raskin, V. (1968). O semantičeskoj rekursii /On semantic recursion/. In V. A. Zvegincev (Ed.), *Semantičeskie i fonologičeskie problemy prikladnoj lingvistiki* (pp. 268–283). Moscow: Moscow University Press.

Raskin, V. (1971). *K teorii jazykovyx podsistem* /Towards a Theory of Linguistic Subsystems/. Moscow: Moscow University Press.

Raskin, V. (1972). Osnovnye položenija poroždajuščej semantiki /Basic ideas of generative semantics/. *Naučno-Texničeskaja Informaciia* (Series 2), *10,* 25–31.

Raskin, V. (1975). *A concise history of linguistic semantics* (1st ed.). Jerusalem - Tel-Aviv: Hebrew University - Tel-Aviv University.

Raskin, V. (1976). Generation and performance. *Linguistics, 181,* 45–61.

Raskin, V. (1977). Literal meaning and speech acts. *Theoretical Linguistics, 4*(3), 209–225.

Raskin, V. (1978a). Presuppositional analysis of Russian, 1: Six essays on aspects of presupposition. In V. Raskin & D. Segal (Eds.), *Slavica Hierosolymitana* (Vol. 2, pp. 51–92). Jerusalem: Magnes.

Raskin, V. (1978b). Problems of justification in semantic theory. In W. U. Dressler & W. Meid (Eds.), *Proceedings of the 12th International Congress of Linguists* (pp. 224–226). Innsbruck: Institut für Sprachwissenschaft der Universität Innsbruck.

Raskin, V. (1979a). Is there anything non-circumstantial? In A. Margalit (Ed.), *Meaning and use* (pp. 116–122). Dordrecht - Boston: Reidel.

Raskin, V. (1979b). Literal meanings in speech acts. *Journal of Pragmatics, III*(5), 489–495.

Raskin, V. (1979c). Recent trends in Soviet semantics. *Slavic and East European Journal, 23*(1), 114–124.

Raskin, V. (1979d). Semantic mechanisms of humor. In C. Chiarello et al. (Eds.), *Proceedings of the Fifth Annual Meeting of the Berkeley Linguistics Society* (pp. 325–335). Berkeley, CA: University of California.

Raskin, V. (1979e). Theory and practice of justification in linguistics. In P. R. Clyne (Eds.), *The elements: A parasession on linguistic units and levels* (pp. 152–162). Chicago: Chicago Linguistic Society.

Raskin, V. (1980). *A concise history of linguistic semantics,* (2nd ed.). West Lafayette, IN: Purdue University.

Raskin, V. (1981). Script-based lexicon. *Quaderni di Semantica, II*(1), 25–34.

Raskin, V. (1984). *Semantic mechanisms of humor.* Dordrecht - Boston - Lancaster: D. Reidel.

Schank, R. C., & Colby, K. M. (Eds.). (1973). *Computer models of thought and language.* San Francisco: Freeman.

Schank, R. C. (1975a). *Conceptual information processing.* Amsterdam: North-Holland.

Schank, R. C. (1975b). Using knowledge to understand. In R. Schank & B. L. Nash–Webber (Eds.), *Theoretical issues in natural language processing* (pp. 131–135). No place: Bolt, Beranek, and Newman.

Schank, R. C., & Abelson, R. (1977). *Scripts, plans, goals, and understanding.* New York: Wiley.

Searle, J. R. (1969). *Speech acts.* Cambridge: Cambridge University Press.

Searle, J. R. (1975). Indirect speech acts. In P. Cole & J. L. Morgan (pp. 59–82).

Sørensen, H. S. (1970). Meaning and reference. In A. J. Greimas et al. (Eds.), *Sign, language, culture. Proceedings of the Congress on Semiotics, Kazimierz, Poland* (pp. 67–80). The Hague: Mouton.

Staal, J. F. (1967). Some semantic relations between sentoids. *Foundations of Language, 3*, 66–88.

Steinberg, D. D., & Jakobovits, L.A. (Eds.). (1971). *Semantics*. Cambridge: Cambridge University Press.

Stern, G. (1931). *Meaning and change of meaning*. Göteborg: Göteborgs Högskolas Arsskrift.

Strawson, P. F. (1950). On referring. *Mind, 59*, 320–344.

Tannen, D. (1979). What's in a frame? In R. O. Freedle (pp. 137–181).

Ullmann, S. (1951). *The principles of semantics*. Glasgow: Blackwell.

van Dijk, T. A. (1977). *Text and context*. London - New York: Longman.

Weinreich, U. (1966). Explorations in semantic theory. In T. A. Sebeok (Ed.), *Current trends in linguistics* (Vol. 3, pp. 395–477). The Hague: Mouton.

Weizenbaum, J. (1966). Eliza: A computer program for the study of natural language communication between man and machine. *Communications of the association for computing machinery, 9*, 36–45.

Weizenbaum, J. (1977). *Computer problem and human reason: From judgment to calculation*. San Francisco: Freeman.

Wittgenstein, L. (1953). *Philosophical investigations*. Oxford: Blackwell.

Ziff, P. (1964). On understanding 'understanding utterances.' In J. A. Fodor & J. J. Katz, (pp. 390–99).

Zvegincev, V. A. (1960). Ob osnovnoj i predel'noj edinice semasiologičeskogo urovnja jazyka. / On the basic and ultimate unit of the semantic level of language/. In *Omagiu Lui, Al. Graur, in prilejul implinirii a 60 de ani, Bucharest: no pub.*

Zvegincev, V. A. (1964). Očerk istorii jazykoznanija do XIX veka. /An essay on the history of linguistics before the 19th century/. In V. A. Zvegincev (Ed.), *Istorija jazykoznanija XIX-XX vekov v očerkax i izvlečenijax* (7–27). Moscow: Prosveščenie.

Zvegincev, V. A. (1968). *Teoretičeskaja i prikladnaja lingvistika*. /Theoretical and Applied Linguistics/. Moscow: Prosveščenie.

3 Attribution Schemes and Causal Inference in Natural Conversations

Brant R. Burleson
Purdue University

The dominant paradigm informing most current research on naturally occurring conversations views conversation as a complex form of rule-governed behavior (e.g., Coulthard, 1977; Jacobs & Jackson, 1982; Levinson, 1983). Hence, a considerable amount of research has been devoted to identifying and formulating those general rules through which two or more people take turns (e.g., Duncan, 1972; Sacks, Schegloff, & Jefferson, 1974), open and close conversational episodes (Schegloff, 1972; Schegloff & Sacks, 1973), introduce, maintain, and change topics during the course of a conversation (Keenan & Schleffelin, 1976; Sigman, 1983), make their conversational contributions coherent (e.g., Ellis, 1983; Goldberg, 1983), and so on. The goal of identifying the general rules through which conversations are constituted and regulated is perfectly legitimate, and studies pursuing this goal have considerably enhanced our understanding of conversational structures and processes. However, identifying the general rules governing conversational behavior is by no means the only legitimate purpose motivating the detailed analysis of conversational interaction. Conversation is a highly significant form of human *action*. All human action reflects the operation of underlying cognitive structures and processes through which aspects of the world are interpreted and given meaning; thus, beyond providing insight into the rules governing conversational behavior, the analysis of naturally occurring conversations can be an important source of information for studies of human cognitive processes. This chapter maintains that the analysis of natural conversation can illuminate and document the operation of basic social inference processes, especially those processes involved in explaining and assigning causes to the actions of other people. More specifically, the position developed in the following pages suggests that certain natural conversations constitute an important source of data for *attribution theory*.

Attribution theory concerns "the processes by which an individual interprets events as being caused by a particular part of a relatively stable environment," and especially focuses on "how a typical observer infers a person's motivations from that person's actions" (Kelley, 1967, p. 193). The process of inferring the causes of another's behaviors has generally been viewed as a covert, psychological process occurring in the minds of individual perceivers. Thus, both the operation of attributional processes and the content of specific attributions typically have been conceived as internal psychological entities that cannot be directly observed. Consequently, researchers have frequently assumed that the existence and characteristic operation of attributional processes must be inferred from observable behavior. Although it is certainly the case that attributional processes occur covertly within the minds of individuals, it is also the case that people frequently *talk* to one another about why someone acted in some way; indeed, exploring why someone behaved as he or she did is probably one of the most ubiquitous conversational topics. When people talk about why someone behaved as he or she did, attributional processes that are typically covert and private become overt and publicly accessible. Moreover, although the attributions made about others are frequently the product of an individual consciousness, when two or more people collectively interpret the action of another through talk, the resulting attribution assumes the character of a collaboratively constructed social product. Thus, the analysis of conversations in which people talk to one another about why others behave as they do can (a) reveal and make available for detailed inspection cognitive processes that are usually considered to be beyond the purview of direct observation, and (b) provide insight into how the qualities, dispositions, and motives used to characterize others get socially constructed and validated.

Although studies of "motive-seeking" conversations (i.e., conversations in which people talk about why some person acted as he or she did) may aid us in learning more about the nature of attributional processes, it is also possible that knowledge of attributional processes can help shed light on how certain conversations are organized and on how they sequentially unfold. Most discourse analysts have sought to explain the coherence and sequential organization of conversation in terms of highly general or formal structures (see Craig & Tracy, 1983). Such work is important and should be encouraged. However, when people talk, they always talk *about* something. One can speculate that talk within a given topical domain may engage the cognitive schemes utilized to interpret phenomena in that domain, and these engaged schemes may, in turn, have important consequences for how the conversation gets structured. Thus, it is possible that knowledge of the general attributional processes through which the behaviors of others are interpreted may provide a basis for anticipating how conversations about others' actions are structured.

To summarize, the focused analysis of "motive-seeking" conversations may contribute to our understanding of attributional processes, whereas knowledge of attributional processes may help us understand how such conversations are structured and organized. These possibilities are pursued in detail through the extended analysis of a single motive-seeking conversation. Prior to this analysis, some basic principles of attribution theory are reviewed. Although much of the analysis developed in this chapter is speculative and exploratory, a concluding section suggests how several of the notions presented here might be subjected to more rigorous testing.

ATTRIBUTION THEORY: AN OVERVIEW

As just noted, attribution theory is chiefly concerned with how ordinary social actors make inferences about the causes of others' behaviors (for general introductions to the literature on attribution theory, see Schneider, Hastorf, & Ellsworth, 1979; Seibold & Spitzberg, 1981; Shaver, 1975; Sillars, 1982; Wegner & Vallacher, 1977). Perhaps the dominant research tradition in contemporary social psychology, the roots of attribution theory can be traced to the phenomenological social theory of Alfred Schutz (1932/1967) and the early empirical work of Fritz Heider (1958).

Foundations of Attribution Theory

A primary concern of Schutz (1932/1967) was with how perceivers come to understand the causes or motives for another's actions. According to Schutz, there are two basic routes a perceiver can follow in attempting to determine the causes of another's acts: "I can begin with the finished act, and then determine the type of action that produced it, and finally settle on the type of person who must have acted in this way. Or I can reverse the process, and knowing the personal ideal type, deduce the corresponding act" (p. 188). In the former case, where the nature of the act has been satisfactorily identified but the motive or cause for the act is in question, perceivers start with the act and, from knowledge of its nature, work back to the construction of the type of person capable of behaving in that way. In other words, the inferential process moves from an understanding of the type of act observed to a determination of the type of person whose qualities would be realized in the act. The notion that perceivers determine the causes of another's behavior by inferentially moving "from acts to dispositions" underlies virtually all contemporary attribution research. Extending and formalizing the work of Schutz and other writers in the phenomenological tradition, Heider (1958) argued that persons attain a causal understanding of the social world by referring transient actions to relatively stable underlying dispositional properties. The basic framework of Heider's theory is derived from a "naive analysis of action" or explication of how ordinary social actors routinely conceptualize aspects of other's behaviors. Central to Heider's analysis is the assumption that people not only view others' behaviors as caused, but as caused by some combination of personal and environmental forces. Heider distinguishes between two components of personal force, power and motivation. Power, or ability, refers to judgments about whether an observed actor possesses the requisite talents, skills, or resources needed to produce some effect. The other aspect of personal force, motivation or trying, is composed of two distinct components, intention and exertion. Intention pertains to *what* an actor is attempting to do. Exertion refers to the amount of effort expended by an actor in attempting to realize a particular end. Heider argues that the personal force of an actor is a multiplicative relationship between power and motivation because if an actor either possesses no ability or does not try, no effect (i.e., act) can be produced as a result of personal force.

Environmental force refers to aspects of the situation or context that influence the achievement of some end. In some cases, environmental force can be a sufficient cause for some effect. In other cases, environmental forces can play either a facilitative or inhibitory role; that is, environmental forces can work either in conjunction with or against personal forces in the achievement of some end. Because environmental forces may act as a sufficient, necessary, or inhibitory cause or a particular effect, Heider argues that an additive relationship exists between environmental force and personal force with respect to the production of some effect. Significantly, Heider notes that environmental forces can also influence judgments of both ability and effort because the difficulty of a task (i.e., environmental resistance) helps determine the levels of ability and effort believed necessary for the successful completion of a task.

Because environmental forces can be a sufficient cause for some act and further may impact on judgments of ability and effort, Heider suggests that a person's search for the causes of an action proceeds in a *sequential* fashion, beginning with a considerational of environmental forces (see Seibold & Spitzberg, 1981, p. 95; Shaver, 1975, p. 44). That is, in causally interpreting the behavior of another, a person asks: Was the behavior a function of a stable feature of the environment (environmental causality)? Was it a function of chance factors such as transient characteristics of either the environment or actor (impersonal causality)? Or was it an intentional act reflecting relatively stable dispositions of the actor (personal causality)? Thus, at each step in this process, the perceiver assesses the extent to which the causes underlying the other's behavior are a function of environmental forces, personal forces, or some combination thereof.

Current Models of the Attribution Process

In the years since the publication of Heider's *Psychology of Interpersonal Relations* (1958) several elaborations and refinements of attribution theory have been proposed. Particularly worthy of note are three detailed models of the attribution process: Jones and Davis' (1965) correspondent inference model, Kelley's (1967) covariation model, and Kelley's (1972) causal schemata model.

The Correspondent Inference Model.   Jones and Davis' (1965) correspondent inference model represents an effort to describe the specific conditions under which an observer of an act (or its effects) will invoke a personal dispositional quality of the actor to explain the act. These writers argue that many acts produced by people are socially desirable in the sense that they are consistent with social expectations regarding how people should behave. Action consistent with social expectations provides little information about the personal qualities of the acting subjects because perceivers tend to assume that such actions are caused by these expectations (environmental forces). On the other hand, actions that diverge from the socially expected or desirable provide a rich source of information about the personal qualities of the actor. It is under such conditions that a dispositional attribution is likely to occur. Jones and Davis suggest that the more an act diverges from normative expectations, the more likely the act will be attributed to dispositional qualities of the actor. These writers further argue that perceivers' confidence in the veracity of their dispositional attributions increases as a function of the unexpectedness or undesirability of the act. Thus, the more divergent the observed act, the more the perceiver is likely to believe that the act *corresponds* with an inferred dispositional attribute of the actor. It is important to note that the correspondent inference model is applicable only in instances where perceivers assume that the effects of an act were intended by the actor.

The Covariation Model.   The correspondent inference model focuses on attributions based on a single act by an actor. Quite frequently, however, perceivers have available information about multiple acts and multiple actors. In his covariation model, Kelley (1967) describes the types of information perceivers employ in deciding whether an act was caused by dispositional qualities of the actor or aspects of the environment.

Kelley notes that behavior varies as a function of persons (or actors), entities (the target toward which behavior is directed), and context (the time and setting of the behavior). Each of these factors provides information that influence perceivers' attribution processes. *Consistency* information refers to the generality of the actor's behavior across contexts. *Distinctiveness* information pertains to the generality of the actor's behavior across entities. *Consensus* information refers to the generality of other people's behavior toward the entity in the context. The type of attribution invoked to explain another's behavior (internal or external) will vary, according to Kelley, as a function of the consistency, distinctiveness, and consensual status of the behavior. For example, if a perceiver concludes that an actor's behavior exhibits high consistency, low distinctiveness, and low consensus (i.e., the actor behaves in a way that others do not, and further behaves in this way across contexts toward many different entities), then a stable personal disposition of the actor will most likely be invoked as the causal force for the act. If most people, including the actor of interest, consistently behave in a specific way with respect to a particular entity (i.e., high consistency, high distinctiveness, and high consensus), the entity will be imbued with causal force. Finally, if the observed behavior is an infrequent one for the actor (low consistency), others (low consensus), and occurs only with respect to a specific entity (high distinctiveness) in a specific context, a perceiver will most likely conclude that something peculiar to the context caused the act. In summary, Kelley's covariation model provides a framework for anticipating whether causal attributions will be made to the actor or the environment and, if to the environment, whether to the entity or context.

The Causal Schemata Model. Kelley's causal schemata model represents an effort to account for attributions made with respect to single observations of behavior. Kelley assumes that perceivers have a general understanding of the number and nature of causes needed to produce a particular effect. Some effects can result from any one of a number of causes; this situation is interpreted within what Kelley terms a *multiple sufficient cause schema.* Kelley holds that when one or more sufficient causes for the observed behavior is known to be present, the perceiver will discount the efficacy of other potential causes. Kelley terms this rule the *discounting principle.* In particular, Kelley suggests that perceivers are likely to discount the influences of potential internal causes for an action (i.e., personal dispositions) when a sufficient external (environmental) cause is known to be present; the parallel here with the correspondent inference model should be clear.

Kelley holds that perceivers know that some effects can be produced only through the conjunction of multiple causes; this inference pattern is appropriately termed the *multiple necessary cause schema.* For example, attaining a high score on a difficult test is usually assumed to require both a certain amount of native ability and the expenditure of effort. In the absence of either of these causes, the effect (scoring highly) could not be attained. Thus, for events apprehended within the purview of the multiple necessary cause schema, the failure to observe a given effect signals the absence of at least one cause. Significantly, however, the application of this schema alone does not enable the perceiver to determine which cause was absent.

In summary, Kelley's causal schemata model suggests that perceivers first determine which causal scheme applies to an observed event (e.g., multiple necessary causes, multiple sufficient causes, and so on), and then attempt to ascertain which specific cause (or set of causes) is responsible for the event. Obviously, such causes may take the form of either personal dispositions or environmental forces.

Success and Failure Attributions.   In addition to proposing general models of the attribution process, social psychologists have studied a number of specific attributional phenomena. One topic receiving considerable attention in recent years concerns "achievement" or success and failure attributions (Weiner, 1974; Weiner, Frieze, Kukla, Reed, Rest, & Rosenbaum, 1972; Weiner & Kukla, 1970). Weiner and his colleagues (Weiner et al., 1972) note that the environmental forces affecting an achievement outcome can be either stable or variable in nature. For example, the difficulty of a test represents a stable environmental force, whereas chance factors such as conditions under which a test is taken (e.g., level of noise in the testing room) represent a variable environmental force. Similarly, Weiner argues that personal forces can be divided into both stable and variable components. For example, a student's native ability in some academic domain represents a stable personal force whereas the effort expended by the student in studying for a particular exam constitutes a variable personal force.

When combined, the stable/variable distinction and the personal/environmental distinction provide a neat framework for specifying the possible causes of success or failure. That is, a person may be successful on a task because he or she is talented (high ability), worked hard (high effort), had an easy job to do (low task difficulty), or was lucky (chance factors). The specific cause (or set of causes) held by a perceiver to be responsible for a given success–failure outcome depends on the perceiver's knowledge of the actor's past performance (consistency information), the actor's performance on other tasks (distinctiveness information), and how other persons have fared on the observed task (consensus information). For example, consistent success by an actor (high consistency) on tasks where others have met with failure (low consensus) is likely to result in a high ability attribution. On the other hand, if a person accomplishes a task that many others have also accomplished, the success of the actor is likely to be attributed to low task difficulty.

In addition to utilizing consistency, distinctiveness, and consensus information in explaining the causes of others' successes and failures, perceivers also employ certain general attributional tendencies or biases. In particular, perceivers have been found to attribute success to high ability, and failure to high task difficulty (see Frieze & Weiner, 1971). The nature of these biases, then, favors a view of generally competent actors.

In summation, the work of Weiner and his colleagues describes a choice matrix or decisional calculus perceivers employ in explaining the causes of others' successes and failures. Observers are assumed to know that there are only a limited number of factors contributing to success and failure, and are further assumed to employ the information given in a situation in isolating the specific causes leading to a particular achievement outcome. In the absence of such information, observers tend to rely on certain attributional biases that maximize the competence of the observed actor.

CAUSAL INFERENCE IN A NATURAL CONVERSATION

This section analyzes a natural "motive-seeking" conversation. The analysis focuses on (a) how the talk among the conversational participants makes manifest the existence and operation of several attribution schemes, and (b) how some of these attribution schemes serve to sequentially organize the conversation.

The analyzed conversation took place in an office shared by several graduate teaching assistants. The conversation was observed and covertly tape recorded by the author; subsequent to the conversation, the author interviewed the participants and obtained permission to use the recorded conversation for analytic purposes. The following excerpted conversational segments are verbatim transcriptions from the recorded conversation. (A full transcript of the conversation is presented in Appendix A.)

The conversation takes place primarily between two communication graduate teaching assistants, Don and Bob. A third teaching assistant, Shelly, makes two comments during an early phase of the conversation, but does not become involved as a full participant in the interaction. At the time of the conversation, Don and Bob had known each other for 2 years and had shared an office together for slightly over 1 year. Throughout the conversation Don and Bob remain seated at their desks.

Don and Bob both teach freshman-level courses in speech communication and a frequent topic of conversation for them concerns their teaching experiences and problems. In the reported conversation, Don's teaching responsibility is of particular importance. Don teaches a special course for students suffering from speech anxiety or "communication apprehension." In this course, students are permitted to redo any assignments that they happen to fail. Graded on a "pass–fail" basis, students enrolled in this course are required to pass all individual assignments in order to receive a passing grade in the course. On two separate occasions prior to the reported conversation, Don and Bob had discussed a female student who was having difficulty in Don's course. Don opens the conversation by recalling these previous discussions.

Segment 1

U01	Don:	Remember that girl I've been havin' trouble with?
U02	Bob:	Yeah.
U03	Don:	She just took the midterm for the third time and failed it.
U04	Bob:	*Jesus Christ*! (Pause)
U05	Bob:	*Jesus.*
U06	Don:	I have never known a student that could not take a test— *several times*—and not eventually pass it.
U07	Bob:	*Three* times?
U08	Don:	Exactly the same test.
U09	Bob:	The *same* test? The *same* questions?

U10	Don:	(Nods affirmatively.) I just gonna have to insist that she drop the course.
U11	Sherry:	That's, that's beyond me. I mean, that's, that's . . .
U12	Don:	I just can't . . . There's nothing I can do. I'm just gonna have to do whatever's necessary to get her out of the course. She just can't handle it.
U13	Bob:	How can ya . . . Da *da* da da da. *Blah.* How . . . how . . .
U14	Don:	That's my reaction. (Laughs.)
U15	Sherry:	It's beyond . . .— . . . (Pause.)

The aforementioned conversational segment provides an opportunity to examine directly the attribution processes of two persons seeking a causal understanding of another's problematic behavior. In this segment of the conversation, Don and Bob move almost immediately from the identification of problematic act to a consideration of the possible causes of the act. The provocation for such movement is, of course, the recognition and identification of a highly deviant act on the part of Don's student. The act requiring interpretation and explanation is identified by Don in U03 (failing the midterm for the third time), and the highly deviant nature of this act is developed throughout the remainder of this segment. Bob's cursing and intonational patterns in U04–U09, the fragments and nonfluencies in U11–U15, and the specific content of these utterances (e.g., "That's beyond me") all contribute to the characterization of the act as deviant. In particular, Don's explicit statement of U06 ("I have never known a student that could not take a test—*several times*—and not eventually pass it") marks the act as one highly deviant for the type of people known as students.

Don's U03 and U06 are particularly important in that they constitute and specify the nature of the act to be interpreted and explained. That is, the problematic act is not one of simply failing an exam; for an occasional student to fail an exam is not at all an uncommon experience for these teachers. Rather, the problematic act constituted by Don is that of the student failing the same exam three consecutive times. In Schutz's (1932/1967) terminology, a series of polythetic actions (failing three different times) is constituted by Don and Bob as a singular, monothetic act (a triple failure). Thus, it is the act of triple failure that must be interpreted and explained.

Weiner's analysis of success and failure attributions suggests the basic categories the teachers will employ in seeking to interpret and causally explain the student's triple failure. That is, according to Weiner, the teachers should implicitly know that the factors of ability, effort, task difficulty, and luck or chance are relevant to achievement outcomes. Moreover, according to Kelley's causal schemata theory, the teachers should further implicitly know that achieving success on tests is an outcome due to the operation of multiple necessary causes; thus, the teachers should know that failure of an exam is potentially due to any one of several sufficient causes (i.e., low ability, low effort, high task difficulty, or bad luck). Moreover, because failures are events apprehended within the multiple sufficient cause scheme, the discounting principle should be operative. The activation of the discounting principle suggests that the teachers should isolate one sufficient cause as primarily responsible for the student's failure.

Which one of the four potential causes is ultimately held responsible for producing the student's failure is a highly significant matter because each cause implies a different identity (i.e., a different "personal ideal type") for the student, with this inferred identity becoming the basis for Don's future action toward the student. Thus, consistent with Schutz's notion that interpreters begin with the structure of an act and work back to the construction of the type of person capable of producing the act, the central question pursued by Don and Bob through the remainder of the conversation is: "What type of student is capable of flunking the same exam three consecutive times?" Weiner's analysis of achievement attributions suggests that there are four basic answers to this question: (1) a "normal" student facing a tough test (high task difficulty), (2) an "unlucky" student (someone repeatedly malaffected by chance factors), (3) a "lazy" or "irresponsible" student (low effort), and (4) a "stupid" or "slow" student (low ability).

Although Kelley's causal schemata model and Weiner's analysis of achievement attributions suggest possible causes of the student's failure, they do not specify, in the absence of further information, which of these causes will actually be invoked to explain the failure. Jones and Davis' correspondent inference model suggests that highly deviant acts are explained by reference to the personal dispositions of the actor, and there is some evidence that such attributions are considered during this segment of the conversation (e.g., Don's U12: "She just can't handle it"). However, there are problems with this interpretation. As previously noted, Jones and Davis set as a limiting condition of the correspondent inference model the perceiver's belief that the consequences of an act are intended by the actor. Clearly, the teachers do not believe that the student intended to fail the exam. Moreover, Don's assertion in U12 that "she can't handle it," is not an unambiguous personal attribution because, as Heider (1958, pp. 84–90) notes, the concept of "can" contains implicit references to both ability and task difficulty (i.e., one "can" do something only if ability exceeds task difficulty). In addition, when other information is unavailable, perceivers, as previously noted, have a general tendency to attribute failure to high task difficulty. Hence, it is conceivable (at least from Bob's perspective) that high task difficulty may account for the student's failure. Thus, additional information is needed about the student and task before a firm cause for the triple failure is settled on consensually. Such information seeking is exhibited in the following segment.

Segment 2

U16   Bob: I mean, you know, if you were changing the questions and
                   changing the items and making an essay exam and a multiple

		choice another time, something like that—yeah. Did she ever—did she—did anybody ever tell her what the right answers were? So she could study or anything, or—
U17	Don:	Well, I didn't wanta just go over the test and say "here are the right answers," and then have her take it again.
U18	Bob:	Sure, sure. 'Course not. You know. But she could—did she have a copy of the test so she could study the stuff?
U19	Don:	She has—I gave quizzes which, you know, cover the material. So she's got copies of the quizzes which led up to the midterm, and some of the questions on that midterm are just lifted off the quizzes. Just exactly the same as those quizzes.
U20	Bob:	And you did go over those quizzes, right?
U21	Don:	Oh yes, yes I did. And she still missin' those that are exact copies of the ones on quizzes that she's got copies of.

* * * * * * * * * * * * * * * * * * *

U27	Bob:	Everybody else's passed it, I presume.
U28	Don:	Oh, everybody passed it the first time, except her.
U29	Bob:	Was her score noticeably below everybody else's?
U30	Don:	Yeah, yeah.

* * * * * * * * * * * * * * * * * * *

U31	Bob:	Has she been getting any higher on these trials? I mean, is she getting any closer? (Chuckles.)
U32	Don:	Nope. First one she made a 60, second time she took it she made a 50, and the third time she took it she made a 60.
U33	Bob:	What do you have for passing, 70?
U34	Don:	Seventy.
U35	Bob:	Jesus, man.

It should be recalled that, according to Heider, in the absence of clear-cut information about the causes underlying another's act, perceivers will often begin interpreting the act by considering environmental force explanations for others' behavior. The three conversational excerpts just reported appear to represent efforts by the teachers to investigate the possibility that environmental forces (i.e., task difficulty or luck) may have been responsible for the student's triple failure.

In the first excerpt (U16–U21), Bob explores the possibility that test difficulty may have been high for the student because the test was composed of material that the student did not expect to have to know: U16: "Did anybody ever tell her what the right answers were? So she could study or anything?"; U20: "And you did go over those quizzes, right?" If the test was composed of unfamiliar material, then the test might be held as responsible for the student's failure. This potential explanation is rendered untenable, however, because Don's answers to Bob's questions make it clear that he adequately prepared the student for the exam: U19: "I gave quizzes which, you know, cover the material"; U21: "And she still missin' those that are exact copies of the ones on quizzes that she's got copies of." Thus, the notion that the test was difficult because it was composed of unfamiliar material cannot be maintained.

However, even if the midterm exam was based on material covered by Don in quizzes, it is possible that the exam itself might be intrinsically difficult. In the second excerpt (U27–U30) Bob explores this possible explanation by seeking information about how others performed on the exam: U27: "Everybody else's passed it, I presume"; U29: "Was her score noticeably below everybody else's?" In these questions, Bob appears to be seeking what Kelley's covariation model terms *consensus information*. If the student's failure is a high consensus behavior— that is, if many other students have also had real trouble with the midterm exam—then the difficulty of the exam can be invoked to explain the student's behavior rather than the factors of luck or personal attributes. The facts reported by Don in U28 and U30 (that all other students passed the exam the first time and that the failing student's score was noticeably lower than all other scores) establish that failing the exam is a low consensus behavior. Coupled with the knowledge that the test was not composed of unfamiliar material, the low consensus behavior of the student means that the stable environmental force of task difficulty cannot be invoked to explain the student's behavior.

Continuing an exhibition of reliance on covariation principles, the third excerpt (U31–U35) establishes the student's behavior as consistent with respect to the entity (i.e., the test) across contexts. This excerpt is important for it establishes the student's behavior as *highly* consistent; she not only has failed the test three times, she has failed to make any noticeable improvement over the test-taking trials. This high degree of personal consistency over trials is significant because it completely eliminates the remote possibility that the student's behavior is due to contextual or chance factors associated with the individual test-taking situations. Indeed, this excerpt simply makes explicit an understanding taken for granted by Bob and Don from the outset of the conversation: the lightening of contextual (chance) influences may strike once with respect to performance on an exam, but not three times.

The net effect, then, of the three excerpts in Segment 2 is the elimination of environmental forces as possible explanations for the student's behavior. This conclusion appears to have been reached by the interactants through the application of Kelley's covariation model. The stable feature or environmental force, task difficulty, was eliminated through the assessment of consensus information. The variable feature of environmental force, transient contextual or chance influences, was eliminated through the assessment of consistency information. Moreover, the determination that the student's behavior exhibited high consistency and low consensus points directly toward a consideration of personal forces as causes of the behavior. Don and Bob begin to consider personal force explanations for the student's behavior in the following segment.

Segment 3

U37	Bob:	How have her speeches and stuff been?
U38	Don:	Uh, low passing.
U39	Bob:	How'd she do on these quizzes?
U40	Don:	About the same.

* * * * * * * * * * * * * * * * * * *

| U45 | Bob: | I'm just glad I'm not you and I don't have to, uh, to tell her. I mean, cause—cause it seems—you know, she's been in here several times, and it seems like she's *tryin'*. |
| U46 | Don: | Yeah. Well, I'm sure she is. (Pause.) But I just think about— she's a second year freshman (ticking points off on fingers), she's taking a minimum load, she's had, according to what she's said, just as much trouble with all her other classes that she's having with mine. And uh, it just doesn't make sense to me to keep her in this kind of grade-oriented, pressurized institution. She can't handle the work load, the material. I think at, uh, this point the best thing I can do for her is to help her get out of my class. |

Don and Bob know that if the student's behavior cannot be explained on the basis of environmental forces, it must be attributed to the operation of personal forces. According to Weiner, Don and Bob should know that two personal forces, lack of ability or lack of effort, are sufficient to cause failure. Thus, in Segment 3 the teachers begin to evaluate which of these personal forces is to be regarded as the cause for the student's triple failure.

In Segment 2 Don and Bob evaluated consistency and consensus information pertaining to the student's performance. In the first excerpt of Segment 3 (U37–U40), Bob appears to be seeking information about the *distinctiveness* of the student's failure of the midterm exam. Distinctiveness pertains to the similarity of an actor's behavior across entities (e.g., tests, quizzes, speeches). If the student's failure of the midterm exam exhibits low distinctiveness (i.e., if she has also failed many other *types* of assignments), then it would be reasonable to infer that a stable feature of personal force (i.e., low ability) is responsible for failure of the midterm. Thus, Bob's questions in U37 and U39 seem directed at establishing whether the student had the necessary ability to perform in Don's course.

Don's answers to Bob's queries (U38 and U40) suggest that the student's behavior with respect to the midterm exam is at least moderately distinctive:

although she has repeatedly failed the exam, she has at least passed other assignments (speeches and quizzes). In the absence of other information, a highly distinctive behavior usually implies that something about the entity (in this case, the midterm exam) is responsible for causing the observed behavior. However, in the present circumstance, the teachers *do* have access to other information; Bob and Don have already determined that the entity (i.e., difficulty of the midterm) cannot be held responsible for the student's failure because the failure was an extremely low-consensus behavior (all other students passed the exam the first time). The high consistency and low consensus of the student's behavior means that environmental forces (whether stable or variable) cannot be invoked to explain the triple failure of the midterm, and the moderately high distinctiveness of this behavior (she *has* passed other assignments) suggests that the stable aspect of personal force is also not responsible for the failure. This means that the variable personal force of effort is likely to be responsible for the student's failure of the midterm; perhaps she repeatedly failed the midterm because she did not work (*try*) hard enough to pass it.

Kelley's discounting principle suggests that at this point in the conversation Bob and Don should settle on low effort as an explanation for the student's failure; recall that the discounting principle stipulates that when an act is apprehended within the multiple sufficient cause scheme, the act will be explained on the basis of the sufficient cause (or causes) known to be present, and the influence of other potential causes will be discounted. But the teachers do not settle on lack of effort as an explanation for the student's behavior. Indeed, in the second excerpt (U45–U46), expended effort on the part of the student is directly asserted by Bob (U45: " . . . it seems like she's *tryin*"). This attribution of effort is clearly acknowledged by Don in his U46 ("Yeah. Well, I'm sure she is."). Moreover, Don's U46 goes on to state explicitly that the student does not have the necessary ability to pass the test ("She can't handle the work load, the material.").

Why is it that the teachers fail to follow the discounting principle by proceeding to consider a low-ability explanation for the student's behavior when a low-effort explanation seems to have been established in the prior excerpt (U37–U40)? Effort is a *variable* personal force; as such, effort attributions most cogently account for behavior that is inconsistent across situations. However, Bob and Don have previously determined that the student had behaved in a *highly* consistent manner with respect to the exam; she failed it three times and her performance had not improved over the test-taking trials. Thus, it appears that the teachers fail to follow the discounting principle because they implicitly recognize that a variable personal force (low-effort) explanation for the student's behavior conflicts with the previously determined consistency of this behavior. Given a low-consensus behavior, behavioral consistency points to a stable personal force (ability) as a causal mechanism whereas behavioral distinctiveness points to a variable personal force (effort) as a causal mechanism. The student's behavior with respect to the midterm is only *moderately distinct* (she achieved only *low* passing on other assignments) while being *highly consistent*. These facts not only explain why the discounting principle is not followed and low ability surfaces explicitly as an account for the student's failure, they also suggest that the conflict between low effort and low-ability attributions will be resolved in favor of the low-ability explanation. The resolution between these conflicting explanations is achieved in the following segment.

Segment 4

U47	Bob:	. . . Uh, but to blow the same exam *thrice*—is she just— I just *gotta* ask this question—is she just plain *stupid*?
U48	Don:	That's—
U49	(Uninterpretable talk-over.)	
U50	Bob:	I mean, you know, is she an idiot?
U51	Don:	Yeah, I think she's just dumb. That's the only thing I can figure out.
U52	Bob:	Does she study? I mean, do you think—
U53	Don:	—She claims she does, and I'm, I'm sure she does.
U54	Bob:	One would think so. I mean, you know, I can't imagine her just tryin'—thinkin' she could breeze through it, especially after she'd blown it twice. The first time, yeah, you could understand, but you'd figure study the second time and then especially the *third* time. (Pause.) The thing of it is,—this, this just sounds so cruel and elitist—but, you just don't encounter very many dumb people.
U55	Don:	No, not not at a college of this quality. Certainly not. It's a real shame. (Pause.)

In this segment, Don and Bob finally establish a firm explanation for the student's triple failure of the midterm exam—her lack of ability. However, this explanation is not established without some difficulty and hesitation.

In Segment 3, both lack of effort and lack of ability were pointed to as potential explanations for the student's behavior. Lack of effort did not appear to be an entirely plausible explanation because it conflicted with the known consistency of the student's behavior. Moreover, a low-effort explanation is inconsistent with the fact noted by Bob in U45 that "she's been in here several times, and it seems like she's *tryin'*." Thus, Don's assertion in U46 ("she just can't handle it") and Bob's question in U47 ("is she just plain *stupid*?") reflect the only cause still available capable of accounting for the student's behavior—low ability. Don's immediate and firm support in U51 of Bob's low-ability inference ("Yeah. I think she's just dumb") appears to establish solidly low ability as the cause of the student's triple failure.

However, the teachers, and especially Bob, appear quite uncomfortable with the causal attribution of stupidity. The attribution of stupidity is only hesitantly put forth (note Bob's apparent reluctance to posit this explanation in U47, "I just *gotta* ask this question"). Moreover, even though Don strongly confirms the low-ability explanation of U51 ("Yeah, I think she's just dumb"), Bob returns consideration to a low-effort explanation in U52 ("Does she study?"). Such hesitation and reconsideration can be explained by the real infrequency of a pronounced lack of ability in most students encountered by Bob and Don. It appears that in Don and Bob's experience it is much more likely for students to perform poorly because of low effort rather than low ability. This interpretation is directly supported by Bob and Don's exchange in U54–U55: "You just don't encounter very many dumb people." "No, not, not at a college of this quality." Because failure by students is much more frequently due to low effort than to low ability, the low-effort explanation is not to be sacrificed easily. Hence, the low-effort explanation is finally surrendered only when Don explicitly claims effort on the student's part in U53 ("She claims she does, and I'm, I'm sure she does") and when Bob, in U54, reasons that the variable nature of effort cannot be rationally invoked to explain the highly consistent pattern of three failures ("I can't imagine her just tryin'—thinkin' she could breeze through it, especially after she'd blown it twice"). Indeed, Bob's comments in U54 explicitly recognize that the variable personal force of effort can only meaningfully account for behavior that is exceptional with respect to the actor, but cannot account for a behavioral pattern that is consistent with an actor ("The first time, yeah, you could understand that, but you'd figure study the second and then especially the *third* time"). When it deviates from behavioral consensus, personal consistency in behavior is most parsimoniously explained in terms of stable personal forces, and the stable personal force that causes failure is low ability. Thus, with the conclusive elimination of a low-effort explanation in U53–U54, the low-ability explanation is the only remaining alternative capable of accounting for the student's behavior. This segment of the conversation thus ends with Bob and Don reaching the consensual agreement that the student's triple failure was caused by her lack of ability.

Interestingly, although the low-ability explanation had been projected by Don as early as U12, it is not until U54 that low ability is *consensually established* as the cause for the student's failure. Through their interaction, then, Bob and Don have *jointly constructed* a specific identity for the student and, moreover, have *collaboratively validated* the appropriateness of this identity by collectively eliminating other possible explanations for the student's behavior. The resulting personal attribution (that the student is "stupid" or lacks ability) thus is an *intersubjective* attribution, one carrying the force of social consensus.

CONCLUSION

The conversation just reported displays in an explicit and public way the attribution processes of two persons seeking a causal explanation for another's behavior. We are able to *see* in Don and Bob's talk the definition of the student's failure as an event falling under the multiple sufficient cause scheme, the participants' usually implicit knowledge of the conditions affecting success and failure outcomes, and the joint application of covariation principles in the effort to determine which of several possible causes is most responsible for the student's triple failure. Thus, examination of Don and Bob's talk reveals the presence and operation of several specific attribution processes. More generally, the conversation displays, in Schutz's (1932/1967) terms, how interpreters define and constitute the structure of an act, and then how interpreters "work back" from the structure of a constituted act to a determination of the type of person capable of producing the act. Moreover, analysis of the conversation reveals that the *outcome* of the collaborative, publicly conducted attribution process (i.e., the attribution that the student's failure was due to her low ability) is a product that was socially constructed, tested, and verified.

Don and Bob's conversation helps us observe usually covert attribution processes; however, it also appears that aspects of the sequential organization of the conversation were guided by general attributional schemes. Recall that Heider's (1958) work suggests that a perceiver's search for the causes of another's behavior proceeds in a *sequential* fashion (see p. 66). In general, perceivers are thought first to consider stable environmental causes for behavior, then transient environmental causes, and finally stable personal causes. Don and Bob's conversation appears to follow this pattern. A stable environmental cause for the student's triple failure (i.e., test difficulty) was considered in early portions of the conversation (U16–U21, U27–U30). Next, transient environmental causes (i.e., luck or chance factors) received attention (U31–U35). Then, variable personal force explanations (i.e., lack of effort) for the student's act were considered and dismissed (U45–U46, U54). Finally, Don and Bob discuss and endorse a stable personal force (low ability) as the sufficient cause for the student's act (U46, U47–U55). Determining whether motive-seeking conversations generally follow this pattern—a pattern quite consistent with the principles of attribution theory—will require more rigorous research designs and a much larger data base. However, the sequence in which issues appear in Don and Bob's conversation suggests that topical sequences in motive-seeking conversations may parallel the sequence in which perceivers mentally consider possible explanations for another's behavior. More generally, the topical pattern in Don and Bob's conversation suggests that *substantive* aspects of conversational topics may play important roles in how conversations are structured and organized.

From its inception, an underlying principle of attribution theory has been that ordinary actors can be usefully viewed as "naive psychologists" who possess "scientist-like" aspects. Recently, however, the "man as scientist" metaphor has been subject to trenchant criticism. Considerable empirical evidence indicates that ordinary actors are sometimes very poor scientists indeed. Among other things, they continue to maintain beliefs that have been empirically falsified, ignore base-rate information in assessing probabilities, infer causation on the basis of simple correlation, base inferences on illusory correlations, and appear quite ignorant of formal logic and principles of statistical decision theory (see Nisbett & Ross, 1980). Although naive psychologists are thus sometimes given to making very fallible inferences, it is interesting to note that Don and Bob's conversational search for the cause of the student's failure appears to proceed in a relatively rational and careful manner. That is, Don and Bob compare the student's performance with others' performance on the exam, assess the consistency of the student's performance over test-taking trials, compare the student's performance on the failed midterm with her performance on other class assignments, relate the student's performance in Don's class with her performance in other classes, and consensually reach the conclusion that the student's failure was caused by her lack of ability only after assessing the merit of competing explanations. Throughout the conversation, then, Don and Bob appear to possess certain scientist-like aspects: They derive alternative hypotheses for the student's failure from a general (albeit implicit) theory of achievement outcomes, assess the merit of each of these hypotheses in light of the available evidence, and ultimately invoke one of these hypotheses to account for the student's behavior only after the reasonably careful consideration of alternatives. Moreover, these rational practices are directly observable in Don and Bob's talk. Recognition of the sometimes substantial inferential errors made by ordinary "scientists" should not blind us to their rational practices.

Although attribution processes are usually thought of as covert, and thus not directly observable, the analysis offered in this chapter suggests that the detailed examination of natural conversations provides a potentially useful approach wherein attribution processes *can* be directly observed. Of course, the utility of conversational analysis as a basis for the study of attribution processes may be limited by the difficulty in collecting and/or the rarity of conversational specimens of the sort analyzed in this chapter. If, however, researchers are willing to sacrifice a degree of "naturalness," existing methodologies already employed in person-perception research can be adapted to generate the kind of conversational data examined in this study. Researchers of impression formation processes have frequently employed an "inconsistent information paradigm" in the study of information integration processes (e.g., Nidorf & Crockett, 1965; Press, Crockett, & Delia, 1975). In this paradigm, subjects are provided with several passages of information describing a character who engages in seemingly inconsistent acts (e.g., sitting with an isolated newcomer at lunch, then publicly ridiculing a peer's failure of a test); subjects are then asked to write an impression of the character, explaining why that person acts as he or she does. However, instead of being asked to write personal impressions of the inconsistently acting character, pairs of subjects could be instructed to talk about why the character acted as he or she did and decide among themselves on a motivation for the character's act. These conversations could be tape recorded and transcribed so as to supply data for the examination of publicly manifested attribution processes. Having subjects engage in such motive-seeking conversations is a very natural task for, as previously noted, one of our most common activities is *talking* about why others act as they do.

APPENDIX A: TRANSCRIPT OF A
CAUSE-SEEKING CONVERSATION

U01	Don:	Remember that girl I've been havin' trouble with?
U02	Bob:	Yeah.
U03	Don:	She just took the midterm for the third time and failed it.
U04	Bob:	*Jesus Christ!*
U05	Bob:	(Pause.) *Jesus.*
U06	Don:	I have never known a student that could not take a test—*several times*—and not eventually pass it.
U07	Bob:	*Three* times?
U08	Don:	Exactly the same test.
U09	Bob:	The *same* test? The *same* questions?
U10	Don:	(Nods affirmatively.) I just gonna have to insist that she drop the course.
U11	Sherry:	That's, that's beyond me. I mean, that's, that's . . .
U12	Don:	I just can't. . . . There's nothing I can do. I'm just gonna have to do whatever's necessary to get her out of the course. She just can't handle it.
U13	Bob:	How can ya. . . . Da *da* da da da. *Blah.* How—how—
U14	Don:	That's my reaction. (Laughs.)
U15	Sherry:	It's beyond. . . . — . . .
U16	Bob:	I mean, you know, if you were changing the questions and changing the items and making an essay exam and a multiple choice another time, something like that—yeah. Did she ever—did she—did anybody ever tell her what the right answers were? So she could study or anything, or. . . .
U17	Don:	Well, I didn't wanta just go over the test and say "here are the right answers," and then have her take it again.
U18	Bob:	Sure, sure. 'Course not. You know. But she could—did she have a copy of the test so she could study the stuff?

U19	Don:	She has—I gave quizzes which, you know, cover the material. So she's got copies of the quizzes which led up to the midterm, and some of the questions on that midterm are just lifted off the quizzes. Just exactly the same as those quizzes.
U20	Bob:	And you did go over those quizzes, right?
U21	Don:	Oh yes, yes I did. And she still missin' those that are exact copies of the ones on quizzes that she's got copies of.
U22	Don:	(Pause.) I just don't see that I can do anything for her. I just have—I know the day has passed for dropping the course, but I just gotta—
U23	Bob:	—Does she know she failed it?
U24	Don:	No.
U25	Bob:	Oh. . . . I don't envy you, man. What are you gonna say to her?
U26	Don:	I'm just gonna say "you failed it again. This is the last straw. I'm gonna get you out of this class." I don't know how I'm gonna do it. If necessary, I'm gonna lead her around by the hand and do whatever's necessary to get her petitioned out of my class. Cause—I don't—I gonna—I'm just gonna *fail* her! It's pointless. If she can't pass the midterm in three tries, there's no way she's gonna pass the final.
U27	Bob:	Everybody else's passed it, I presume.
U28	Don:	Oh, everybody passed it the first time, except her.
U29	Bob:	Was her score noticeably below everybody else's?
U30	Don:	Yeah, yeah.
U31	Bob:	Has she been getting any higher on these trials? I mean, is she getting closer? (Chuckles.)
U32	Don:	Nope. First one she made a 60, second time she took it she made a 50, and the third time she took it she made a 60.
U33	Bob:	What do you have for passing, 70?
U34	Don:	Seventy.
U35	Bob:	Jesus, man.
U36	Don:	I just feel sorry for her. I really wish we had a farm or community college to send her to or something.
U37	Bob:	How've her speeches and stuff been?
U38	Don:	Uh, low passing.
U39	Bob:	How'd she do on these quizzes?
U40	Don:	About the same.
U41	Bob:	But, but those don't count in terms of whether or not—
U42	Don:	—They don't count. You're right.
U43	Bob:	Oh, man.
U44	Don:	What do you do, you know? What do you do?
U45	Bob:	I'm just glad I'm not you and I don't have to, uh, to tell her. I mean, cause—cause it seems—you know, she's been in here several times, and it seems like she's *tryin'*.

U46	Don:	Yeah. Well, I'm sure she is. (Pause.) But I just think about—she's a second year freshman (ticking points off on fingers), she's taking a minimum load, she's had, according to what she's said, just as much trouble with all her other classes that she's having with mine. And, uh, it just doesn't make sense to keep her in this kind of grade oriented, pressurized institution. She can't handle the work load, the material. I think at, uh, this point the best thing I can do for her is to help her get out of my class.
U47	Bob:	Yeah, she oughta get out of the University, instead, uh, stickin' around and havin' her ego crushed. Man, what's it goin' to do to her self-concept? I mean, what—the thing is, my self-concept would be just utterly devastated when I blew an exam. And then to blow—But, I mean, you know, uh—That only happened twice in college, once in math class and once in my history class at midterm. And those were basically signals to get off my ass and do something. Uh, but to blow the same exam *thrice*—is she just—I just *gotta* ask this question—is she just plain *stupid*?
U48	Don:	That's—
U49	(Uninterpretable talkover.)	
U50	Bob:	I mean, you know, is she an idiot?
U51	Don:	Yeah, I think she's just dumb. That's the only thing I can figure out.
U52	Bob:	Does she study? I mean, do you think—
U53	Don:	—She claims she does, and I'm, I'm sure she does.
U54	Bob:	One would think so. I mean, you know, I can't imagine her just tryin'—thinkin' she could breeze through it, especially after she'd blown it twice. The first time, yeah, you could understand, but you'd figure study the second and then especially the *third* time. (Pause.) The thing of it is—this, this just sounds so cruel and elitist—but, you just don't encounter very many dumb people.
U55	Don:	No, not, not at a college of this quality. Certainly not. It's a real shame. (Pause.)

REFERENCES

Coulthard, W. (1977). *An introduction to discourse analysis.* London: Longman.
Craig, R. T., & Tracy, K. (Eds.). (1983). *Conversational coherence: Form, structure, and strategy.* Beverly Hills, CA: Sage.

Duncan, S., Jr. (1972). Some signals and rules for taking speaking turns in conversations. *Journal of Personality and Social Psychology, 23*, 283–292.

Ellis, D. G. (1983). Language, coherence, and textuality. In R. T. Craig & K. Tracy (Eds.), *Conversational coherence: Form, structure, and strategy* (pp. 222–240). Beverly Hills, CA: Sage.

Frieze, I., & Weiner, B. (1971). Core utilization and attributional judgments for success and failure. *Journal of Personality, 39*, 591–605.

Goldberg, J. A. (1983). A move toward describing conversational coherence. In R. T. Craig & K. Tracy (Eds.), *Conversational coherence: Form, structure, and strategy* (pp. 25–45). Beverly Hills, CA: Sage.

Heider, F. (1958). *The psychology of interpersonal relations*. New York: Wiley.

Jacobs, S., & Jackson, S. (1982). Conversational argument: A discourse analytic approach. In J. R. Cox & C. A. Willard (Eds.), *Advances in argumentation theory and research* (pp. 205–237). Carbondale, IL: Southern Illinois University Press.

Jones, E. E., & Davis, K. (1965). From acts to dispositions: The attribution process in person perception. In L. Berkowitz (Ed.), *Advances in experimental social psychology* (Vol. 2, pp. 219–266). New York: Academic Press.

Keenan, E. O., & Schieffelin, B. B. (1976). Topic as a discourse notion: A study of topic in conversations of children and adults. In C. N. Li (Ed.), *Subject and topic* (pp. 335–384). New York: Academic Press.

Kelley, H. H. (1967). Attribution theory in social psychology. In D. Levine (Ed.), *Nebraska symposium on motivation* (Vol. 15, pp. 192–238). Lincoln: University of Nebraska Press.

Kelley, H. H. (1972). Causal schemata and the attribution process. In E. E. Jones et al. (Eds.), *Attribution: Perceiving the causes of behavior* (pp. 1–26). Morristown, NJ: General Learning Press.

Levinson, S. C. (1983). *Pragmatics*. London: Cambridge University Press.

Nidorf, L. J., & Crockett, W. H. (1965). Cognitive complexity and the integration of inconsistent information in written impressions. *Journal of Social Psychology, 79*, 165–169.

Nisbett, R., & Ross, L. (1980). *Human inference: Strategies and shortcomings of social judgment*. Englewood Cliffs, NJ: Prentice-Hall.

Press, A. N., Crockett, W. H., & Delia, J. G. (1975). Effects of cognitive complexity and perceiver's set upon the organization of impressions. *Journal of Personality and Social Psychology, 32*, 865–872.

Sacks, H., Schegloff, E., & Jefferson, G. (1974). A simplest systematics for the organization of turn-taking for conversation. *Language, 50*, 696–735.

Schegloff, E. A. (1972). Sequencing in conversational openings. In J. A. Fishman (Ed.), *Advances in the sociology of language* (Vol. 2, pp. 91–125). The Hague: Mouton.

Schegloff, E. A., & Sacks, H. (1973). Opening up closings. *Semiotica, 8*, 289–327.

Schneider, D. J., Hastorf, A. H., & Ellsworth, P. C. (1979). *Person perception* (2nd Ed.). Reading, MA: Addison-Wesley.

Schutz, A. (1967). *The phenomenology of the social world* (G. Walsh & F. Lehnert, Trans.). Evanston, IL: Northwestern University Press. (Original work published 1932.)

Seibold, D. R., & Spitzberg, B. H. (1981). Attribution theory and research: Formulization, review, and implications for communication. In B. Derbin & M. J. Voight (Eds.), *Progress in the communication sciences* (Vol. 3, pp. 85–125). Norwood, NJ: Ablex.

Shaver, K. G. (1975). *An introduction to attribution processes*. Cambridge, MA: Winthrop.

Sigman, S. J. (1983). Some multiple constraints placed on conversational topics. In R. T. Craig & K. Tracy (Eds.), *Conversational coherence: Form, structure, and strategy* (pp. 174–195). Beverly Hills, CA: Sage.

Sillars, A. L. (1982). Attribution and communication: Are people "naive scientists" or just naive? In M. E. Roloff & C. R. Berger (Eds.), *Social cognition and communication* (pp. 73–106). Beverly Hills, CA: Sage.

Wegner, D. M., & Vallacher, R. R. (1977). *Implicit psychology: An introduction to social cognition.* New York: Oxford University Press.

Weiner, B. (Ed.). (1974). *Achievement motivation and attribution theory.* Morristown, NJ: General Learning Press.

Weiner, B., Frieze, A., Kukla, L., Reed, S., Rest, R., & Rosenbaum, M. (1972). Perceiving the causes of success and failure. In E. E. Jones et al. (Eds.), *Attribution: Perceiving the causes of behavior* (pp. 95–120). Morristown, NJ: General Learning Press.

Weiner, B., & Kukla, A. (1970). An attributional analysis of achievement motivation. *Journal of Personality and Social Psychology, 15,* 1–20.

4 A Developmental Analysis of Children's Narratives[1]

Beth Haslett
University of Delaware

Narratives have been studied from an increasing variety of perspectives. Long studied by literary critics (Smith, 1980), narratives have been analyzed more recently for their importance in socialization and enculturation (Gardner, Winner, Bechhofer, & Wolf, 1978; Polanyi, 1979), in conversations (Beach, 1983; Burton, 1981), and in the processing and storing of complex information (van Dijk, 1977a, b; 1980a, b). Narratives provide more explicit, limited texts for analysis than do conversational texts whose interpretation relies on more indirect, variable knowledge structures (van Dijk, 1980b). In addition, narrative structures may be studied in a wide range of contexts, including both oral and written modes of communication (Haslett, 1983; Tannen, 1979). The purpose of this chapter is to analyze the narrative structures used by children in their storytelling and, in particular, to assess developmental changes in these structures. In what follows, I first present a brief theoretical overview of approaches to narrative comprehension and production, especially among children. Secondly, I present and discuss the results of my analysis of children's original narratives, and finally discuss the implications of this line of research for the acquisition of communicative competence and for models of human communicative processes.

---

[1]There has been a proliferation of terms with respect to terms representing the way in which humans organize their knowledge: *frames, scripts, schemas,* and *superstructures* are some terms recently developed. For the sake of simplicity and consistency, I shall use the term *schema* throughout this chapter. For interesting discussions of the derivation of these terms and their differences, see van Dijk (1980a) and Tannen (1979).

COMPREHENSION AND PRODUCTION OF
NARRATIVES

Researchers investigating narrative structure have developed multiple approaches to this problem area. Generally, research is primarily concerned with either comprehension or production of narrative. Although some, like van Dijk, Kintsch, and Nelson, argue that both comprehension and production are controlled by the same hierarchical cognitive processes, few discuss narrative comprehension and production as related processes, and most focus their attention on either comprehension or production. For these reasons, it seems most useful to discuss narrative comprehension and production as relatively distinct research areas.

Comprehending Narratives

Models of narrative structure have been developed primarily through studies on recalling, recognizing, and summarizing stories. According to Glenn (1978), common assumptions underlying all these approaches are that:

1. Behavior described in stories is purposive: These purposive behaviors cluster in sequences (i.e., episodes) and are central to the story meaning.
2. Episodes include the following behavioral sequence: A character is motivated to follow a certain plan of action: then takes this action and certain consequences follow.
3. Readers/listeners structure story information into episodes.

In addition, Artificial Intelligence (AI) researchers have been attempting to model narrative structures in order to program "understanders" capable of interpreting stories. For the purposes of this chapter, we focus on those narrative models dealing with how information is processed and organized—that is, on the cognitive and semantic aspects of narratives rather than their implications for AI research. Given that the focus of this chapter is the development of narrative schemas among children, the emphasis on the cognitive, semantic, and linguistic aspects seems especially appropriate. The work of Rummelhart (Rummelhart, 1975; Rummelhart & Ortony, 1977) van Dijk and Kintsch, and deBeaugrande and Colby are of primary importance in this regard.

Van Dijk and Kintsch (van Dijk, 1976a, 1976b; 1977a, 1977b; 1980a, 1980b; van Dijk & Kintsch, 1977; Kintsch, 1974, 1977) have worked extensively on how knowledge is represented in memory, and how this knowledge representation influences discourse comprehension. According to van Dijk and Kintsch (1977), sentences are interpreted in light of their verbal and nonverbal context. They argue that we interpret and recall new information according to socially and cognitively established schemata. These schemata provide us with frames of interpretation for processing complex information.

Van Dijk (1972, 1977a, 1980a) has developed the concept of *macrostructures,* which represents the overall global semantic organization of a discourse. Several macrostructures may characterize a discourse, and the most general, abstract macrostructure is the macrostructure for a given discourse (van Dijk & Kintsch, 1977). Semantic mappings, called *macrorules,* are needed to build up more global macrostructures from the individual propositions in a given discourse. Although van Dijk's work has concentrated on the global organization of meaning (macrostructures) of a discourse, he has also been concerned with the overall structure of particular types of discourse (e.g., narratives, ads, newspaper stories, etc.).

Macrostructures deal with content and meaning, whereas *superstructures* deal with the overall characteristic organization of a particular type of discourse. The semantic organization of a discourse is systematically related to the superstructure of that discourse (van Dijk, 1980b). For example, a narrative's *resolution* (a superstructure category of narratives) contains the point or concluding action of a narrative. Or, in conversation, *greetings* (a superstructure conversational category) usually express a mutual acknowledgment by the interactants and, if they do not know one another, usually introductory information is exchanged. In this chapter, the primary emphasis is on children's developing knowledge of narrative superstructure—that is, on understanding the form of narratives. As van Dijk points out, however, both semantic and schematic (superstructure) representations are necessary in understanding and processing complex information; in what follows, both aspects are discussed although schematic rather than semantic representations of narrative structure are emphasized.

Narrative Structures: Some Alternative Viewpoints

All theories of narrative structure focus on the form or overall organizing structure of a given narrative. Theorists differ in the structural categories they propose as well as in the ordering, importance, and level of specificity of these categories. Most would agree that an appreciation of narrative structure is required by communicators for effective comprehension and production of narratives, and indeed much of the work on narrative structure has been motivated by a desire to model underlying cognitive processes in comprehension and production of complex information.

Van Dijk's Model of Narrative Structure. In every narrative, whether it is a story in a conversation or a novel, there are basic categories that form the narrative superstructure, and are listed here (van Dijk, 1980b):

1. *Setting*—expresses the general features of the original situation, time and location; characterizes the main participants.

2. *Complication*—expresses an event or action, and must be of significance; typically, such events may be dangerous, interesting, unexpected, and so forth.

3. *Resolution*—expresses the result or outcome.

4. *Evaluation*—expresses a global mental or emotional reaction with respect to the narrative.

5. *Coda* or *Moral*—expresses a conclusion for future action (e.g., "Next time I'll drive more carefully.")

These categories may be very brief or lengthy, depending on the complexity of the narrative, the narrator's purpose, cultural conventions, and so forth.

Van Dijk (1980b) suggests that these categories are hierarchically ordered in the following way:

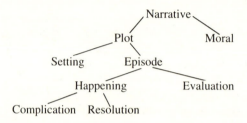

As van Dijk (1980b) points out:

> This structural graph should be defined in terms of *formation rules*, which specify the rank and ordering of the various categories. Such rules would be partially *recursive*. For instance, we may have stories with different, successive episodes, several Complications, and (successful or unsuccessful) Resolutions. For specific discourse types we finally have *transformation* rules, which allow certain categories to be deleted under specific conditions or to change place.
>
>   . . .certain types of discourse (viz., stories) have a global schematic structure and that this structure consists of a number of hierarchically related narrative categories. These categories are the functional slots for the 'content' of the discourse. Since the categories do not usually hold for individual sentences of a text, we must assume that the typical content of superstructure categories are *macrostructures* . . . We have already briefly observed that the Resolution category requires human (re)-action and that the Complication category should contain interesting events.
>
> Note that the narrative categories indeed have a *conventional* nature. First, the ordering could be different. A Moral could appear at the beginning as well. Second, there is no need to provide the personal Evaluation of a Happening or, in general, to tell only about interesting events. Of course, as we have seen before, the conventional nature of the categories holds for those discourse types that are well-established; the original communicative, pragmatic, cognitive, or social factors remain as the general basis and explanation of the categories. (pp. 115–117)

DeBeaugrande and Colby: Story-Telling Rules.   Although models of narrative structure have isolated similar abstract structures, deBeaugrande and Colby (1979) comment that "it is still not clear how and why event units are selected and arranged by narrators, or identified and processed by an audience" (p. 44). Like van Dijk, deBeaugrande and Colby propose an action basis for narratives; they state that the "*narrated world* is a progressive system in which *events* and *actions* occur and bring about changes from one *state* to the next" (1979, p. 45). Beyond this, however, narratives must be interesting and thus "there must be substantial uncertainty about state-event-state chaining if the audience is to participate actively" (1979, p. 45). These events/actions are presented from various characters' viewpoints, and the motives, goals, and plans of these characters may conflict with one another.

In order to construct narratives deBeaugrande and Colby (1979, pp. 45–46) argue that narrators follow the set of story-telling rules listed here:

1. Identifying at least one character.
2. Creating a problem state for the character.
3. Identifying a goal state for the character.
4. Initiating a pathway from the problem and state toward the goal state.
5. Blocking attainment of the goal state.
6. Marking a transition point.
7. Creating a terminal state which clearly expresses a match or mismatch with the goal state.

These rules are recursive, so they may be applied to different characters (e.g., protagonist and antagonist) and to multiple episodes.

DeBeaugrande and Colby (1979) thus view narration as "complex activities of planning and predicting" (p. 49). The narrator has to plan action sequences for characters, relate these actions to some goal, and anticipate audience reaction to these action sequences. In addition, some information may be deleted or unexpected information added to create and maintain interest in the narrative. Viewed in this way, narrator and audience both attempt to solve the character's problem.

Comprehension and production of narratives, of course, depend on and are constrained by human information-processing strategies (Thorndyke, 1977). Much of van Dijk and Kintsch's research discusses the limitations of these processes in recall and recognition of narratives. DeBeaugrande and Colby suggest that narrative comprehension may be influenced by processing strategies, such as planning and problem-solving capacities, processing depth, and processing ease. Such concerns are especially critical when assessing children's comprehension and production of narratives. We next turn to the research on the comprehension and production of narratives by children. Because the processes of narrative comprehension and production are believed to be similar (van Dijk, 1977a), we shall discuss the skills children bring to bear on both.

Children's Processing of Narratives.   A substantial number of studies have investigated children's ability to comprehend and recall stories. A study by Poulsen and Kintsch (cited in van Dijk & Kintsch, 1977) found that 4-year-olds gave good descriptions when story pictures were shown in their natural order; when the order of story pictures was scrambled, children were unable to figure out the pictures and regressed to simple labelling of the picture. Brown and Smiley (1977) found that young children do not understand what is most important or central in a story. Yussen, Buss, Matthews and Kane (1980) found that second graders fail to identify key propositions in a story grammar. Stevens (1981) found that second graders could recognize errors in the ordering of propositions in a story, although older children (fifth graders) were better at explaining what the problem was.

Yussen (1982) found striking age differences in two aspects. The first difference reflects children's restricted ability to correctly *sequence* narrative information. According to Yussen (1982) "These findings point to a clear limitation in younger children's ability to reorder information in their heads. The problem was later documented to be the result of limited knowledge by the children of how to sequence propositions rather than a problem with holding on to them in memory. We are just beginning to understand the limits of how much children can do when asked to operate upon what is in their heads" (p. 177). A second difference was found in stories children produced when responding to WISC story sets: Children tell "skeletal" stories with little attention given to character motivation, feelings, or logical connectives. The reasons for this storytelling style were not clear.

The general sociocultural frame of reference the children bring to bear on storytelling also influences their understanding and production of narratives (Cook-Gumperz & Green, in press). Heath (1983), in an ethnographic story of three different communities, found that patterns of language use in each community profoundly influenced their children's approach to literacy. Each community acknowledged books as authoritative sources of information, but each community used books (a mode of taking information from the environment) in distinct ways. By age 2, middle-class children ascribed fiction-like features to objects in their fantasy stories. They also announced their stories, often using formulaic openings (e.g., "Once there was . . .," etc.), and borrowed episodes from books. At age 3, they assumed the "audience role"—listening, storing information, and asking questions about the story. In contrast, working-class children viewed stories as an account of something, or a lesson to be learned; they did not decontextualize their knowledge.

Thus far, we have examined the structural categories of narratives and some interrelationships among those structural categories. These categories reflect the manner in which narrative information is understood, stored, and recalled. Thus, they represent cognitive processing of complex information; as such they are influenced by general human cognitive capabilities, such as age, ease and depth of processing, task demands, and so forth. We have also seen that children's ability to comprehend and produce narratives is limited by their cognitive capacities. We next turn to two developmental studies exploring the links between children's cognitive abilities and their narrative abilities. Botvin and Sutton-Smith (1977) deal primarily with the development of narrative structure among children, whereas Applebee (1978) focuses on the global meaning of stories as reflected by the level of children's cognitive capabilities.

Botvin and Sutton-Smith.   Botvin and Sutton-Smith analyzed the spontaneously told stories of 220 children, from ages 3 through 12. The stories were analyzed into their action sequences by Propp's (1958) analysis which had been modified by Botvin and Sutton-Smith. Botvin and Sutton-Smith (1977) categorized stories according to the following levels:

1. Level I—narratives lack coherence and structural unity; events are associated in a fragmented, unorganized way.
2. Level II—narratives are characterized by one primary plot unit.
3. Level III—narratives are internally expanded through the presence of secondary plot units which provide intermediate actions.
4. Level IV—narratives contain at least two or more primitive episodes (i.e., an action sequence) that are conjoined.
5. Level V—narratives are composed of two or more coordinated, developed episodes, in which the intermediate action sequences have been expanded.
6. Level VI—one dyadic structure is embedded in another, and thus there is subordination and hierarchical organization in these dyads.
7. Level VII—similar to Level VI, but contains multiple embedding.

Their results found that structural complexity increased with age, and thus the hypothesized order of acquisition from Level I to Level VII was confirmed. Structural complexity was also significantly correlated with narrative length, and both correlated significantly with age. However, when the effect of age was partialled out, the relationship between narrative length and structural level appears to be due to the child's ability to use increasingly complex narrative structures. The order of narrative acquisition appears to parallel that of analogous linguistic structures, and thus suggests that both skills maybe rest on similar underlying cognitive structures. Although Botvin and Sutton-Smith used spontaneously told stories, they used only fantasy stories; in some cases, these stories were based on television programs and book themes.

Applebee.   Applebee's research (1978) analyzed the stories of young children for their grammatical and plot complexity. With the effect of age partialled out, Applebee found that the complexity of the story corresponded to different methods of structuring the plot. Applebee (1978) pointed out that:

> The succession of ways of organizing a story bears a complex relationship to the overall complexity of the comprehension and production task facing the child. Looking only at the modes of organization, each stage is more complex than the previous one, and is correspondingly more difficult to master . . .
>   . . . there is an interplay between form and content in which increasingly complex material is dealt with through the expedient of organizing it more thoroughly . . . From the least to most complex, the six major stages of narrative form found here are heaps, sequences, primitive narratives, unfocused chains, focused chains, and true narratives. Each in turn represents a progressively more complex combination of two basic structuring principles, centering and chaining. By recognizing that these can apply recursively to ever-larger units of discourse, they can be seen to underlie adult uses of language in the spectator role, as well as the children's uses from which they were derived. (p. 68)

Although Applebee's work contributes to understanding how complex events may be organized, several major weaknesses confound the results of the study. First, Applebee himself notes that several of the story types seem to overlap (sequences and focused chains, focused chains and primitive narratives). Second, the stories were not analytically separated into original stories, reports of personal experience, and re-telling of stories. Re-telling well-known stories was a significant proportion of the stories analyzed. However, re-telling reflects the original story plot as written by adults, not the narrative scripts children are developing. The re-telling reflects the child's memory of and meaning for the story, but it is not clear how that may relate to the child's developing scripts for narratives. Finally, Applebee used data from the Pitcher and Prelinger (1963) study, in which children were given probes to prompt them in their storytelling (i.e., "What happened next?"). Although these probes may not influence the content of the stories, it seems likely that they influenced the length and structure of the stories. The work of William Labov (Labov & Waletsky, 1967; Labov, 1972) constructed a model of narrative scripts that was based on the narratives of black preadolescents. As can be seen, Labov's model also deals with the entire narrative script, rather than just the plot complexity as does Applebee, although Labov does not articulate a developmental model.

Labov's Narrative Script.   Labov developed his model of narrative scripts on the structural similarities he found among the oral narratives of black English speakers. A completely developed narrative, according to Labov, consists of the following structural elements:

1. *Abstract*—which serves as a short summary of the story;
2. *Orientation*—which serves to identify the setting and characters in the story;
3. *Complicating Action*—which serves to detail the sequence of events and action in the story;
4. *Evaluation*—which reveals the point of the story (i.e., it lets the listener know why the story is "tellable");
5. *Resolution*—which gives the end result of the actions or events; and
6. *Coda*—which serves to finish or signal completion of the story (i.e., "That's it!").

The two most important script elements are the complicating action and evaluation: the complicating action reveals what is happening and the evaluation highlights the story's reportability. As Labov (1972) pointed out:

The narrators of most of these stories were under social pressure to show that the events involved were truly dangerous and unusual, or that someone else really broke the normal rules in an outrageous and reportable way. Evaluative devices say this to us: this was terrifying, dangerous, weird, wild, crazy; or amusing, hilarious, wonderful; more generally, that it was strange, uncommon, or unusual—that is, worth reporting. (p. 371)

Labov's analysis is particularly powerful because it reveals a narrative script that is found in everyday conversation as well as in literature. As Pratt (1977) stated:

The oral narrative of personal experience is a speech act exceedingly familiar to us all, regardless of what dialect we speak. We all spend enormous amounts of conversational time exchanging anecdotes . . . We are all perfectly aware of the "unspoken agenda" by which we assess an experience's tellability. We know that anecdotes, like novels, are expected to have endings. We know that for an anecdote to be successful, we must introduce it into the conversation in an keep the point of the story in view at all times, and so on . . . and when narrative speech acts fail, we can almost always say why: the experience was trivial, the teller long-winded, or we "missed the point." (pp. 50–51)

Pratt (1977) also stated that:

All the problems of coherence, chronology, causality, foregrounding, plausibility, selection of detail, tense, point of view, and emotional intensity exist for the natural narrator just as they do for the novelist, and they are confronted and solved (with greater or lesser success) by speakers of the language every day. (pp. 66–67)

Labov's analysis also focuses on syntactic devices associated with narratives. According to Labov, narrative syntax consists mainly of simple clauses with the following structure:

Conjunc. + simple subj. + verb + obj. + locative adverbial + temporal locative
"And + the girl + hit + the old man + in the jaw + then."

Because Labov's narrative script emphasizes the importance of evaluation, he discusses evaluative devices that narrators use and the strategies available to the narrator for use in story evaluation. Labov details four evaluative devices: *external comments* (the storyteller stops the narrative action and tells the listener what the point is); *embedded evaluation* (the storyteller quotes the feeling as occurring during the narrative action itself), *evaluative action* (the storyteller relates what people did rather than what they said) and *suspending action* (the storyteller stops the narrative and expresses emotion or sentiment about what's happening). Syntactic devices that perform an evaluative function include intensifiers, comparators, correlatives, and explicatives.

In summary, narrative schemas have influenced both production and comprehension of stories. Children's narrative schemas are limited by their cognitive and linguistic skills. However, studies of children's narrative competence have not clearly tested children's narrative abilities because the stories analyzed were elicited by probes or included stories based, in part, on episodes from popular books or television episodes. Several scholars (deBeaugrande & Colby, 1979; Haslett, 1983) have called for the study of original, spontaneous narratives so that narrative competence may be more directly assessed. Such narratives attempt to meet the communicative demands of clarity, cohesion, and interest in everyday interactive settings; as such, these narratives overcome the objections raised about the simple, artificial stories produced by story grammars (deBeaugrande & Colby, 1979; Heath, 1983; Yussen, 1982).

Two broad questions are investigated. First, what are the structural categories children use in their stories, and how are they functionally related? In particular, do children's stories express coherent connections between events, and do they have a point? Second, what are the linguistic strategies children use in constructing their stories—do they use specific markers (e.g., then, next, etc.), formulaic expressions (e.g., "Once upon a time there was . . .". etc.), and evaluative language (e.g., intensifiers, etc.)? The structural categories will be analyzed by using Labov's narrative model; this model was selected because it is a functionally based model derived from everyday stories, and also deals with grammatical features of stories.

The children serving as subjects in the present study ranged in ages from 4 to 8. This age range is of particular interest because they are shifting from preoperational to concrete operational thinking (Piaget, 1926) and because the older children will be attending school and thus be exposed to early reading/

writing training. During this age span, children's ability to understand complex relationships increases as does their ability to classify objects/events (Wood, 1981). Linguistic skills also develop more complexity and organization during this time (Brown, 1973). As children become cognitively and linguistically more mature, it is hypothesized that the structural complexity of narratives increases. This structural complexity will be expressed by an increasing number of narrative events, but also in narratives that provide some background information for listeners (i.e., orientation), and commentary on character feelings and motivation (i.e., Labov's evaluative category). Generally, then, children will develop an increasing ability to produce a well-formed narrative.

METHOD

Subjects. Forty children served as subjects in the present investigation. Ten 4-year-olds (5 male, 5 female), ten 5-year-olds (5 male, 5 female), ten 6-year-olds (5 male, 5 female) and ten 7-year-olds (5 male, 5 female) served as subjects. This age range was selected because it represented the transition period from preoperations to concrete operational thought, and from egocentric to sociocentric thought and communication.

Data Collection. The data analyzed in the present study were part of a larger study relating the oral and written language of young children. During a 1-week period in late January, children were asked to tell a story to a research assistant as well as to write stories. These oral stories were tape recorded by the research assistant. For half of the subjects, oral stories were first and then stories were written: The order was reversed for the remainder of the subjects. If children seemed reluctant to talk, the research assistant used the probe question, "Is there anything else you want to tell me about this story?" to encourage the subject. This phrasing of the question gave the subject an encouraging response to his or her story, but left it up to the child as to whether the story should be continued.

Data Analysis. Because the purpose of the study was to investigate children's development of narrative scripts, only those narratives that originated from the child (i.e., original narrative or dreams) were included in the present study. Such stories would provide the strongest test for the development of narrative scripts because other narratives would be "scripted" by the sequence of events that actually happened to the child (i.e., personal experience narrative) or by a ready-made plot (i.e., re-telling of popular stories).

The experimenter analyzed each story for the presence of the structural elements of Labov's narrative script model. Chi-square tests and *t* tests for significance of differences as a function of age were done. Because the age range represented a transition period cognitively for the children, subjects were grouped into two groups, with the midpoint of this age span (i.e., from 4 to 7) serving as the dividing line. Thus, 4- and 5-year-olds were analyzed as one group, and 6- and 7-year-olds were analyzed as the other group.

RESULTS

Analysis of young children's original narratives according to Labov's narrative script model revealed significant developmental differences across narratives. Preoperational children had significantly less complicating actions in their stories: 4- and 5-year-olds had a mean of 8.9 complicating actions per story whereas the 6- and 7-year-olds had a mean of 18.4 complicating actions per story ($df = 38$, $t = 2.8$, $p < .005$). The 6- and 7-year-olds used evaluative structures significantly more frequently than did the younger subjects ($df = 1$, $x^2 = 3.8$, $p = .05$). Orientation was used significantly more by the 6- and 7-year-olds than by the 4- and 5-year-olds ($df = 1$, $x^2 = 4$, $p < .05$). There were no significant differences across the two groups in their use of abstracts, codas, and resolutions.

DISCUSSION

The results of the present investigation supported the claim that the structural elements of children's narratives varied as a function of age. Children in the concrete operational stage had significantly more complicating action and included evaluative elements and orientations significantly more frequently than did preoperational children. Greater use of evaluative devices and orientations by older children was believed to reflect the children's shift from egocentric to sociocentric thought and communication: They need to articulate their own perspective because the listener's perspective may differ from theirs. Older children's greater complexity in their narratives, both in terms of number of complicating actions and the organization of the stories, was believed to reflect their ability to categorize and arrange elements hierarchically; this characterizes the thinking of children in the concrete operational stage. The qualitative analysis of prototypical stories for each age that follows further contributes to our understanding of children's narrative structures, particularly in terms of the linguistic strategies utilized in story-telling and story cohesion.

Four-Year-Olds.   Following are several prototypical narratives by 4-year-olds. Each narrative has been divided into its structural elements and evaluative language used in the narratives has been underlined. The first story represented one of the most complex and well-formed of the stories among these children.

Orientation	And my next *scary* dream was that a witch and a monster came up the stairs and a ghost scared me up in my bed.
Complicating Action	And I had to jump out the window.
	And the witch scared [me] far, far away.
	I had to, she scared me *so much*.
	I ran to the, I ran to the desert.
Resolution	And then a cobra killed me.
Coda	And that's my dream.

The narrative began with a brief orientation that told the listener that this was a scary dream, involving a witch and a monster. Following this orientation, a series of complicating events occurred; these events followed logically and temporally from one another and used linguistic markers like *then* and *next*. The narrative also was cohesive because all events were integrated with one another, and moved toward a final resolution. The motives for actions were given and thus the action's implications were clarified: for example, the child ran far away because of his fear of the witch. This narrative also contained an evaluation of the action (i.e., "she scared me *so much*") and evaluative language, the intensifier *so much*.

The following story, told by another 4-year-old, demonstrated less complexity and well-formedness.

Orientation	One time there was a little bumble bee.
Complicating Action	And the bumble bee stinged a little girl.
	And the little girl ran to her house.
	And there was a beetle crawling up her leg.
	And a butterfly came.
Resolution	And it helped.

The narrative's complicating actions were not integrated: There was a list of events, some of which were related (i.e., the bee stinging and the girl running into the house) and others which were not (i.e., the beetle and the butterfly). The statement "it helped" could be interpreted as both an evaluative statement and a resolution. However, if it is interpreted as a resolution, the listener is not clear about what was helped or about what was doing the helping. The consequence of the story, its resolution, was not clear and the story's tellability, its interest value, was not given. The story apparently was of some interest to the storyteller!

All of these stories exemplified the simple syntactic structure Labov found in narrative texts. Adjacent clauses were linked temporally or causally, although such relatedness was not sustained over the course of the narrative and thus overall coherence was often lacking. Two structural elements contributing to text cohesion, evaluation, and resolution, were typically missing or unclear. The dream narrative was tellable because "scary dreams" qualify as being "strange" or "unusual" in Labov's sense: the evaluative justification for the other narrative was problematic because the point of the story was not implicit within the text itself.

Five-Year-Olds.   Narratives by the 5-year-olds were more complex than those by 4-year-olds; the sequence of actions seemed to be clearer although 5-year-olds, like the 4-year-olds, had difficulty establishing overall text cohesion as the following narrative demonstrated.

Orientation	Little old man, he had a house.
Complicating Action	And he [unclear] on the roof. His whistle blew.
Evaluation	He sure had a noisy house.
Complicating Action	Then one day he went to a teacher.
	And he says "What should I do?"
	They said "Buy a cow."
	The cow did no good.
	They said "Buy a chicken."
	But the chicken didn't do any good.
	They said "Buy a donkey."
	The donkey didn't do any good.
	They went to the teacher and they said, "Let all the animals go, let them all go."
Resolution	Then he had a quiet house.
Coda	That's my whole story!

Although this story has a number of complicating actions, it lacks coherence because the actions are not connected—the listener does not know why certain actions are being done. As Clark and Clark (1977) point out:

> One thing people commonly do in comprehension is draw the obvious implications . . . People seem to draw these inferences easily and automatically . . . Most implications are based wholly or partially on world knowledge in conformity with the reality principle . . . In comprehending prose passages, people not only draw implications as each sentence comes along, but also create new representations, unrelated to any single sentence, to capture the global situation being described . . . The global representation is based on all the information taken together embellished by knowledge of the world according to the reality principle. (pp. 158–161)

A global representation of the narratives of the 4- and 5-year-olds—one that reflects a narrative's cohesiveness—was not possible because the implications to be drawn from the text were incomplete, inconsistent (as demonstrated in the previous story) or unclear. This may be attributed, in part, to the cognitive abilities of the preoperational child. Piaget (1962) observed that "To say that child thought is syncretistic means . . . that childish ideas arise through comprehensive schemas and through subjective schemas, i.e., schemas that do not correspond to analogies or causal relations that can be verified by everybody (p. 227).

Six-Year-Olds.   The 6-year-olds demonstrated the following significant advances in their skill in fulfilling the communicative demands of oral narratives: the use of direct dialogue in narrative, the use of evaluation to reflect the sentiments and feelings of the characters, and the use of "surprise" endings that violate the expectations set up earlier in the narrative.

The following narrative exemplified the use of direct dialogue and a surprise ending:

Orientation	Once there was a man and a woman
Complicating Action	And once the woman said, "Don't go into that one room." She said.
	Then one night they went to the door.
	And this man was going to open it. He did.
	And the woman said—then they heard this—
	"Rah, rah, rah, bang, bang!"
	And then the woman said, "Let's go back to our bedrooms."
	Then the next night, woman was going to open it.
	And then they heard this *Rah! rah! bang! bang!*
	And then the man said "Let's us go back."
	Then the third night, they went to the door.
	And they *didn't hear nothing.*
	And then—and they *both* were going to open it.
	And then they opened this—the door,
	There was *this huge* monster with *one huge* eye.
	Then they ran, and *they ran,* and *they ran, and they ran, ran.*
	And they had to catch their breath.
	And then the monster was catching up, *catching up.*
Resolution	He caught up.
	And then he said, "Tag, you're it!"

The resolution of the story was unexpected because the listener's normative script would anticipate that monsters chase people to inflict bodily harm, not to play tag. The boy who told this story broke into a big laugh upon telling the punch line, demonstrating his own enjoyment of the unexpected. Also of interest was the use of intensifiers and of repetition to heighten the drama of the narrative, and thus enhance the story's tellability or interestingness.

The following narrative demonstrated the use of an unanticipated resolution as well as the use of evaluation that reflected the sentiments of the main character in the narrative. The use of phrases such as "you see" and "And well, one day" clearly marked the storyteller's movement out of the text's complicating action—suspending this action and commenting upon it—before returning to the complicating action. This evaluation, in effect, served a meta-communicative function for the narrative.

Orientation	Well, one day there was a little boy and he was telling someone a story and he had *all kinds* of friends.
Complicating Action	And one man he didn't like was grumpy. He didn't like him *at all.* And he didn't like noise. He didn't like cats or dogs or cars or even trucks.
Evaluation	Because noise, you see, the noise was bothering him a lot and he sleeps in the morning. So he doesn't like to have noise bothering him in the morning 'cause everyone else is up and he doesn't like it when everyone else is up.
Complicating Action	And, well, one day a man came on down And he was going to work right there in the middle of two windows. And he started drilling up the sidewalk.
Evaluation	Yuk! And the man didn't like it.
Complicating Action	And then one day the boy went to the store. And he saw some earmuffs. And he paid for them. And then he went back to the window. And he knocked on it. And then he gave him the earmuffs.
Resolution	And he said, "Put those earmuffs on your ears and then you won't hear anything and you can sleep.

Narratives like the two previous stories were the norm for the 6-year-olds. However, some children still presented disjointed narratives in which the listener was set down in the midst of complicating action, with indefinite references being used and linkages between complicating actions missing, as the following story reveals.

There was a, wait, there was a haunted house and there was a ghost all of his friends didn't like him, they used to live with him, but they scooted him out 'cause they didn't like him. So at the haunted house there was a gold hanging off the door and the robber came and took the gold and his friends thought and it was their gold so the ghost saw the robber and he duck and he threw it and the robber tried to throw it away, he was watching out the window, he threw it away and he put it back on the door and he threw the robber into the trap; he dead. The end.

Seven-Year-Olds.   The narratives of the 7-year-olds were more complex than those of the 6-year-olds, typically involving a series of episodes within the narrative. In addition, the narratives appeared more cohesive with the implications of a series of events flowing directly from one another.

This narrative exemplified a complex narrative structure, incorporating several distinct episodes and using direct dialogue to convey action.

Title	Lisa and the Grumpet
Orientation	Once there was a *little girl* named Lisa.
Complicating Action	She woke up one day.
	And her sister said, "Don't make so *much* noise! Don't knock over the Goldfish bowl!"
Evaluation	She was tired of being told what to do.
Complicating Action	She went downstairs.
	Her mother said, "Don't wear that old shirt!
	Pull up your socks! And don't forget you have a piano lesson today."
	Her father said—she went into where her father was.
	Her father said, "Pull up your socks!
	And tie your shoelace."
	And went off to work without saying goodbye.
	Then Lisa went outside.
	She said, "I'm gonna tell myself what to do!"
	And she did.
	She walked *and walked and walked.*
	And then she sat down and said, [unclear]
	And then she said, "there I run away."
	Then she heard a *little noise.*
	And then something [unclear] her.
	"Ouch," said Lisa.
	"I Grumpet, I Grumpet, I Grumpet!" yelled the Grumpet.
	"You sat on my front yard and squashed it.
	"I'm sorry I squashed your front yard," said Lisa.
	Then the Grumpet looked at her.

	"Now what am I going to do?"
	"I told you I'm sorry I squashed your front yard."
Evaluation	"When you squash somebody's front yard you are supposed to tell them the story of your life."
	"Oh, I didn't know that," said Lisa.
Complicating Action	And then she said, "I'm tired of being told what to do. And I don't like it anymore."
	And then the Grumpet yelled, "Don't tell me the story of your life."
	He shouted, "I'm supposed to tell you the story of my life." Then he started talking.
	He said, "My Uncle George never told me to take my vitamin pill. He *never* said not to spill the milk. He *never said* to not knock over the Goldfish bowl. Nothing. He just sat and [unclear].
Evaluation	And Lisa said, "Oh you sound like my mother!"
	He goes, "You sound like my Uncle George."
	"I love you," said Lisa.
	"I love you, too!" said the Grumpet.
Complicating Action	And they went home.
	And then they had lunch.
Evaluation	Lisa was *so* happy, she ate *all* her lunch.
Complicating Action	The Grumpet ate *all* his lunch.
Resolution	And then they were happy ever after.

This narrative was striking in its similarity to formats used in children's books. This may, in part, reflect the child's experiences in reading and writing in school. However it may be learned, such detailed structuring of narratives reveals a finely tuned appreciation of narrative form. There were a number of distinct series of actions (Lisa's morning exchanges with her family, Lisa's running away and meeting the grumpet, the story exchange, and the final action of reciprocal liking and going home). Each action series was logically and temporally ordered, and thus develops coherently. Although some of the rationale for actions were not plausible (i.e., squashing a grumpet's yard means you tell your life story!), at least a rationale outlining the act's implications was given. Such rationales were missing in the younger children's narratives.

A final excerpt from one 7-year-old's narrative reveals a fascinating evaluative element, in which the storyteller has a dialogue with the listener concerning how these narrative events might have occurred. (The evaluative component is set off by slash marks.)

Once there was a terrible, terrible island. There were volcanos and monsters and horns and stingers and even bugs and none of them like each other. /They weren't brothers or sisters or anything! They were just plain old monsters. You would think how they were born. Well, they were just brought up out of the ground. Now you don't know how they could just come out of the ground and I don't know either. This is what happened/ . . .

The child, in the midst of her narrative, is puzzled about how all these things came about and realized her listeners were as well. The narrator thus acknowledges the lack of a frame of reference for interpreting these events.

Narrative Reportability.   An increasing appreciation of the reportability of narratives was found when the content of the children's narratives were examined. The older children demonstrated a clear understanding of the need to tell a story that was interesting, strange, or unusual. Among the 4-year-olds, half the narratives concerned animals and their activities; however, the activities reported were the mundane, routine activities of eating, walking in the forest, and so forth. Among the 5-year-olds, 70% of the stories concentrated on animals and their activities. In contrast, at 6, a marked shift in narrative topics was found with three monster stories and five danger/adventure stories being told: All clearly acceptable because of their dramatic nature. Among 7-year-olds, seven danger/ adventure narratives and two special-occasion narratives were told. With increasing age, there was a greater acknowledgment that narratives need to be reportable to justify the extended talking turn that storytelling allows the speaker. The greater use of evaluative devices among older children also intensified the appeal of their narratives.

Structural Complexity.   Complicating action was found to increase with age, both in terms of the number of complicating events and in terms of the organization of these complicating actions. Children in the concrete operational stage demonstrated a superior ability to organize narratives through their ability to classify events and, in particular, through their ability to specify the relationships among events (see, for example, the narrative about the earmuffs, or Lisa and the Grumpet).

When the narratives are evaluated according to Applebee's developmental sequence, the following patterns emerged: The majority of narratives by the 4-year-olds were primitive narratives; the majority of 5-year-olds told unfocused chain narratives and the majority of the 6- and 7-year-olds told true narratives. In true narratives, clear, coherent global representations for the narrative were possible. In fact, some of the 6- and 7-year-olds created humor through violating the implications set up earlier in their narratives. In true narratives, furthermore, it seems likely that children will emphasize different organizational patterns to foreground specific events or characters. Thus, it may not be possible to specify a single predominant organizational strategy because several may appear in a given story. The 6- and 7-year-olds seemed to demonstrate the ability to use diverse structural patterns within a single narrative (e.g., in the narrative of Lisa and the Grumpet, the storyteller switched from a focus on a series of events to a focus on the Grumpet to a focus on their feelings—thus the listener moves from an action focus to a character focus and then to an evaluative focus). This skill in utilizing different structural patterns is believed to reflect the child's growing decentration of thought, and increased linguistic skills for expressing more complex relationships among events and objects (see, for example, Haslett, 1983).

When the development trends found in this study are compared with those of Botvin and Sutton-Smith, we find the hierarchical order of complexity is similar, although the children in this study appeared to achieve, at the same age, more complex stories than their counterparts in the Botvin and Sutton-Smith study. In particular, some 6- and 7-year-old subjects achieved stories on Level VI.

CONCLUSION AND IMPLICATIONS

Like other scholars, I have argued in this chapter that the structural analysis of narratives needs to incorporate research on story telling by people in everyday situations. Formal story grammars are often very abstract and generate stories that are relatively simple and uninteresting (Yussen, 1982). Furthermore, as van Dijk (1980a) reminds us, narrative structures are only one aspect of what narration represents; we must take into account the cognitive capabilities and the socio-cultural backgrounds of both narrator and audience.

In particular, this study has demonstrated the value of a structural approach, such as that of Labov, which emphasizes the relationships among categories and their functions, and analyzes the linguistic strategies operating in narratives. The results of the present study indicate that with increasing age, children's narrative structures increase in complexity. Additionally, children's ability to coordinate narrative events—to make them coherent and express a point—also increases with age. Put another way, children's scripts for narratives become increasingly well-formed and cohesive. Finally, the qualitative analysis developed here reveals some skills and failures among children's story-telling ability that produce additional insights into narrative comprehension and production.

Children develop their narrative skills with an increasing recognition of both narrative structure and the implied communicative demands of narratives, such as reportability, intepretive frames of reference and the like. Children's developing cognitive and linguistic abilities permit them to express this knowledge in their narratives. The relationship among linguistic, cognitive and narrative skills is undoubtedly multi-faceted and reciprocal; linguistic markers such as *now* and *then* facilitate a narrative's coherence, while at the same time, the understanding of how such markers function in narratives facilitates the use and understanding of those devices in general.

Two cautions should be noted. First, the use of a certain linguistic structure does not necessarily imply that children have mastered its use. With regard to narratives, we must keep in mind that children may be imitating certain structures without full understanding of its usages. Orientations, for example, especially among the 3-and 4-year-olds may be largely imitation that stems from being read stories with formulaic orientations like *one day* or *once upon a time*. Similarly, the use of *and* may function only as a connective, rather than as a cohensive device. Any analysis of children's communicative competence, then, must carefully qualify how, when, and for what purposes certain linguistic features are used. These qualifications, I believe, can be most accurately done by analyzing children's everyday, naturalistic communication over a range of diverse contexts.

Second, children's narrative skills must be evaluated in light of sociocultural variables as well as cognitive and linguistic abilities. For example, Heath (1983) found that children's attitudes toward literacy are influenced by their sociocultural group. Another important factor is the communicator's tacit world knowledge that constrains both linguistic production and comprehension. Raskin's work (this volume) develops a semantic theory that rests upon a schema-based representation of world knowledge. Although Raskin's model is not a developmental model, we need to consider children's semantic representation of their world knowledge and its impact on narrative comprehension and production. Clearly, such semantic knowledge plays a critical role in metaphor, sarcasm and fantasy. And in assessing this semantic knowledge, researchers must look at children's knowledge as it develops in its own right rather than viewing it as a more primitive, simplified representation of adult semantic knowledge. Children's ability to switch topics and to connect unrelated events, for example, appears to indicate that their sense-making attempts need to be assessed without reference to any adult model that presupposes an adult's tacit semantic ability.

ACKNOWLEDGMENT

I wish to gratefully acknowledge the support of an Interdisciplinary Research Grant from the College of Education, University of Delaware, granted to myself, Dr. Joanne Golden, and Dr. Carol Vukelich. Their assistance in the data collection and data analysis for the project is also gratefully acknowledged.

REFERENCES

Applebee, A. N. (1978). *The child's concept of story*. Chicago: University of Chicago Press.
Beach, W. (1983). Background understandings and the situated accomplishment of conversational telling-expansions. In R. Craig & K. Tracy (Eds.), *Conversational coherence: Studies in form and strategy*. Beverly Hills, CA: Sage.

Botvin, G., & Sutton-Smith, B. (1977). The development of structural complexity in children's fantasy narratives. *Developmental Psychology, 13,* 377–388.

Brown, A. L., & Smiley, S. S. (1977). Rating the importance of structural units of prose passages: A problem of metacognitive development. *Child Development, 48,* 1–8.

Brown, L. (1973). *A first language.* Cambridge: Harvard University Press.

Burton, D. (1981). *Dialogue and discourse.* London: Routledge, Kegan, Paul.

Clark, H., & Clark, E. (1977). *Psychology and language.* New York: Harcourt Brace Jovanovich.

Cook-Gumperz, J., & Green, J. (in press). Sense of story: Influences on children's storytelling ability. In D. Tannen (Ed.), *Cohesion in oral and written communication.* Norwood, NJ: Ablex.

deBeaugrande, R., & Colby, B. (1979). Narrative models of action and interaction. *Cognitive Science, 3,* 43–66.

van Dijk, T. A. (1976a). Philosophy of action and theory of narrative. *Poetics, 5,* 287–338.

van Dijk, T. A. (1976b). Narrative macrostructures. Logical and cognitive foundations. *PTL, 1,* 547–568.

van Dijk, T. A. (1977b). Semantic macro-structures and knowledge frames in discourse comprehension. In M. Just & P. Carpenter (Eds.), *Cognitive processes in comprehension* (pp. 3–32). Hillsdale, NJ: Lawrence Erlbaum Associates.

van Dijk, T. A. (1977a). *Text and context. Explorations in the semantics and pragmatics of discourse.* London: Longman.

van Dijk, T. A. (1980a). *Macrostructures.* Hillsdale, NJ: Lawrence Erlbaum Associates.

van Dijk, T. A. (1980b). Story comprehension. *Poetics, 9,* 1–3.

van Dijk, T. A., & Kintsch, W. (1977). Cognitive psychology and discourse. In W. Dressler (Ed.), *Current trends in textlinguistics.* New York: deGruyter.

Gardner, H., Winner, E., Bechhofer, R., & Wolf, D. (1978). The development of figurative language. In K. Nelson (Ed.), *Children's language: Vol. 1.* New York: Gardner Press.

Glenn, C. (1978). The role of episodic structure and of story length in children's recall of simple stories. *Journal of Verbal Learning and Verbal Behavior, 17,* 229–247.

Haslett, B. (1983). Children's strategies for maintaining cohesion in written and oral stories. *Communication Education, 32,* 91–104.

Heath, S. B. (1983). What no bedtime story means: Narrative skills at home and school. *Language in Society, 7,* 49–76.

Kintsch, W. (1974). *The representation of meaning in memory.* Hillsdale, NJ: Lawrence Erlbaum Associates.

Kintsch, W. (1977). *Memory and cognition.* New York: Wiley.

Labov, W. (1972). *Language in the inner city.* University Park, PA: University of Pennsylvania Press.

Labov, W., & Waletsky, J. (1967). Narrative analysis: Oral versions of the personal experience. In *Essays on the Verbal and Visual Arts: Proceedings of the 1966 Annual Spring Meeting of the American Ethnological Society.* Seattle: University of Washington Press.

Piaget, J. (1926). *The language and thought of the child.* New York: Harcourt & Brace.

Piaget, J. (1962). *Comments on Vygotsky's critical remarks.* Cambridge, MA: MIT Press.

Pitcher, E., & Prelinger, E. (1963). *Children tell stories.* New York: Interna-Universities Press.

Polanyi, L. (1979). So what's the point? *Semiotica, 25,* 207–236.

Pratt, M. L. (1977). *Toward a speech act theory of literary discourse.* Bloomington: Indiana University Press.

Propp, V. (1958). *Morphology of the folk tale.* Austin: University of Texas Press.

Rummelhart, D. (1975). Notes on a schema for stories. In D. Bobrow & D. Collins (Eds.), *Representation and understanding.* New York: Academic Press.

Rummelhart, D., & Ortony, A. (1977). The representation of knowledge in memory. In R. Anderson, R. Spiro, & W. Montague (Eds.), *Schooling and the acquisition of knowledge* (pp. 99–136). Hillsdale, NJ: Lawrence Erlbaum Associates.

Smith, B. (1980). Afterthoughts on narrative. *Critical Inquiry, 1,* 213–236.

Stevens, B. (1981). *Children's awareness of juxtaposed stories.* Unpublished master's thesis, University of Wisconsin—Madison.

Tannen, D. (1979). What's in a frame? Surface evidence for underlying expectations. In R. Freedle (Ed.), New directions in discourse processing. Norwood, NJ: Ablex.

Thorndyke, P. (1977). Cognitive structures in comprehension and memory of narrative discourse. *Cognitive Psychology, 9,* 77–110.

Wood, B. (1981). *Children and communication.* Englewood Cliffs, NJ: Prentice-Hall.

Yussen, S. (1982). Children's impressions of coherence in narratives. In B. Hutson (Ed.), *Advances in reading and linguistic research: Vol. 1.* London: JAI Press.

Yussen, S., Buss, R., Matthews, S. R., II, & Kane, P. (1980). Developmental changes in judging important and critical elements of stories. *Developmental Psychology, 16,* 213–219.

5 Scripts, Story Grammars, and Causal Schemas

Sally Planalp
University of Illinois

The preceding chapters by Raskin, Burleson, and Haslett represent a broad range of concerns for the study of language and discourse. As a set they encompass interpreting (Raskin), producing (Haslett), and collaborating on discourse (Burleson). They include several forms of discourse—sentences (Raskin), ordinary conversation (Burleson), and narratives (Haslett). The content of the discourse ranges from scary dreams and monsters (Haslett), to reasons for failing an exam (Burleson), to anything that could be said in a sentence (Raskin). Yet in spite of the range of issues represented in the three chapters, they all share a concern for how knowledge is used in discourse processing, a concern that transcends function, form, and content.

Unraveling the interplay between human knowledge and discourse is a task that goes beyond even those issues raised in the chapters by Raskin, Burleson, and Haslett. It may be the most pervasive and difficult problem confronting anyone studying discourse. It may also be the most important. Certainly it will require the coordinated efforts of scholars working on different aspects of the problem, using different research tools and different perspectives. Raskin, Burleson, and Haslett have made their separate contributions; I try to provide some coordination. Rather than discussing each piece in isolation, I place them within the broader research effort, raise issues and controversies, and hopefully draw out some useful criticisms and new directions for each. First I sketch the role of world knowledge in discourse processing drawing on several theoretical frameworks in order to set up a context for discussion of the three chapters. Then I focus on one specific issue found in each chapter as a more direct way of setting each piece within the general framework. Specifically, Raskin's work is linked to other efforts to specify what knowledge is needed to comprehend discourse and how it is used. Haslett's piece is tied to problems in defining the relationship between knowledge of discourse forms and other world knowledge. Finally, Burleson's piece is the impetus for discussing how knowledge serves as a guide to producing texts, especially conversations.

OVERVIEW OF RESEARCH ON KNOWLEDGE
AND DISCOURSE PROCESSING

It is hard to deny the importance of knowing something for producing and comprehending texts. Our intuitions tell us that we need to know something about aardvarks before we can talk or write stories about them, and that the more we know about aardvarks the better we are able to comprehend what others say and write about them. The problem is that we can, and ordinarily do, communicate on topics other than aardvarks. Does this mean that to study discourse we must study everything people know? The answer obviously cannot be an unqualified "yes" because we are studying discourse now without sophisticated models of world knowledge but it cannot be an unqualified "no" either, because the limits are visible on the horizon. Consider, for example, three processes that are central to comprehending texts—producing coherence, making inferences, and deriving gists. Impressive research progress has been made in all three areas, most of it within the last decade. Obviously a great deal can be learned without considering world knowledge in depth, but some basic and bothersome questions remain.

In the case of coherence, research has uncovered a wide repertoire of cohesive devices (Halliday & Hasan, 1976; Schegloff & Sacks, 1973), many types of coherence relations (deBeaugrande, 1980; Schank, 1977), and social consequences of being incoherent (Planalp & Tracy, 1980; Tracy, 1982; Vuchinich, 1977). In all three cases, world knowledge plays an important if sometimes unrecognized role. All the cohesive devices in the world (including pronouns, conjunctions, repetition, question–answer pairs) will not produce coherence when they run contrary to world knowledge (Mosenthal & Tierney, 1984) (e.g., Jane bought some scurvy, then went home to paint his house with it). Many kinds of relations are possible (such as causal, temporal, and functional connections), but world knowledge is necessary to determine that there is a relationship between Vitamin C and scurvy and that a Vitamin C deficiency causes scurvy but not vice versa. And one person's incoherence may be another person's obvious connection, depending on what each knows (the Limeys didn't have that problem).

A similar case can be made for the importance of world knowledge for making inferences and deriving gists. Research has revealed types of inferences (Warren, Nicholas, & Trabasso, 1979), when they are made (Goetz, 1979) and how they are used strategically (Harris & Monaco, 1978), but the content of the inference depends on world knowledge. Similarly, deriving gists involves either applying sets of condensing rules to a text (van Dijk, 1977), applying a conventional text structure (Rumelhart, 1975) or both. The condensing rules themselves depend on knowledge of categories and their instances and of goals and goal-oriented action (van Dijk, 1977). A conventional text structure (such as a story grammar) will give the elements of a gist (setting, characters, plot, resolution) but the reader must draw upon world knowledge to determine how those elements are instantiated in any particular story (e.g., Vulcan is a setting but Spock is a character). Thus it is impossible to derive the gist of a text without using world knowledge, just as it is impossible to make it coherent or to draw inferences from it.

Clearly the role of world knowledge cannot be ignored if discourse processing is to be fully understood, but the task is formidable. It entails modeling everything that people know (because anything that is known can be talked about) and determining how that knowledge is used to move from idea to text in producing texts or from text to idea in interpreting them. The only reasonable way to attack a task of such magnitude is to divide it into smaller, more tractable pieces that will ultimately fit together. This is exactly what is happening with work on world knowledge and discourse processing. Specific areas of focus, formulations of problems, terminology, and methods may vary from study to study but the ultimate goal is the same. In fact, when the overall research effort is examined in light of that goal it seems more coherent and complete than the individual research programs that make it up. For example, a basic distinction that can be used to organize work on world knowledge and discourse processes is the distinction between what knowledge people have (content and structure) and how that knowledge is used in interpreting and producing texts (processing). No line of research deals exclusively with content/structure or with processing but the focus tends to be on one or the other. Even though it is widely recognized that no model or theory of processing can be fully specified without constraints on content/structure and vice versa (Anderson, 1978), it seems to be equally widely assumed that effort is best devoted to one or the other now, leaving a sophisticated synthesis for the future. Thus, the overall research effort is balanced by lines of research that are complementary and should ultimately converge.

Focus on How Knowledge Is Used

The first of two basic approaches to studying discourse and world knowledge is to set aside issues of content and structure in order to focus on how knowledge is used in comprehending and producing messages. Within that approach three specific tactics are taken. One is to sketch the structure of knowledge in broad outline and build a processing model that accounts for important conceptual distinctions and experimental data. Another is to build a more detailed model of processing by relying on the intuitions of human coders for the knowledge component. The third is to identify global individual differences in knowledge and to trace their effects on processing.

Ortony's (1978) work on comprehension and memory for texts is an example of the first tactic. It is a broad theoretical effort devoted to modeling comprehension and memory. Knowledge is represented as a network of associations both between and within concepts—a semantic network—across which activation spreads. Ortony uses his model to distinguish between comprehension (activating related concepts) and memory (retrieving a record of formerly activated concepts) and then to account for a number of subtle experimental findings such as context effects on comprehension, inferences at both comprehension and recall, and loss of memory for exact wording and gist. In a sense, the processing component of Ortony's model (spread of activation) is no more refined than his knowledge component (semantic network), but the focus of his thinking is on memory and comprehension (and whatever subprocesses are involved in them) rather than on the nature of the knowledge in semantic memory.

The second tactic that focuses on processing is represented by the research program of van Dijk and Kintsch (1983). Their model is broad enough to cover comprehension, memory, and production of a number of discourse forms yet is detailed enough to explain established data and generate new predictions concerning memory (Kintsch & van Dijk, 1978) and readability (Miller & Kintsch, 1981). The knowledge component, however, is finessed by using human coders to identify propositions and connections between them. Kintsch and van Dijk recognize that their knowledge base is "ad hoc and intuitive" and a major limitation of their model (van Dijk & Kintsch, 1983, p. 8) but they are currently working to overcome it by incorporating simple knowledge structures (Miller & Kintsch, 1981).

The third tactic for studying how knowledge is used is to identify individual differences in knowledge and to trace their effects on processing. In principle, any individual difference might be studied but practice has been limited to identifiable (or manipulable) differences in expertise for a given domain of knowledge. For example, Miyake and Norman (1979) trained subjects in text editing and found that those with moderate levels of expertise (relative to the task) asked more questions. Those that found the task too easy had nothing to ask; those that found it too hard did not "know enough to know what was not known." In a similar vein, Fiske, Kinder, and Larter (1983; Fiske & Kinder, 1981) studied relative experts and novices with regard to political knowledge and found that experts inferred and recalled more inconsistencies in stories about the political orientations of countries than did novices. Spilich, Vesonder, Chiesi, and Voss (1979; Chiesi, Spilich, & Voss, 1979) undertook the most sophisticated studies of expertise (in this case for baseball) and found differences in the ability to recognize and recall events, group them into sequences, link them to general goals, and anticipate outcomes. They have also gone one step beyond other studies of individual differences by describing how their findings could be incorporated into Kintsch and van Dijk's model and used to refine it.

To summarize, work that focuses on processing steers clear of modeling the knowledge used in discourse by using abstract frameworks, human intuition, or global individual differences as stand-ins for well-articulated models world knowledge. It tells us very little about what people must know about the world in order to understand and produce texts, but a great deal about how they use whatever knowledge they have. It is the crucial first step toward modeling comprehension, memory, and production processes in discourse. As is widely acknowledged, the next step must be to incorporate explicitly defined knowledge into those processing models.

Focus on Structure and Content of Knowledge

The second basic approach to studying knowledge in discourse, one that complements work that focuses on processing, is to determine what knowledge is needed to interpret and produce texts (content) and how that knowledge is structured. Within this approach, two interlocking tactics are used. The first begins with a text and infers what knowledge would make it comprehensible. The second begins with a plausible knowledge structure and tests for its existence by appeal to effects on discourse processing.

Investigators that begin with a text and infer what knowledge would make it comprehensible must of necessity pick small, manageable texts. A brief look at two research examples demonstrates why. Labov and Fanshel (1977) gave themselves the seemingly unambitious task of analyzing five very short episodes of a 15-minute psychotherapeutic conversation. The knowledge needed "simply" to elaborate each speaker's intentions and draw out what each remark implied for the ongoing interaction involved knowledge of speech acts, emotions, and personal relationships that took nearly 400 pages to describe. More impressive still is Schank and Abelson's (1977) pioneering attempt to explicate the knowledge structures involved in basic comprehension of very simple stories. They had to include knowledge of words, stereotyped actions, plans, goals, role and personal relationships, even the meaning of life. The problem is that people draw on such vast stores of interrelated knowledge in comprehending and producing even the simplest and shortest texts, it is very difficult to make the task manageable.

One productive way around the problem is to isolate relatively self-contained units of knowledge that could be used to comprehend simple texts or limited aspects of complex texts. These appear in the literature under several labels—*frames, schemas, scripts, story grammars*—but all refer to partially isolable knowledge structures that are used to comprehend texts[1] (Anderson, 1981).

---

[1]There is as yet no standard usage for these terms. For example, knowledge structures that are used to put together a coherence picture of what is being said are called *schemas* (Bartlett, 1932), *frames* (Charniak, 1982) and *scripts* (Raskin, this volume). Hewes and Planalp (1982) have tried to sort out similarities and differences among the terms as most investigators use them.

Frames and schemas are generic labels for a wide variety of knowledge structures. For example, when frames are postulated to explain context recognition (Charniak, 1982) or descriptions of films (Tannen, 1979), they can refer to knowledge of anything from theft to magic acts. Schemas also come in many forms—self-schemas (Markus, 1977), political schemas (Fiske & Kinder, 1981), and relational schemas (Planalp, 1983). Scripts refer more specifically to knowledge of stereotyped action sequences that make it possible to understand stories about routine events such as going to a restaurant or to a class lecture (Schank & Abelson, 1977). Finally, story grammars refer to knowledge of the components of stories (such as setting, theme, plot, and resolution) that make it possible to comprehend and produce simple stories.

By analyzing texts, one can conclude that people must have something like a schema, script, frame, or story grammar to comprehend and produce texts, but that is not enough. The precise content and structure of the knowledge must be specified and submitted to independent tests for its existence. Such tests are based on the assumption that people have a single knowledge base that they use to perform a number of cognitive functions[2]. A knowledge structure can then be postulated on the basis of one process (e.g., inference) and verified using other processes (e.g., attention, memory, or message production). For example, Schank and Abelson (1977) demonstrated that their computer program found scripts useful in "comprehending" texts, but they did not demonstrate that people have and use scripts. Bower, Black, and Turner (1979), however, submitted scripts to several independent tests. They found that human subjects could agree on the constituents of scripts, their hierarchical organization, and linear ordering. When subjects were asked to read stories about scripted actions, they tended to confuse actions that were explicitly stated with actions not stated but consistent with the script (the standard test of inference) and remembered actions in the order expected from the script rather than in the order they happened in the text. Finally, they found that reading time for adjacent sentences in the story varied with their distance apart in the script. As evidence for the existence and use of scripts, Bower, Black, and Turner's (1979) evidence is difficult to deny and has been supported by other processing measures as well (Haberlandt & Bingham, 1982).

Because scripts and story grammars have similar structures (hierarchical and linear), the evidence for story grammars parallels that for scripts. Pollard-Gott, McCloskey, and Todres (1979) and Thorndyke (1977) found evidence for hierarchical organizations using cluster analyses and measures of memory,

---

[2]The presumption of a single knowledge store is not only intuitively plausible but also necessary on practical grounds. It seems unlikely that people draw on one knowledge store to talk about baseball and another store to comprehend what others say about it. Moreover, if there were knowledge structures for each minor cognitive process, we would have to model all human knowledge several times over. The most thorough discussion of this assumption specifically applied to discourse processing is found in Reiser and Black (1982).

respectively. Mandler (1978) and Stein and Glenn (1979) found evidence for linear ordering in memory inversions. Stein and Glenn also found that inference was guided by story grammars.

Research on schemas and frames is much more sketchy and less well integrated with the discourse processing literature than the script and story grammar work. One notable exception is Spiro's (1980) test of Heider's (1958) balance theory as a schema. He asked subjects to read a story about a couple who were considering marriage but had either similar or different views about whether to have children, then surreptitiously slipped them information later about whether the couple actually had or had not married. Errors in recall for information in the original story were consistent with a balance schema (i.e., those who married were remembered as agreeing and those who never married were remembered as disagreeing).

To summarize work on the content and structure of world knowledge used in discourse processing, there are two distinguishable but interrelated lines of research. The first considers what knowledge would be necessary to comprehend or produce messages. The second gathers evidence for or against specified knowledge structures by looking for their effects on cognitive processes. At this point it should be clear how work that focuses on processing complements work on the content and structure of knowledge. Obviously processing cannot take place unless there is something to process and knowledge without processing is useless. Less obvious is the way refinements in one area feed work in the other. A knowledge structure may be posited to perform some process; it is then tested using other processes; the results may lead to further refinement of the knowledge structure, and so on. In this way, the two lines of research interleave both as important aspects of discourse processing and as interrelated components to be developed together. In the next section of this chapter, I use this overview of work on discourse processing and world knowledge as a context for considering issues relevant to the chapters by Raskin, Haslett, and Burleson in greater detail.

SCRIPTS, STORY GRAMMARS, AND CAUSAL SCHEMAS

Raskin on Scripts

Of the three chapters, Raskin's has the broadest sweep and is almost a macrocosm of the work I have reviewed. His goal is to model comprehension of any sentence, regardless of form or content. He argues that the only way to reach that goal is to combine sophisticated structures of world knowledge (in his terminology, a script-based lexicon) with a processing component (combinatorial rules). He also recognizes that sentences are comprehended both as parts of larger units of discourse and as events occurring in an informative world, so that contextual influences must be an integral part of any model of sentence comprehension. Those observations capture many of the important challenges researchers studying discourse processing have faced in the last decade. Because Raskin's work has so many ties to a wide variety of research in discourse processing I turn to that work to assess its validity and limitations.

Although Raskin's approach to sentence comprehension may be controversial among linguists, much of the current work in psycholinguistics, cognitive science, and discourse processing reflects the same basic commitments. As discussed in the previous section of this paper, courageous attempts have been made to model whatever knowledge is needed to comprehend texts. It is also widely recognized that sophisticated models of world knowledge are only half the picture, the other essential component being processing functions. The commitment to studying sentences in context is both explicitly articulated (Winograd, 1977) and by now almost taken for granted in conducting research. Not only have Raskin's basic commitments been adopted, but experimental work has been in large measure consistent with his theory.

Consider, for example, work on ambiguous sentences. Raskin's work incorporates two seemingly contradictory phenomena—that at least two compatible combinations of meaning are possible for ambiguous sentences (by definition) but that normally only one meaning comes to mind. His solution to the problem is to build a model that generates several (if not all) possible meanings from which a choice is made based on compatibility of meanings within the sentence and between sentence and obvious context(s). In fact, there is experimental evidence that people do just this. Swinney (1979) showed that multiple meanings of words were accessed but that one meaning was chosen based on context within one-half second, below the level of awareness. Oden (1978) also demonstrated that people use relative sensibleness (in Raskin's terms, degree of fit between combinations) to choose the appropriate meaning of ambiguous sentences and draw on semantic information to resolve syntactic ambiguities. Gibbs (1979) extended the work to the influence of extra-linguistic contexts on intepretations of pragmatically ambiguous remarks (such as "Must you open the window?) that could be interpreted as a request for action (or in this case inaction) or as a request for information. In short, experimental evidence generally confirms Raskin's view of how ambiguous sentences are interpreted.

Unfortunately, other work has also confirmed the degree of difficulty involved in elaborating the theory beyond Raskin's general outline. As discussed earlier in this chapter, specifying what knowledge is needed to comprehend texts is a monumental task fraught with practical and theoretical difficulties and Raskin's theory ultimately requires that it all be specified. In addition, work on how knowledge is used has uncovered complexities that are not readily apparent in Raskin's theory. For example, specifying the processes by which sentences are interpreted in context has proven to be very difficult. Combinatorial rules cannot be expanded to encompass context because they would create a combinatorial explosion. That is, if whole texts were interpreted in the same way Raskin indicates that sentences are, there would be an astronomical number of combinations that are theoretically possible. (As an illustration, if "The paralyzed bachelor hit the colorful ball" had 64 potential combinations and 25 compatible ones, what would *War and Peace* have?) Obviously people cannot hold that much information in short-term memory before making an interpretation (van Dijk & Kintsch, 1983). What seems to happen instead is that tentative interpretations are developed immediately and are used as long as they generate plausible interpretations of subsequent discourse. But a host of new problems arises when one tries to specify how tentative interpretations are developed in the first place (Charniak, 1982), how they are used to interpret subsequent discourse (Anderson & Shifrin, 1980; Kozminsky, 1977; Rumelhart & Ortony, 1977), and what the limits of reinterpretation are (Anderson & Pichert, 1978). In short, acknowledging that context guides interpretations still leaves a number of complex processes to be specified.

Haslett on Story Grammars

The next chapter of this set, Haslett's piece on children's narratives, illustrates a very different approach to studying the use of world knowledge in discourse. Whereas Raskin has developed a general abstract model of sentence comprehension, Haslett has focused on one specific form of discourse (the story) and on one specific form of knowledge (the story grammar) in order to test empirically how children's abilities to tell stories develop. Because Haslett's work is such a fine representative of the larger body of work on story grammars, it can be used, like Raskin's, to draw out general issues and problems, especially those pertaining to the relationship between knowledge of discourse forms and world knowledge in general.

No other form of discourse has been studies as extensively as stories and no other form or world knowledge has been studied as extensively as the story grammar[3] particularly in the last decade. At least six different story grammars have been postulated (Labov, 1972; Mandler & Johnson, 1977; Rumelhart, 1975; Stein & Glenn, 1979; Thorndyke, 1977; van Dijk, 1980) and studies that have tested how they are used by both adults and children are too numerous to cite. Yet this state of affairs is not entirely welcome from the perspective of studying knowledge structures. Understandable as it may be to find relatively autonomous lines of research in a rapidly developing area, all those story grammars cannot be different and yet be correct. The unfortunate results of story grammar proliferation are that effort has been wasted in virtual duplication of research, story grammars have not been refined by clashes with one another, and the research as a whole gives the false impression that any story grammar is as good as any

---

[3]There is some difference of opinion about whether story grammars are narrative structures (i.e., properties of texts) or knowledge structures. Because nearly all tests of story grammars involve analyses of cognitive processes rather than analyses of texts, they seem more plausible as knowledge structures, but for a different view see Mandler (1983).

other. In an effort to remedy this situation, Pollard-Gott, McCloskey, and Todres (1979) submitted two story grammars to a contrastive test that suggested refinements in each, but no one has followed their lead.

A second issue that plagues research on story grammars is the relationship between story grammars and other forms of world knowledge. The basic question is whether the knowledge people use to interpret and produce stories is knowledge of stories per se or knowledge of the narrated world (see Haslett, this volume). Put simply, to produce or comprehend a story about a boy's pet aardvark, do we need to know about stories or is it sufficient to know about boys and aardvarks? This issue has been debated at length (*Behavioral and Brain Sciences*, 1983; *Cognitive Science*, 1979, 1981) and positions fall all along the continuum. Mandler and Johnson (1980) argue that story grammars are not reducible to world knowledge, Garnham (1983), Black and Wilensky (1979; Wilensky, 1983) argue that they are completely reducible, and van Dijk and Kintsch (1983) argue that they are partially reducible. Regardless of how the debates are ultimately resolved, the point is an important one. As I argued earlier, world knowledge is interrelated in complex ways that make it difficult for a researcher to study only one identified knowledge structure and ignore the rest. Whether or not story grammars can be isolated, their relationship to other knowledge is an important consideration.

This is especially true for developmental studies of story grammars like Haslett's. Presumably, children's knowledge of story structure does not develop independently from the rest of their knowledge and their cognitive skills, so it is incumbent upon those who study the development of story grammars to tie their work to established theories of social and cognitive development. The first step in that direction should be to choose a story grammar to study, as Haslett chose Labov's. As indicated earlier, the existing literature provides no sound basis for choosing one over another. The second step should be to generate and test predictions about the relationship between the development of story grammar skills and other cognitive skills, as Haslett has done in relating her findings to Piaget's stages. Without precise linkages we run the risk of learning only that children learn to comprehend and tell stories better as they get older without learning how or why. Finally, the issue of whether story grammars are reducible to other forms of world knowledge could also be addressed in a developmental context. By investigating whether changes in the use of story grammars covary with similar changes in other linguistic and non-linguistic domains, developmental theorists may be able to determine whether story skills are only one of many related skills that change in childhood or whether they are a special case driven by different processes and subject to different influences.

Burleson on Causal Schemas

Burleson's chapter on attributional processes in conversation, the third of this set, represents still another way of studying how world knowledge is used in discourse. In one sense, his work is very similar to Haslett's work on children's narratives because both are concerned with how knowledge guides the organization of discourse. The difference is that Haslett deals with a knowledge structure that guides only one form of discourse, whereas Burleson deals with general knowledge that is used in all domains of life. Burleson's piece definitely is not a microcosm of the literature on causal attributions because they are rarely studied by looking at discourse. Certainly there are some notable exceptions (Sillars, 1980a, 1980b) but they are overshadowed by the mountains of research on attribution that are not grounded in discourse (for a recent review see Harvey & Weary, 1984).

Burleson's analysis is a fascinating example of people using attribution theory in everyday life. The conversation is a textbook case of people discovering a phenomenon that needs explaining, working through information relevant to competing explanations and choosing the one that fits the data best. But in case one is tempted to conclude that people are better intuitive scientists than was thought, it should be noted that Burleson's analysis is based on a single conversation, on a single topic, produced by learned and articulate participants who have all the information they need to arrive at a causal attribution. If conditions had been different, their attributional processes might not have been so exemplary. Systematic sampling of a wider range of conversations may have revealed many more examples of attribution driven by prior assumptions, stereotypes, or careless reasoning. As Burleson notes, conversation analysis could be fruitfully extended to other conversational contexts and integrated with other literature that has examined what provokes spontaneous attribution searches (Wong & Weiner, 1981), what information is gathered to test competing explanations (Garland, Hardy, & Stephenson, 1975) and how the best explanation is chosen (Kruglanski, Hamel, Maides, & Schwartz, 1978).

Beyond the limitations of this particular study lies the more basic question of how one determines what knowledge and processes have guided the production of naturally occurring texts. Although it is tempting to assume that people say what occurs to them and that the rules of conversation reflect the rules of thought (Schank, 1977) it is also obvious that they do not, otherwise there would be no deception, dissembling, or diplomacy. Thus Burleson's conclusion (Burleson, this volume) that attribution processes can be directly observed in conversation is unwarranted. Like scripts, story grammars, and other types of schemas, causal schemas cannot be observed directly but only indirectly using a variety of techniques, none of which is perfect but which can provide converging evidence as a set. A more circumspect conclusion would be that conversation analysis is a source of indirect evidence about attributional processes that has been neglected.

One reason it is not safe to assume that the rules of conversation reflect the rules of thought is that they also reflect the rules of society. Social constraints often prevent people from saying what they think. In the case of the conversation that Burleson analyzed, the participants may have been motivated to present themselves in a favorable light (Baumeister, 1982) instead of (or in addition to) being motivated to accurately assess the causes of the student's failure. After all, a good teacher should not write off a student's failure to stupidity but should take any reasonable measures to help the student succeed. Seen from this perspective, the topical sequences in the conversation may not have paralleled the reasoning processes of the participants but instead may have been attempts to create the impression that a socially undesirable attribution had not been made lightly. There is some evidence in the conversation for this interpretation. For example, early in the conversation Don, the instructor, seems to have already arrived at the conclusion that he will have to insist that the student drop the course (U10) because she just can't handle it (U12) and there are several indications that both participants feel uncomfortable with the causal attribution of stupidity (Burleson, this volume). Thus the data from this conversation may indicate more about what attribution processes are socially acceptable than what processes social actors actually use to determine causality. If this conversation had taken place in a setting where sexism was acceptable, it might have moved quickly to public explanations based on "known facts" about women's abilities even if each participant had reasoned to the explanation privately in exactly the same way Burleson suggests they did.

CONCLUSIONS

In this chapter I have sketched some of the existing literature on the use of world knowledge in discourse processing and have used the chapters by Raskin, Haslett, and Burleson as focal points for discussing certain issues in greater detail. In doing so I have held all three authors responsible for the work of their fellows more than would normally be fair. No single piece of research can engage all the problems in an area, nor does anyone expect it to. Nevertheless, it is important to understand how each piece of research fits in the larger effort and how the assumptions of one become the hotly debated issues or tested hypotheses of another. In this way, the coordinated efforts of a number of theorists and researchers can make important gains even against problems as difficult as understanding the use of world knowledge in producing and comprehending discourse.

REFERENCES

Anderson, J. R. (1978). Arguments concerning representations for mental imagery. *Psychological Review, 85*, 249–277.
Anderson, J. R. (1981). Concepts, propositions, and schemata: What are the cognitive units? In J. Flowers (Ed.), *Nebraska symposium on motivation, 1980,* (Vol. 28, pp. 121–162). Lincoln, NE: University of Nebraska Press.
Anderson, R. C., & Pichert, J. W. (1978). Recall of previously unrecallable information following a shift in perspective. *Journal of Verbal Learning and Verbal Behavior, 17,* 1–12.

Anderson, R. C., & Shifrin, Z. (1980). The meaning of words in context. In R. J. Spiro, B. C. Bruce & W. F. Brewer (Eds.), *Theoretical issues in reading comprehension* (pp. 331–348). Hillsdale, NJ: Lawrence Erlbaum Associates.

Bartlett, F. C. (1932). *Remembering*. Cambridge: Cambridge University Press.

Baumeister, R. F. (1982). A self-presentational view of social phenomena. *Psychological Bulletin, 91*, 3–26.

Black, J. B., & Wilensky, R. (1979). An evaluation of story grammars. *Cognitive Science, 3*, 213–230.

Bower, G. H., Black, J. B., & Turner, T. (1979). Scripts in memory for text. *Cognitive Psychology, 11*, 177–220.

Charniak, E. (1982). Context recognition in language comprehension. In W. G. Lehnert & M. H. Ringle (Eds.), *Strategies for natural language processing* (pp. 435–454). Hillsdale, NJ: Lawrence Erlbaum Associates.

Chiesi, H. L., Spilich, G. J., & Voss, J. F. (1979). Acquisition of domain-related information in relation to high and low domain knowledge. *Journal of Verbal Learning and Verbal Behavior, 18*, 257–273.

deBeaugrande, R. (1980). *Text, discourse and process: Toward a multidisciplinary science of texts*. Norwood, NJ: Ablex.

van Dijk, T. A. (1977). Semantic macro-structures and knowledge frames in discourse comprehension. In M. A. Just & P. A. Carpenter (Eds.), *Cognitive processes in comprehension* (pp. 3–32). Hillsdale, NJ: Lawrence Erlbaum Associates.

van Dijk. T. A. (1980). *Macrostructures* . Hillsdale, NJ: Lawrence Erlbaum Associates.

van Dijk, T. A., & Kintsch, W. (1983). *Strategies of discourse comprehension*. New York: Academic Press.

Fiske, S. T., & Kinder, D. R. (1981). Involvement, expertise and schema use: Evidence from political cognition. In N. Cantor & J. Kihlstrom (Eds.), *Cognition, social interaction, and personality* (pp. 171–190). Hillsdale, NJ: Lawrence Erlbaum Associates.

Fiske, S. T., Kinder, D. R., & Larter, W. M. (1983). The novice and the expert: Knowledge-based strategies in political cognition. *Journal of Experimental Social Psychology, 19*, 381–400.

Garland, H., Hardy, A., & Stephenson, L. (1975). Information search as affected by attribution type and response category. *Personality and Social Psychology Bulletin, 1*, 612–615.

Garnham, A. (1983). What's wrong with story grammars. *Cognition, 15*, 145–154.

Gibbs, R. W. (1979). Contextual effects in understanding indirect requests. *Discourse Processes, 2*, 1–10.

Goetz, E. T. (1979). Infering from text: Some factors influencing which inferences will be made. *Discourse Processes, 2*, 179–195.

Haberlandt, K., & Bingham, G. (1982). The role of scripts in the comprehension and retention of texts. *Text, 2*, 29–46.

Halliday, M. A. K., & Hasan, R. (1976). *Cohesion in English*. London: Longman.

Harris, R. J., & Monaco, G. E. (1978). Psychology of pragmatic implication: Information processing between the lines. *Journal of Experimental Psychology: General, 107*, 1–22.

Harvey, J. H., & Weary, G. (1984). Current issues in attribution theory and research. *Annual Review of Psychology, 35*, 427–459.

Heider, F. (1958). *The psychology of interpersonal relations*. New York: Wiley.

Hewes, D. E., & Planalp, S. (1982). There is nothing as useful as a good theory . . .: The influence of social knowledge on interpersonal communication. In M. E. Roloff & C. R. Berger (Eds.), *Social cognition and communication* (pp. 107–150). Beverly Hills, CA: Sage.

Kintsch, W., & van Dijk, T. A. (1978). Toward a model of text comprehension and production. *Psychological Review, 85*, 363–394.

Kozminsky, E. (1977). Altering comprehension: The effect of biasing titles on text comprehension. *Memory and Cognition, 5*, 482–490.

Kruglanski, A. W., Hamel, I. A., Maides, S. A., & Schwartz, J. M. (1978). Attribution theory as a special case of lay epistemology. In J. H. Harvey, W. Ickes, & R. F. Kidd (Eds.), *New direction in attribution research* (Vol. 2, pp. 299–333). Hillsdale, NJ: Lawrence Erlbaum Associates.

Labov, W. (1972). *Language in the inner city*. University Park: University of Pennsylvania Press.

Labov, W., & Fanshel, D. (1977). *Therapeutic discourse*. New York: Academic Press.

Mandler, J. M. (1978). A code in the node: The use of a story schema in retrieval. *Discourse Processes, 1*, 14–35.

Mandler, J. M. (1983). What a story is. *The Behavioral and Brain Sciences, 6*, 603–604.

Mandler, J. M., & Johnson, N. S. (1977). Remembrance of things parsed: Story structure and recall. *Cognitive Psychology, 9*, 111–151.

Mandler, J. M., & Johnson, N. W. (1980). On throwing out the baby with the bathwater: A reply to Black and Wilensky's evaluation of story grammars. *Cognitive Science, 4*, 305–312.

Markus, H. (1977). Self-schemata and processing information abut the self. *Journal of Personality and Social Psychology, 35*, 63–78.

Miller, J. R., & Kintsch, W. (1981). Knowledge-based aspects of prose comprehension and readability. *Text, 1*, 215–232.

Miyake, N., & Norman, D. A. (1979). To ask a question, one must know enough to know what is not known. *Journal of Verbal Learning and Verbal Behavior, 18*, 357–364.

Mosenthal, J. M., & Tierney, R. J. (1984). Cohesion: Problems with talking about text. *Reading Research Quarterly, 19*, 240–244.

Oden, G. C. (1978). Semantic constraints and judged preference for interpretations of ambiguous sentences. *Memory and Cognition, 6*, 26–37.

Ortony, A. (1978). Remembering, understanding, and representation. *Cognitive Science, 2*, 53–69.

Planalp, S. (1983). *Relational schemata: An interpretive approach to relationships*. Unpublished Ph.D. dissertation, University of Wisconsin—Madison.

Planalp, S., & Tracy, K. (1980). Not to change the topic but . . .: A cognitive approach to the management of conversation. In D. Nimmo (Ed.), *Communication yearbook IV*, pp. 237–258. New Brunswick, NJ: Transaction-I.C.A.

Pollard-Gott, L., McCloskey, M., & Todres, A. K. (1979). Subjective story structure. *Discourse Processes, 2*, 251–281.

Reiser, B. J., & Black, J. B. (1982). Processing and structural models of comprehension. *Text, 2*, 225–252.

Rumelhart, D. E. (1975). Notes on a schema for stories. In D. G. Bobrow & A. Collins (Eds.), *Representation and understanding: Studies in cognitive science* (pp. 211–236). New York: Academic Press.

Rumelhart, D. E., & Ortony, A. (1977). The representation of knowledge in memory. In R. C. Anderson, R. J. Spiro & W. E. Montague (Eds.), *Schooling and the acquisition of knowledge* (pp. 99–135). Hillsdale, NJ: Lawrence Erlbaum Associates.

Schank, R. C. (1977). Rules and topics in conversation. *Cognitive Science, 1*, 421–444.

Schank, R. C., & Abelson, R. P. (1977). *Scripts, plans, goals, and understanding*. Hillsdale, NJ: Lawrence Erlbaum Associates.

Schegloff, E. A., & Sacks, H. (1973). Opening up closings. *Semiotica, 8*, 289–327.

Sillars, A. L. (1980a). The sequential and distributional structure of conflict interactions as a function of attributions concerning the locus of responsibility and stability of conflicts. In D. Nimmo (Ed.), *Communication yearbook IV* (pp. 217–235). New Brunswick, NJ: Transaction-I.C.A.

Sillars, A.L. (1980b). Attributions and communication in roommate conflicts. *Communication Monographs, 47*, 180–200.

Spilich, G. J., Vesonder, G. T., Chiesi, H. L., & Voss, J. F. (1979). Text processing of domain-related information for individuals with high and low domain knowledge. *Journal of Verbal Learning and Verbal Behavior 18*, 275–290.

Spiro, R. (1980). Accommodative reconstruction in prose recall. *Journal of Verbal Learning and Verbal Behavior, 19,* 84–95.

Stein, N. L., & Glenn, C. G. (1979). An analysis of story comprehension in elementary school children. In R. O. Freedle (Ed.), *New directions in discourse processing* (Vol. 2, pp. 53–120). Norwood, NJ: Ablex.

Swinney, D. A. (1979). Lexical access during sentence comprehension: (Re)Consideration of context effects. *Journal of Verbal Learning and Verbal Behavior, 18,* 645–659.

Tannen, D. (1979). What's in a frame? Surface evidence for underlying expectations. In R. O. Freedle (Ed.), *New directions in discourse processing* (Vol. 2, pp. 137–181). Norwood, NJ: Ablex.

Thorndyke, P. W. (1977). Cognitive structures in comprehension and memory of narrative discourse. *Cognitive Psychology, 9,* 77–110.

Tracy, K. (1982). On getting the point: Distinguishing "issues" from "events," as aspect of conversational coherence. In M. Burgoon (Ed.), *Communication yearbook IV* (pp. 279–301). New Brunswick, NJ: Transaction-I.C.A.

Vuchinich, S. (1977). Elements of cohesion between turns in ordinary conversation. *Semiotica, 20,* 229–257.

Warren, W. H., Nicholas, D. W., & Trabasso, T. (1979). Event chains and inferences in understanding narratives. In R. O. Freedle (Ed.), *New directions in discourse processing,* (Vol. 2, pp. 23–52). Norwood, NJ: Ablex.

Wilensky, R. (1983). Story grammars versus story pronts. *The Behavioral and Brain Sciences, 6,* 579–623.

Winograd, T. (1977). A framework for understanding discourse. In M. A. Just & P. Carpenter (Eds.), *Cognitive processes in comprehension* (pp. 63–88). New York: Wiley.

Wong, P. T. P., & Weiner, B. (1981). When people ask "why" questions, and the heuristics of attributional search. *Journal of Personality and Social Psychology, 40,* 650–663.

II METHODOLOGICAL ISSUES AND THE ANALYSIS OF DISCOURSE

6 Building a Case for Claims About Discourse Structure

Sally Jackson
University of Oklahoma

Discourse analysis aims to discover rules, patterns, properties, and structures of natural discourse. Although many data sources and analytic procedures might be used in discourse analysis, the general approach of the discourse analyst can be described as the method of analytic induction (Denzin, 1970). Analytic induction is a method of both discovery and testing. The process of analytic induction begins with collection of a set of examples of the phenomenon being studied. The examples are used to build, inductively, a hypothesis. The hypothesis may be about the properties of a class, the rules that generate a pattern of interaction, the sequential characteristics of a kind of interaction, or some other empirical issue. An initial test of the hypothesis is its adequacy as an account of the examples. But this is only a preliminary step. The method of analytic induction is driven by a falsificationist attitude, which subjects any hypothesis about discourse structure to critical examination. The method of analytic induction requires that empirical claims be tested through active, procedurally diverse search for counterexamples.

A good example of analytic induction can be found in Nofsinger's (1975) analysis of the demand ticket. A set of conversational occurrences is identified (through observation and through construction of hypothetical examples), and a set of rules is proposed as an analysis of the belief conditions implied in the issuing of a demand ticket. Further, each rule is tested through demonstration that deviation from the rule produces a noticeable abnormality in the conversation. Not only is each individual rule testable, but so is the set as a whole. We can note, as a purely empirical matter, that the rules are not quite right, because they fail to differentiate between well-formed demand tickets and sequences such as this hypothetical exchange:

Mike: "What would you like to do this evening, Mary?"
Mary: "Hey, Mike?"
Mike: "Yes?"
Mary: "What I'd really like to do is hit balls at the driving range."

By finding ways in which the hypothesis is wrong, we can refine and improve our formulation of the rules. In this case, a revised formulation would include a condition on when a demand ticket should not be issued (specifically, when a space and an audience for the remark already exist—analogous to the rule proposed by Labov & Fanshel, 1977, that a request should not be issued if the hearer would be expected to do the requested act even in the absence of the request). This process of hypothesis/counterevidence/reformulation is the means by which facts about discourse structure must be established.

The method of analytic induction is a rigorous form of empirical demonstration. It is capable of producing forceful arguments for claims about discourse structure. But in the popular image of discourse analysis, analytic induction is regarded, along with all qualitative methodology, as a "soft" methodology, and discourse analytic findings are regarded as nonempirical, nonmethodical, or, at best, preliminary to testing. In part, the popular image of discourse analysis reflects widespread and serious errors in the practice of analytic induction. But equally, it reflects a fundamental flaw in the way social scientists have come to think about their methods. This chapter lays out a general perspective on methodology. From this perspective, analytic induction can be defended in principle. However, the practice of analytic induction by communication researchers rests on the same misconceptions about method as do its critiques by traditional social scientists. The main thrust of the chapter is to suggest ways in which discourse analytic research can profit from a more sophisticated appreciation of the role of methodology in empirical studies.

METHOD AS ARGUMENT

Critics of analytic induction ask what is methodical about this method. Experimental methods can be neatly summed up in terms of a small body of principles: Use a control group, assign subjects randomly to treatments, avoid confounding the independent variable with any other possible causal variable, and so on. Survey methods, too, have their small body of methodological principles: Sample randomly from the target population, use multiple indicators for variables where possible, and so on. No such principles can be found in the literature on analytic induction. To many critics, the lack of an organized body of principles indicates a lack of method. The flaw in this sort of thinking is that it confuses methodology with specific concrete procedures.

This discussion begins by drawing a distinction between two views of method. One view of method takes specific design and analysis procedures as rules to be followed in doing research. If the rules are followed, the results will be considered scientifically acceptable; otherwise not. The rules may evolve over time, as we become aware of new ways in which supposedly correct procedure leads to false conclusions. Thus, the discovery of experimenter effects in some lines of research may lead to a rule that both experimenters and subjects be "blind" to the treatment condition of the subject. Though wrong, this view of methodology does have some practical benefits, because it routinizes within a community of researchers safeguards that might be overlooked by the individual researcher.

The second view takes methodology to be a way of generating arguments for empirical claims. Specific design and analysis procedures are seen not as guarantors of correct conclusions, but as routinized solutions to argumentative problems. The study of methodology is the study of a Generalized Skeptic—an intellectual stance from which empirical claims can be subjected to maximal scrutiny. This view of methodology differs most sharply from the first view in treating procedural rules as being standard but substitutable lines of argument. Procedural rules are seen as the products of a deeper generative structure, which may also generate alternative procedures for specific research problems.

Where bodies of methodological rules exist, they can be seen to spring from deeper principles as standard solutions to anticipated counterarguments. For experimental methodology, this is particularly obvious, because experimental research is wed to one unified class of empirical claims, all of which impose the same general burden of proof. The experimental method is specifically geared to the problem of generating arguments for causal claims; it developed out of an abstract conceptual position on causality best represented in the writing of John Stuart Mill (see Nagel, 1961, pp. 316–324).

What social scientists refer to as principles of experimental inquiry are actually specialized lines of argument that can be routinely used to support statements about the causes or effects of behavior. The basic form of an experiment— manipulation of one variable while holding others constant—can be seen to be one specific variant of Mill's Method of Difference. The Method of Difference, along with the Method of Argument, the Method of Concomitant Variation, and the Method of Residues, represent the sorts of evidence needed to justify calling something a cause. Social scientific experiments have a standard feature not present in experiments generally—replication of the basic experimental procedure across a large number of individual persons. This principle represents a field-specific response to the problem of using human beings as cases for study. Because no two can be assumed to differ in all respects but one or to be identical in all respects but one, neither the Method of Agreement nor the Method of Difference can be applied at the individual level (see Nagel, 1961). Random assignment of replications to treatment groups is a standard line of argument for equality of aggregate response prior to treatment. Campbell and Stanley (1966) explicitly defend control groups and randomization as ways of ruling out counterarguments against causal interpretations of human responses. For the argument that change following treatment may have resulted from organismic processes unconnected with the treatment (history, maturation, and so on), the standard response is lack of comparable change in a control group. For the argument that differences between treatment and control groups may have resulted from inequality existing even prior to treatment, the standard response is replication of the effect across many individual cases and lack of bias in the assignment of cases to groups. Use of a control group and use of randomized replications are general solutions to argumentative problems, specifically, built-in refutations of rival causal claims. It is important to note that none of these design features is indispensable: The "method" is in analysis of what has to be proven, not in any specific, concrete way of proving it. Once the possible rival claims are clearly understood, the standard lines of argument against them can be replaced by other lines of argument. For example, time series designs offer resources for arguing against organismic processes as explanations of change following treatment, even without an independent control group (Cook & Campbell, 1979). Causal modelling offers resources for arguing against spuriousness of covariation without the use of randomized replications (Heise, 1975; Kenny, 1979). Thus, what are often thought of as methodological absolutes are clearly only routinized solutions to standard argumentative problems, solutions that are replaceable by other forms of argument.

Consider, likewise, principles of survey sampling. On the need for random selection of cases, all surveyors agree, and on the desirability of large samples, most agree. The reason is not that large random samples guarantee correct descriptions of the population; on the contrary, random samples of all sizes guarantee incorrect descriptions of the population in some proportion of all surveys. The importance of random sampling is that it undercuts challenges to the fairness and representativeness of the specific sample observed. A random sample allows the surveyor to simultaneously acknowledge and discount the argument that his or her sample of cases doesn't adequately represent the population. Like rules of experimental design, random sampling is an argumentative resource, not a guarantor of correct description.

Our most widely accepted methodological principles have clear connections to the argumentative problems associated with particular kinds of claims. Many quantitative researchers treat these principles as methodological absolutes, applicable across all types of empirical claims: survey researchers who critique experimenters for failing to randomly sample people, and experimenters who refuse to accept perfectly defensible causal claims because the data are "only correlational." But however routinized a methodological principle becomes, the fact remains that its overall rationale and its situated applicability depend on the contribution it makes to defense of specific, concrete empirical claims.

Unlike experimentation and survey methodology, analytic induction offers no standard research designs, no widely accepted criteria for validity of observation, no body of principled or practical wisdom to guide selection of cases for study. In short, analytic induction offers no pre-existing argumentative structure into which empirical claims can be slipped. But this does not mean that it has no method, nor does it mean that the claims are non-empirical. What is means is that, for the present at least, researchers and critics must confront each claim on its own individual merits, asking of each, what alternative claims could the data support? What reason is there to prefer the claim as stated over its alternatives? What additional data would be required to rule out the alternatives? What effect could the selection of cases have had on the conclusion? In the best applications of analytic induction, these issues have clear meaning. Conclusions generated by analytic induction can be evaluated, criticized, refuted, repaired— all with respect to data. That analysts can systematically resolve empirical disputes is evidence that analytic induction is indeed methodical. Its findings are no more the product of individual subjectivity than the findings of experimenters or surveyors.

If we view methodology as a way of generating arguments about empirical claims, rather than as a set of procedural guarantors of truth, we must search for methodological principles at a level deeper than the concrete steps in a research process. The deeper principle behind experimentation is the nature of causality and the meaning of a causal claim. Mill's experimental method is a conceptually grounded analysis of the specific sorts of evidence required to advance or refute a causal claim. The deeper principle behind analytic induction might be characterized as the nature of social structure. No one analysis of social structure has achieved universal acceptance, but relative to any particular theory of structure, the evidence required to identify a structure can be derived from the conceptualization of structure. A clear analysis of what is being claimed about discourse will in every case clarify the evidence needed to support the claim.

As a leading example, consider the claim that a set of events are governed by a particular rule. What does it take to verify or falsify the claim? For the concept of rule, several abstract analyses have been offered (e.g., Cushman & Whiting, 1972; Shimanoff, 1980; Sigman, 1980). To the extent that these analysts adequately represent what the rules analyst is claiming, they generate for the rules analyst the sorts of evidence needed to demonstrate the correctness of a claim about any particular rule. Consider, for example, Sigman's social perspective on rules. Nothing in Sigman's analysis of rules requires that any particular rule will find widespread application, so no proposed rule needs evidence based on its frequency of use. On the other hand, Sigman argues strongly that rules must be social constructions, rather than individual constructions, so that evidence of sharedness is an important element in the defense of a proposed rule. One common strategy for establishing sharedness, especially for interpretive rules, is to point to the fact that any natural language user can see a particular case as having a particular feature. Labov (1975) argues that argument in linguistics depends on a general assumption, held tentatively, that natural language users share the intuitions of the analyst. Sometimes consensus on how to interpret a case does not, in fact, exist. To the extent that the analyst's case hinges on such consensus, we must be prepared to meet such problems with back-up arguments (see Labov, 1975). If an analyst is wrong in thinking that what he or she sees in a case can be seen by any other observer, claims based solely on the analyst's intuitions will fail. Had Emmanual Schegloff (1980) been the only person able to see "Are you busy?" as leading up to something, his analysis of pre-sequences would have been refuted at once. The presumed recognizability of a feature by all observers is acceptable evidence of a shared interpretive structure, possibly a rule.[1]

The history of other methodologies suggests that standardization in analytic induction will arise from a process of claim and counterclaim. Initially, users of analytic induction must confront the world with few tools other than clear conceptualizations of what they have discovered and minds capable of anticipating counterarguments. Among some users of analytic induction, a normative constraint on counterarguing has developed, so as to suppress the evaluation and criticism that are most needed if this method is to progress. Schwartz and Jacobs (1979) note that among conversation analysts, skepticism about the grounds for a claim is explicitly discouraged, unless supported by concrete data that contradict the claim. They contrast the conversation analysts' attitude toward criticism with conventional social science and its "what if" mentality—which they characterize as allowing for a claim to be "wholly invalidated" by niggling objections to the methodology of the study or by rival hypotheses that fit the data no better than the claim as stated. The "what if" mentality puts the burden of proof on the analyst; Schwartz and Jacobs' alternative puts the burden of proof on the skeptic, and further requires that any critique of research be based on competing data. But an empirical argument consists not only of data (observations of phenomena), but also of some sort of warrant. To preclude critique on other than empirical

---

[1]Shimanoff's view of rules differs substantively from Sigman's, with the consequence that she identifies a quite different set of empirical issues as being raised by any claim about the form or content of a rule. In Shimanoff's view, for example, rules must be about behavior, and further, must be prescriptive or normative. This view of rules is responsible for the interest among communication researchers in issues like what happens when a communication rule is "broken." Cushman and Whiting's conceptualization of rules presents still another set of empirical issues requiring other forms of argument. Adler (1978) analyzes the consequences of the Cushman and Whiting conceptualization for the problem of testing claims about rules. Notice that an analyst looking for what Sigman would call a rule cannot reasonably be expected to follow methodological suggestions developed from other conceptualizations of rules—at least not until the field settles the (non-empirical) issue of the nature of a rule.

grounds is to preclude the possibility of scrutinizing whatever warrants the inference from data to claim. That isn't a good idea. Building strong arguments for empirical claims *requires* attention to possible counterarguments, whether supported by data, or supported merely by logic. The point of observation and analysis is to build an argument that will satisfy a reasonable skeptic, and to close ranks against reasonable skepticism is to abandon rationality. If criticism on nondata grounds is suppressed, the research community will have no means by which to develop strong general lines of argument comparable to those embodied in principles of experimental design or principles of sampling, no means by which to arrive at a general understanding of its conceptually necessary burden of proof.

Method is more than an arbitrary set of conventions scientists use to judge some factual claims acceptable and others unacceptable. It is a way of generating arguments for the correctness of individual factual claims. Discourse analysts cannot build a sound body of knowledge by agreeing among themselves not to argue about one another's findings. Analytic induction is capable of generating strong arguments for empirical claims, but only if researchers accept their legitimate burden of proof.

BUILDING ARGUMENTS THROUGH ANALYTIC INDUCTION

Let us not trivialize the method of analytic induction by trying to reduce the method to superficial rules for collecting and transcribing conversation. No doubt these are important technical issues for discourse analysts, just as the problem of getting a random sample within a community is an important technical issue for survey research. But data sources and transcribing conventions do not define the practice of discourse analysis or of analytic induction, any more than the use of random-digit dialing defines the practice of surveying. More importantly, preoccupation with these technical issues is diverting attention from what it is that ails discourse analytic research. Recognizing method as a way of generating arguments for empirical claims concentrates attention on broader issues of argumentative structure.

As should be clear from the preceding discussion, the most important determinant of argument structure is the nature of the claim being offered. Unfortunately, not only are the claims made about discourse very diverse, but also, many are not at all well thought out or even explicitly formulated. These problems are discussed in the first section of this part. Beyond the quality of the claims, the next most important feature of empirical arguments is the nature of the evidence. The form of evidence most in dispute is examples of dialogue, and their treatment by discourse analysts is the topic of the second and third sections.

Empirical Claims About Discourse Structure

Clark (1979) has argued very persuasively that we should view the quality of a research question or hypothesis as a central issue in experimental methodology. Not only does the quality of the question constrain the importance of the answer, but also, more subtly, it affects the quality of the research. Clark argues that a conceptually coherent research question is a major preventive to poor research design because a well-formed question will suggest what is needed for a well-formed answer. Although Clark directed her remarks specifically to experimenters, a strictly analogous argument can be made for the role of empirical claims in analytic induction. In order to argue effectively for a claim about discourse, an analyst must first be able to state the claim clearly, coherently, and in empirical form. The claim need not be formulated prior to data collection and analysis (see Philipsen, 1977), but until the claim can be formulated, no argument can be offered.

Unfortunately, discourse analysts have done no better than experimenters in producing uniformly coherent claims. Numerous reports have been published, containing conversational data and analysis of a sort, without any identifiable empirical claim. In the popular image of discourse analysis, the typical research report is a series of interesting examples of dialogue separated by an editorial comment or two. And this image is not wholly without basis.

Consider Beach and Dunning's (1982) analysis of *pre-indexing*. No bald on-record statement of the empirical claim occurs, nor is any such claim clearly implicated. A variety of plausible candidate claims can be constructed, but all could be denounced by the authors as not what they meant to say. The paper may make no claim more ambitious than that there is something in conversation we might call pre-indexing, and that it is somehow related to several previously analyzed phenomena. Or at the other extreme, the paper might be making a fairly specific claim like this: "There is a general class of utterances in conversation which serve the function of guiding the interpretaton of later utterances. Members of this class are hints, prompts, teases, conditional disclosures, and small talk." The former claim is obviously not an empirical claim, but merely a proposed name for an as yet unidentified set of events. Only when a claim is made about pre-indexing (such as what objects belong to the set or what functions the set has) are we dealing with an empirical issue. The latter claim is empirical, but incorrect in some rather obvious ways (e.g., conditional disclosures are the main business of an exchange, not a pre to an exchange; small talk, hints, and teases are not subclasses of a broader category of pre-indexing speech acts; in fact, pre-indexing is not a conventional feature of *any* known class of speech acts; etc.). As cooperative communicators, we should probably assume that Beach and Dunning did not intend to make any claim as strong as this or as weak as the first suggestion. But what are we to believe about pre-indexing and how are we to decide whether to believe it? Unless we can pin down what an author is claiming about a set of data, the data themselves cannot function as evidence, but only as vague hints about the researcher's general topic.

How can problems of this sort be avoided? One way to assure that a study makes a clear empirical claim is to insist that the report include a thesis summarizing the findings of the study. An appropriate thesis should refer to what was discovered, not to what was attempted, what was observed, or what was illustrated. Statements that do not qualify as empirical claims include statements about the goal of a research, the value of a theory, the applicability of a method, the meaning of a term, and so on. Statements that do qualify as empirical claims include proposed rules, assertions about the properties of a class of events, assertions about the differences between two classes of events, assertions about the structure of a kind of interaction, and the like. Note, though, that what makes a statement empirical is not its topic or its form, but its illocutionary force: It must commit the speaker to defending the existence of some state of affairs. As has often been noted, this commitment on the part of an analyst is genuine only if the state of affairs can be either true or false, that is, if the statement is falsifiable as well as verifiable. Contemplating the kind of evidence that could invalidate a claim can clarify what a claim amounts to—or can reveal that a claim does not amount to much.

For example, suppose a researcher is interested in confrontation—that is, in conversational episodes in which one person confronts another. The researcher might collect a number of examples of confrontation for detailed analysis, develop a description of each example, and submit the claim that confrontation is a patterned event that occurs in conversation. A moment's reflection, on the issue of falsification, will reveal that the claim is not a very interesting one. How might someone argue *against* the claim? One way would be to deny that the examples are properly regarded as confrontation, which in the extreme case amounts to a denial that confrontation exists as a social category. Another way would be to deny that there is any patterning in the examples—that each is unique and that no common themes run throughout the collection. The counterarguments, by their vacuity and superficiality, highlight the vacuity and superficiality of the claim as formulated. Fortunately, they also suggest ways in which the claim could be made more interesting. Specifically, a more interesting claim could be developed as a formal characterization of confrontation, one that pins down the common pattern (if any) exhibited by the examples. Of particular interest would be analysis of the unique structural or functional properties of confrontation. Incidentally, Bleiberg and Churchill (1975) have proposed such analyses, and Jacobs (this volume) has proposed revisions required to handle counterexamples.

An empirical claim about anything, including discourse structure, is a claim that can be either right or wrong. If it does not make much sense to ask if a researcher's conclusions are right, then the researcher probably does not have much to say at the empirical level. And obviously, if the researcher does not have much to say, how well it gets said is simply not important.

Examples as Evidence for General Claims About Discourse

Perhaps the most salient characteristic of discourse analytic research is the use of examples drawn from conversation or other discourse as data. Most discourse analytic research in communication relies on qualitative rather than quantitative description, but the more fundamental departure from traditional social scientific research is the focus on units of discourse rather than on people as cases for study. Experimenters observe a number of individually uninteresting people in order to make general claims about individual human processes; discourse analysts observe a number of individually uninteresting messages in order to make general claims about rules or other social structures.[2] In the popular image of discourse analysis, it is the specific collection of examples that are the analyst's principal concern. This is roughly equivalent to the idea that in a typical experiment, it is the specific sample of human respondents that are the experimenter's principal concern. Analytic induction does not require, nor does it justify, preoccupation with particular transcripts or other texts. The widespread view that analytic induction is a case study method is simply wrong.

Some discourse analytic studies, to be sure, take as their task the explication of some particular discourse. But these are aberrant, not prototypical, examples of discourse analytic research. For example, Hawes (1976) reports a study of "how writing is used in talk," that turns out to be an analysis of how a particular written report was used for relational and instrumental ends by the members of a particular organization. No general claims or explanatory principles are advanced; instead, detailed description of the members' talk about the report is used as a basis for interpretation of the functioning of the organization. The applied focus of the project, and not the method of analytic induction, accounts for the case study approach taken by Hawes.

How can examples serve as evidence for general claims? Sometimes they can't. Certain kinds of claims just have to have a different sort of evidence (see also Jacobs, this volume). Quantitative claims, even vague and casual ones, require quantitative evidence. These include claims about what usually happens, what frequently happens, or what typically happens. Claims about individual or situational variations in discourse likewise require evidence other than examples. A claim that men and women use different speech styles cannot be supported

---

[2]Curiously, experiments designed to support general claims about messages have, in the overwhelming majority of cases, examined only one individually uninteresting message of any given type (see Jackson & Jacobs, 1983).

by showing examples of male and female speech. Instead, evidence must be gathered which reflects the variability among individual women and men, and that permits comparison of the frequency of certain features in women's speech with the frequency of those features in men's speech.[3]

Examples might serve as evidence for many other sorts of claims about discourse, however. Presumably, examples will never close the books on any particular issue, but like other forms of evidence, we may reasonably expect them to provide the basis for a prima facie case for structural claims.

One sort of claim examples might support concerns features that may or must be present in certain kinds of episodes. Jackson and Jacobs (1980) and O'Keefe and Benoit (1982) have claimed that argument is characterized by overt disagreement. The alternative claim, backed by a large professional literature on public standards of rationality, is that argument is characterized by reason-giving. A few examples of naturally occurring argument suffice to show that reason-giving without disagreement is something other than argument, whereas disagreement without reason-giving is indeed recognizable as argument, so that examples will serve well to support one characterization of an argument over its alternative.

A second sort of claim that examples might support concerns the existence of a rule or the events permitted or prohibited by a rule. Such claims occur frequently in the literature on conversational sequencing. To show that a rule exists requiring an answer following a question, the sort of evidence needed is demonstration that anything other than an answer following a question will receive special interpretive treatment designed to account for why no answer was given. Non-answers following questions must be interpreted as preliminaries to the answer (Garvey, 1977), as replacements for the answer (Bowers, 1982; Nofsinger, 1976), or, if all else fails, as errors or rule violations. A few clear examples suffice to show that non-answers following questions do in fact get this sort of special interpretive treatment—that is, they are easily recognizable as contingent queries, indirect answers or replacement answers, or rule violations. This can be explained easily if a queston–answer rule exists (or if something like a question–answer rule exists at a deeper level of organization, as suggested by Jacobs & Jackson, 1983; Levinson, 1981).

A third sort of claim for which examples might serve as evidence concerns the organizational basis for interaction. An example of this sort of claim appears in a theoretical argument advanced by O'Keefe, Delia, and O'Keefe (1980). They set out alternative general views of the organizational basis for conversation and use a single well-chosen example to argue that whatever rules organize conversation cannot operate simply on a linear, turn-by-turn basis. To show that any particular remark may be responsive not to its preceding remark but to some

---

[3]Lakoff (1975) acknowledges the need for sampling and measurement to support claims about actual differences in the behavior of men and women, but does not provide data of this sort.

much earlier utterance requires only one example, provided that the one example exhibits an underlying organization observers can recognize as having pervasive applicability in conversation.

A fourth sort of claim concerns the interpretive prerequisites for communication, such as Grice's (1975) claims about conversational implicature and Clark and Haviland's (1977) claims about the given–new contract. Each of these analyses suggests that the intelligibility of conversation depends on the existence of shared interpretive principles. To show that conversationalists assume other's remarks to be guided by a set of conversational maxims, Grice offers a series of examples whose commonsense meanings can be shown to depend on inferences from such assumptions. The existence of conversational implicature, which is evident from a few well-chosen examples, is evidence for socially shared interpretive structures. Clark and Haviland, similarly, argue that unless the given–new contract is assumed to exist, it is difficult to explain certain inferences people automatically make in comprehending discourse. That people make these inferences is what the examples show.

In all of these cases, the examples are more than mere illustrations of something. The examples serve as evidence for general claims, either by establishing a social fact that remains unexplained if the claim is untrue, or by ruling out the logical opposite or theoretical alternative to the claim. The opportunity for examples to serve as evidence depends, as noted in the previous section, on formulation of a claim that can be either consistent or inconsistent with the examples. As in traditional social scientific research, the problem may be tackled by setting out a null claim and offering examples to show why it cannot be true.

The major weakness in the way discourse analysts have used examples is the tendency to use examples in a strictly confirmatory fashion. A claim is offered, and examples are presented that seem to confirm the claim. This is an inherently weak form of argument (amounting to the fallacy of affirming the consequent) because the examples may match the claim only incidentally (see Jacobs' comments, this volume, on Bleiberg & Churchill's, 1975, characterization of the structure of confrontation). Contrastive use of examples, in which the consequences of critical variations may be observed, allows for stronger and more persuasive defense of claims. Nofsinger's (1975) analysis of the demand ticket relies on comparison of well-formed and ill-formed cases to show that each clause of his proposed rule is necessary to generate acceptable demand tickets. Jackson and Jacobs (1980), claiming to have identified necessary features of conversational argument, use contrastive examples of non-arguments that are similar to arguments in all respects except the absence of one of the necessary features. In both cases, the contrastive examples are as important to the argument as are the directly confirmatory examples (see Jacobs, this volume).

Where contrastive examples are not available or not relevant, an analyst can support confirmatory examples with argument from absence of disconfirming examples. The trick here is to show that a disconfirming case could be recognized, if it were to occur. Sacks, Schegloff, and Jefferson (1974) note a variety of things that could occur in conversation, but ordinarily don't (extended simultaneous talk, speaker transitions at within-unit pauses, etc.). That certain theoretical possibilities don't occur can be evidence for a rule. To exploit this form of argument, the analyst must be able to formulate the sort of things which, if they occurred, would disconfirm the claim, the point being to show that the analyst is not blind to negative cases. Unless an analyst can formulate clearly what sorts of things would count as disconfirmation, the use of examples which seem to confirm the claim will have little credibility.

When offered as support for claims about discourse structure, examples should be treated not as illustrations, but as evidence. This means they should be sufficient to establish the correctness of the claim, and they should be responsive to reasonable challenges to their representativeness and validity. Strong claims about the structure of discourse will not build themselves; the analyst must expect to do much more than to simply display the examples as though only one conclusion could be drawn from them.

Natural and Hypothetical Examples as Evidence

Assuming that examples can serve as evidence for a claim, are there special classes of examples that are inherently better than others? Within some lines of research on discourse structures, only naturally produced conversation is studied, whereas within other lines of research, arguments are often built on hypothetical examples constructed to make a point. Although many discourse analysts have tried to insist that only naturally produced conversation is worthy of study (e.g., deBeaugrande, 1980; McLaughlin, 1984; Nofsinger, 1977; Schwartz & Jacobs, 1979), a view of method as a way of generating arguments suggests that the sort of data one should use (natural or hypothetical) depends on the sort of claim one wants to make.

Clear advantages come from collecting and analyzing naturally produced talk. People's intuitions about language and communication are known to be idealized, and at least some aspects of their language and communication behavior are known to be produced without awareness of how they are produced. Conversation analysts have argued that the patterns exhibited in actual talk would not be accepted as credible if offered as hypothetical examples—that is, that actual talk is not well represented by people's idealizations of it. Naturally produced discourse displays how people use language, not how they think they use it. Perhaps no individual speaker is aware of behavioral synchrony, yet microanalysis of many diverse behaviors shows this process to be important (e.g., Condon & Ogston, 1967; Kendon, 1970). Or again, perhaps no individual speaker can explain how, in a group of conversationalists, the transition from speaker to speaker is accomplished, yet detailed description of natural conversation shows turn-taking to be an orderly process accomplished through specific verbal and nonverbal devices (see Duncan, 1972, 1973; Sacks, Schegloff, & Jefferson, 1974; Wiemann & Knapp, 1975). Whether these patterns represent rules or regularities is arguable, but what is not arguable is that their discovery was possible only through examination of natural conversation, and any demonstration of their existence likewise depends on observation of what actually happens in conversation.

But hypothetical talk has advantages, too. Some of the most influential ideas in discourse analysis have been developed from and supported by hypothetical examples of talk. Grice's (1975) cooperative principle and Searle's (1975) analysis of indirect speech acts represent significant empirical advances based wholly on examination of a variety of hypothetical examples.[4] The evidence supplied by the examples in these cases has to do not with what occurs in the behavior of individual speakers, but with what can occur within a set of socially shared constraints. Obviously, if a claim is to be made about the nature of these constraints, hypothetical talk is good data.

Another way of saying this is that hypothetical talk, like natural talk, presents us with facts to be explained. The recognizability of a common pattern in several hypothetical discourses, for example, is a fact about the structure of the discourses or a fact about the intuitions of the observer or both, just as the repeated occurrence of a pattern in natural conversations is a fact about the interactions or a fact about the interactants or both. If we want to make claims about rules, structures, social schemata, and the like, hypothetical talk serves as well or better

---

[4]In commenting on an earlier version of this essay, McLaughlin (1984) remarked that neither Grice (1975) nor Searle (1975) should be counted as empirical contributions because both offer global conceptual frameworks consistent with any number of empirical positions. I find no strong basis for this charge, either in the works themselves or in the way they have been received by the field. Both Grice and Searle seem to be empirical enough to falsify, and on some counts at least, the falsification could be accomplished through hypothetical counterexamples. Searle makes at least three sorts of empirical claims, all capable of being false: claims about the substance of speech act rules, claims about what sorts of utterances can and cannot be used as indirect speech acts, and claims about the manner in which an utterance can be interpreted as an indirect speech act. On at least one of these issues, Searle's claim is on the verge of conclusive falsification, since numerous analyses have shown that interpretation of an utterance as an indirect request does not necessarily involve rejection of the "literal" interpretation of the utterance (Ervin-Tripp, 1976; Gibbs, 1980). Grice offers a set of hypothesized interpretive structures (Maxims) and a theory of how these maxims can be used to construct meanings beyond what is actually said (implicature). Both the maxims and the process of implicature have been attacked on empirical grounds. Keenan (1976) reports that the maxims do not in fact hold in some cultures. Whatever implications this has for the prospects of Grice's theory as a general theory of communication, it does seem to rule out the idea that Grice has simply articulated a truism. The process of implicature as described by Grice has fared about as well as Searle's account of how indirect speech acts are recognized: The claim that implicature depends on a violation of a maxim is evidently empirical, though not quite right (see, e.g., Kaufer, 1981). Clearly, both Grice and Searle *could* be wrong. Also clearly, other discourse analysts have a fairly concrete notion of what sorts of facts would be needed to confirm or disconfirm these analyses. The generality, abstractness, and durability of these ideas should not be mistaken for in principle nonfalsifiability.

than natural talk, for a number of reasons. First, hypothetical talk allows us to construct context as well as text, so that contextual influences on interpretation can be controlled. Second, hypothetical talk allows us to construct cases to fit detailed specifications, so that we may inspect interactional patterns which are well-formed but rare. Third, hypothetical talk allows us to construct ill-formed cases, to use contrastively in verifying or falsifying hypothesized rules. The acknowledged limitation on the use of hypothetical talk is that it may reflect idiosyncrasies of the analyst or partial awareness of the actual constraints on behavior. For this reason, hypothetical examples are reasonable only when they represent clear cases of a phenomenon, on which all observers may be assumed to agree. But even accepting this restriction, hypothetical examples are widely usable.

The data used in any particular study should be evaluated, not on the basis of fit with an absolutistic but arbitrary standard, but on the basis of fit with the kind of claim being made. Obviously, hypothetical examples ought not be used to support claims about behavioral regularities or about individual or situational variations in discourse. For example, if an analyst wishes to claim that ellipsis is characteristic of talk among intimates, hypothetical examples such as this one offered by Berger and Bradac (1982) would not be useful as evidence, even if the "clear case" criterion were satisfied:

John:	Hi.
Mary:	Of course she did. You know that she did and you should reciprocate.
John:	Right.
Mary:	Now don't invent excuses, a simple note of congratulations will suffice.
John:	Yes.
Mary:	Good idea, a telephone call would be better.
John:	Right.
Mary:	An even better idea! Good for you! She would love you to visit and to bring those funny little candies that she likes so much. (p. 107)

Assuming that a claim about intimacy and ellipsis is more likely to be a claim about a behavioral regularity than about a rule, the sort of evidence needed to support the claim is comparative analysis of discourse actually produced within intimate and nonintimate dyads (or alternatively, longitudinal analysis of the discourse produced by individual dyads as they progress toward intimacy). On the other hand, if it were seriously claimed that a social or relational rule exists permitting or requiring elliptical expresson among intimates, a few hypothetical examples could go a long way toward rendering the claim untenable. If hypothetical examples can be constructed showing the same sort of ellipsis occurring among strangers, or if intimate dialogue can be constructed without ellipsis, we would want to say that something other than the intimacy of the relationship accounts for ellipsis.[5] To support the specific, limited counterclaim that it is not intimacy, but certainty of assumptions about shared context-relevant beliefs that give rise to ellipsis, hypothetical examples are indeed pertinent. Examples from naturally occurring talk would do as well, assuming that the analyst could find the sort of critical instances needed, but notice that data on regularities would not be pertinent in this context, because uneven frequencies of ellipsis in different relationship types is consistent with both explanations—from the view that ellipsis results from certainty, any covariation between intimacy and the occurrence of ellipsis would be recognizable as a consequence of the association of intimacy with increasing knowledge of the other's perspective (as Berger and Bradac themselves acknowledge).

As a second example, consider several sorts of claims made about codes and code-switching (see Ervin-Tripp, 1971, for a review of literature on all issues discussed here). Naturally produced conversation is probably required to support the claim that people systematically vary their syntax and vocabulary depending on the status and familiarity of their addresses. Naturally produced conversation is certainly required to support the claim that particular classes of people "hypercorrect" their speech in particular situations. But naturally produced conversation is emphatically not necessary to demonstrate to a reasonable reader that something like "co-occurrence rules" must exist, because any native speaker of English can readily see that the last of the following hypothetical remarks, though grammatical, is not well-formed:

Pardon me, miss. I could not help noticing your lovely hair.

---

[5]Rommetveit (1974) discusses the issue of ellipsis at some length, and provides all the ammunition needed to kill the idea that it is intimacy per se that provides the basis for ellipsis. He comments:

> *ellipsis . . . appears to be the prototype of verbal communication under ideal conditions of complete complementarity in an intersubjectively established, temporarily shared social world.* Full sentences—and even sequences of sentences—may be required in order to make something known, however, under conditions of deficient complementarity and less than perfect synchronization of intentions and thoughts. (p. 29, emphasis in original)

As an example, he offers a situation in which two football fans, by virtue of seeing the same dramatic play, assume themselves to share a common reality. A comparison of the two possible comments below not only shows that ellipsis is permissible, but also that it is in some sense preferable:
Magnificent!
That tackling performed by the slim, funny-looking quarterback was magnificent!
We might easily construct any number of examples of ellipsis, even the outlandish sort of ellipsis constructed by Berger and Bradac, by stipulating a context in which both participants may be assumed to be aware of and focused on the same set of features. The more certain the mutual focus, the more reasonable the ellipsis. The appearance that intimacy has anything to do with ellipsis is due to the willingness of the observer to assume that the partners share some specific understanding of the context that is not accessible to the observers, not to any special association between ellipsis and intimate discourse.

Hey, mama! Where'd you get that foxy 'do?
*Pardon me, mama. I could not help noticing your foxy 'do.

As in the first example, claims about speech regularities or about individual or situational variations in speech cannot be supported by hypothetical examples, but claims about clearly defined rules can, at least in part.

Research on discourse structure will not progress by arbitrarily excluding data based on hypothetical talk. The possible abuses of hypothetical examples can be controlled once it is recognized that they, like naturalistic examples, are to function as evidence for empirical claims—so that hypothetical examples which are contrived, idiosyncratic, or ambiguous defeat their own purpose.

CONCLUSION

Many traditional social scientific researchers make the mistake of treating methodological rules as guarantors of truth. That is, they assume that observing the canons of experimental design and statistical inference will guarantee correct conclusions. In similar fashion, we discourse analysts might lapse into thinking that if we transcribe carefully enough, take care to use only naturalistic data, test inductive findings experimentally, or otherwise follow the rules for doing discourse analysis, we can be confident of the correctness of our conclusions. This sort of thinking should be avoided. No set of mere rules will prove to be sufficient guarantors of truth. Methodology is better seen as a way of reasoning about the phenomena, a way of generating arguments for what we believe to be true.

The arguments we have been making for proposed discourse structures have not been uniformly strong. Some genuine advances have been made, but fewer than one would like. The analyses that make the strongest arguments for structural claims are those offering clearly formulated empirical claims and using examples, if at all, as evidence. Weak arguments, resulting from poorly formulated claims and unreflective use of examples to confirm claims, call into question the rationality of the entire research program. This should stop.

We need to become more critical of our own research. We should be losing patience with work that remains forever at the preliminary description phase. If individual researchers are to build strong cases for empirical claims, it is the responsibility of the research community to define for them their burden of proof. Discourse analysts as a group need to develop a critical stance toward structural claims similar to the critical stance toward causal claims embodied in Campbell and Stanley's (1966) threats to the validity of experiments. If discourse analysis is to contribute importantly to communication theory, it must go beyond a mere fascination with the possibility of observing structure in natural conversation.

REFERENCES

Adler, K. (1978). On the falsification of rules theories. *Quarterly Journal of Speech, 64,* 427–438.

Beach, W. A., & Dunning, D. G. (1982). Pre-indexing and conversational organization. *Quarterly Journal of Speech, 68,* 179–185.

Berger, C. R., & Bradac, J. J. (1982). *Language and social knowledge: Uncertainty in interpersonal relations.* London: Edward Arnold.

Bleiberg, S., & Churchill, L. (1975). Notes on confrontation in conversation. *Journal of Psycholinguistic Research, 4,* 273–278.

Bowers, J. W. (1982). Does a duck have antlers? Some pragmatics of "transparent questions." *Communication Monographs, 42,* 63–69.

Campbell, D. T., & Stanley, J. C. (1966). *Experimental and quasi-experimental designs for research.* Chicago: Rand McNally.

Clark, H. H., & Haviland, S. E. (1977). Comprehension and the given-new contract. In R. O. Freedle (Ed.), *Discourse production and comprehension* (Vol. 1, pp. 1–40). Norwood, NJ: Ablex.

Clark, R. A. (1979). Suggestions for the design of empirical communication studies. *Central States Speech Journal, 30,* 51–66.

Condon, W. S., & Ogston, W. D. (1967). A segmentation of behavior. *Journal of Psychiatric Research, 5,* 221–235.

Cook, T. D., & Campbell, D. T. (1979). *Quasi-experimentation: Design & analysis for field settings.* Boston: Houghton Mifflin.

Cushman, D. P., & Whiting, G. C. (1972). An approach to communication theory: Towards consensus on rules. *Journal of Communication, 22,* 217–238.

deBeaugrande, R. (1980). *Text, discourse, and process: Toward a multidisciplinary science of texts.* Norwood, NJ: Ablex.

Denzin, N. K. (1970). *The research act.* Chicago: Aldine.

Duncan, S., Jr. (1972). Some signals and rules for taking speaking turns in conversations. *Journal of Personality and Social Psychology, 23,* 283–292.

Duncan, S., Jr. (1973). Toward a grammar for dyadic conversation. *Semiotica, 9,* 29–46.

Ervin-Tripp, S. M. (1971). Sociolinguistics. In J. A. Fishman (Ed.), *Advances in the sociology of language* (Vol. 1, pp. 15–91). The Hague: Mouton.

Ervin-Tripp, S. (1976). Is Sybil there? The structure of some American English directives. *Language and Society, 5,* 25–66.

Garvey, C. (1977). The contingent query: A dependent act in conversation. In M. Lewis & L. A. Rosenblum (Eds.), *Interaction, conversation, and the development of language* (pp. 63–93). New York: Wiley.

Gibbs, R. W. (1980). Spilling the beans on understanding and memory for idioms in conversation. *Memory and Cognition, 8,* 449–456.

Grice, H. P. (1975). Logic and conversation. In P. Cole & J. L. Morgan (Eds.), *Syntax and semantics, Vol. 3: Speech acts* (pp. 41–58). New York: Academic Press.

Hawes, L. C. (1976). How writing is used in talk: A study of communicative logic-in-use. *Quarterly Journal of Speech, 62,* 350–360.

Heise, D. R. (1975). *Causal analysis.* New York: Wiley.

Jackson, S., & Jacobs, S. (1980). Structure of conversational argument: Pragmatic bases for the enthymeme. *Quarterly Journal of Speech, 66,* 251–265.

Jackson, S., & Jacobs, S. (1983). Generalizing about messages: Suggestions for design and analysis of experiments. *Human Communication Research, 9,* 169–181.

Jacobs, S., & Jackson, S. (1983). Speech act structure in conversation: Rational aspects of pragmatic coherence. In R. T. Craig & K. Tracy (Eds.), *Conversational coherence: Form, structure, and strategy* (pp. 47–66). Beverly Hills, CA: Sage.

Kaufer, D. S. (1981). Understanding ironic communication. *Journal of Pragmatics, 5,* 495–510.

Keenan, E. O. (1976). The universality of conversational postulates. *Language and Society, 5,* 67–80.

Kendon, A. (1970). Movement coordination in social interaction: Some examples described. *Acta Psychologica, 32,* 100–125.

Kenny, D. A. (1979). *Correlation and causality.* New York: Wiley.

Labov, W. (1975). *What is a linguistic fact?* Lisse, The Netherlands: Peter de Ridder Press.

Labov, W., & Fanshel, D. (1977). *Therapeutic discourse: Psychotherapy as conversation.* New York: Academic Press.

Lakoff, R. (1975). *Language and woman's place.* New York: Harper & Row.

Levinson, S. C. (1981). Some pre-observations on the modelling of discourse. *Discourse Processes, 4,* 93–116.

McLaughlin, M. L. (1984). *Conversation: How talk is organized.* Beverly Hills, CA: Sage.

Nagel, E. (1961). *The structure of science: Problems in the logic of scientific explanation.* New York: Harcourt, Brace & World.

Nofsinger, R. E. (1975). The demand ticket: A conversational device for getting the floor. *Speech Monographs, 42,* 1–9.

Nofsinger, R. E. (1976). Answering questions indirectly. *Human Communication Research, 2,* 171–181.

Nofsinger, R. E. (1977). A peek at conversational analysis. *Communication Quarterly, 25*(3), 12–20.

O'Keefe, B. J., & Benoit, P. J. (1982). Children's arguments. In J. R. Cox & C. A. Willard (Eds.), *Advances in argumentation theory and research* (pp. 154–183). Carbondale and Edwardsville, IL: Southern Illinois University Press.

O'Keefe, B. J., Delia, J. G., & O'Keefe, D. J. (1980). Interaction analysis and the analysis of interactional organization. In N. K. Denzin (Ed.), *Studies in symbolic interaction* (Vol. 3, pp. 25–57). Greenwich, CT: JAI Press.

Philipsen, G. (1977). Linearity of design in ethnographic studies of speaking. *Communication Quarterly, 25*(3), 42–50.

Rommetveit, R. (1974). *On message structure: A framework for the study of language and communication.* London: Wiley.

Sacks, H., Schegloff, E., & Jefferson, G. (1974). A simplest systematics for the organization of turn-taking in conversation. *Language, 50,* 696–735.

Schegloff, E. A. (1980). Preliminaries to preliminaries: Can I ask you a question? *Sociological Inquiry, 50,* 104–152.

Schwartz, H., & Jacobs, J. (1979). *Qualitative sociology: A method to the madness.* New York: Free Press.

Searle, J. R. (1975). Indirect speech acts. In P. Cole & J. L. Morgan (Eds.), *Syntax and semantics, Vol. 3: Speech acts* (pp. 59–82). New York: Academic Press.

Shimanoff, S. B. (1980). *Communication rules: Theory and research.* Beverly Hills, CA: Sage.

Sigman, S. J. (1980). On communication rules from a social perspective. *Human Communication Research, 7,* 37–51.

Wiemann, J. M., & Knapp, M. L. (1975). Turn-taking in conversations. *Journal of Communication, 25,* 75–92.

7

How to Make an Argument From Example in Discourse Analysis

Scott Jacobs
University of Oklahoma

The most distinctive feature of discourse analytic studies is the method of argument from example. The method works something like this: The analyst displays a number of fragments of discourse and describes particular features that, presumably, can be seen by any reader. The examples can be drawn from any variety of sources (written texts, naturally occurring conversation, computer printouts, the analyst's imagination) without altering their demonstrative power. After having gone through a series of comparisons and contrasts among such displays, the analyst will have documented some claim about the general properties of discourse. The specific features intuited in the examples will have served as evidence for the existence (or nonexistence) of the properties in question.

To anyone trying to understand arguments from example in terms of the paradigms of experimental and survey research, this mode of demonstration must smell pretty fishy. It comes off as nothing more than interesting speculation that happens to get concretely illustrated. How, one wants to ask, could an analyst's subjective *intuitions* about an *example* of discourse ever hope to serve as empirical evidence for some general property of language? How do we objectively verify the existence of the features the analyst claims to see in the examples? And how can we be sure that anyone else shares these intuitions? Don't empirical claims about language use and structure really require systematic sampling and observation of actual linguistic behavior?

Of course, discourse analysts can (and often do) supplement or even replace arguments from example with more traditional methods of demonstration. But this does not reflect some comprehensive skeptical doubt about the ability of examples to in principle meet the burden of proof imposed on discourse analytic claims. The method remains the basic way to make a *prima facie* case for a variety of claims about language use and structure.

Despite their confidence in this pattern of argument, discourse analysts have yet to work out the nature of its logical status and theoretical force. For the most part, discourse analysts have simply taken for granted the validity of the major research exemplars and have tried to model their own work after the patterns of argument they seem to display. Little explicit attention has been devoted to technical considerations of how examples might be reasonably used to defend or challenge claims about the properties of discourse.[1] Methodology in any field ought to be more than a cookbook of conventional procedures authorized by tradition and opinion leaders. Research is conducted best when methodology is understood as a way of generating arguments for empirical claims (Jackson, this volume). Any method will presuppose particular warrants, place a certain burden of proof on the analyst, and emphasize some interests over others. If examples of discourse are to serve as credible and reasonable evidence for claims, the rationale and limits of this method need to be understood.

In this chapter I lay out a rationale for one use of examples to make arguments about discourse. The first section describes an analytic stance guiding this use of examples. The second section applies this stance to answering the skeptical types of challenges just posed and to addressing more technical considerations: What kinds of general claims about patterns of discourse might be profitably pursued with arguments from example and what types of examples are needed to pursue such claims? The third section concretely illustrates these technical considerations by working through a substantive issue—the adequacy of Bleiberg and Churchill's (1975) model of a pattern of argument they call "confrontation."

LANGUAGE GAMES

How discourse analysts conceptualize their subject-matter and the kind of explan-atory puzzle it is taken to pose is central to the rationale behind the use of examples. A metaphor that I have found to be particularly useful for capturing this stance is a view of discourse as a collection of language games (Wittgenstein, 1953). The primary appeal of the metaphor is that it articulates a practical orientation toward the study of language use and structure that is, I think, eminently commonsensical and free from a lot of excess philosophical baggage.

---

[1]O'Keefe (1982) and Searle (1969) do discuss the rationale behind the use of hypothetical examples for which this discussion is much indebted. Jefferson and Schenkein (1978) provide a useful description of how the conversational analyst proceeds, but the analytic requirements of proof through examples remain implicit. The issue of the logical status of examples as evidence has been largely ignored in favor of the related (but different) issue of data sources (cf. Labov, 1975; McLaughlin, 1984; Nofsinger, 1977; Shimanoff, 1980).

The notion that discourse consists of a collection of language games (e.g., argument, conversation, interviewing, demonstrating) suggests a goal-oriented activity involving moves by one or more players, mutual dependence and constraint among moves, and the need for strategy and tactics. More importantly, however, the notion of a language game suggests a social activity defined by rules. Language activities exist at the level of "institutional facts"—facts whose meaning is defined by a system of constitutive rules (Searle, 1969). To speak or hear a language is to presuppose the definitions and requirements given in the rules of that institution. People can engage in language activities and can appreciate the meaning and significance of those activities only because they tacitly know the rules of the game and have the ability to apply that knowledge more or less artfully to the play of the game (both in producing and interpreting moves).

This notion of institutional facts serves as the primary regulative principle behind theory and research in discourse analysis and leads quite naturally to a general explanatory puzzle that is very different from the one ordinarily posed in social science: How is the game played? That question is the fundamental problematic of discourse analysis. The question requires discourse analysts to view their language from a position of "anthropological naivete" and to formulate an explanation that would satisfy the non-native speaker, the visitor from Mars, the dumb computer, or any other novice wanting to know how to make sense of and engage in this activity. As with any game there is a perfectly straightforward answer that can be given by describing what anybody needs to know in order to play rationally and by explaining particular properties or events by deriving them from the rules of the game. It is the sort of explanation that can be found in any chess handbook. Providing a more technical equivalent of this sort of account is a basic aim of discourse analysis.

As with a chess handbook, a completed theory of any language game would lay out the overall point of the activity, the elements or basic components, and the primary rules for making allowable moves. Beyond this primary system of knowledge, a theory of a language game would describe a level of knowledge representing rational play within the rules. The point would be to show how, given the successive application of the rules (move, countermove, and so on) a range of pragmatic consequences follow. Such explanations would be akin to explaining why you can checkmate a lone king with just a knight and a bishop, but not with a knight or a bishop alone. This level of rational play would also include descriptions of conventional patterns and strategies, showing when and how they do and do not work. The parallel here is to the way that chess handbooks describe standard openings and defenses or such strategic rules of thumb as "Place rooks on open files" or "Maintain control of the center." Such patterns and strategies are not required by rule. Rather, they are standardized solutions to the problems presented by the structure of the game.

Although the language game metaphor provides an intuitively appealing framework for thinking about how discourse is organized, it does tend to gloss over the communicative aspects of discourse. The moves of any language game exist only in and through the process of communication. But communication is a practical accomplishment, not simply a conventional one (Bach & Harnish, 1979). Like any game, the moves in a language game have meaning by virtue of their institutionally defined *place* in the structure of the game. But the moves in a language game are conventionally defined in terms of a context of beliefs, knowledge, wants, and intentions that a speaker must express and a hearer must infer—and there are no procedures that guarantee the success of such a process. So, what can and cannot be reliably inferred by the players becomes an important aspect in explaining the practical properties of any pattern of moves—just as swindles and traps in chess can only be explained in terms of implications that one player fails to appreciate.

It should be clear from this discussion of the language game metaphor that the theoretical object of primary concern for the discourse analyst is an abstract system of rules—"the game." It is this system of rules that "generates" an indefinite range of discursive events that may be performed and understood by anyone with the requisite knowledge. The goal of analysis is to explain how play within the game is sensible and orderly. This is done by supplying a technical description of language structures and uses that correspond to the intuitions of players and describes their native "competence" (Chomsky, 1965; Hymes, 1971). This technical description then enters into the explanation of the puzzles posed by discourse.

The attitude here closely parallels that of our handbook author and accounts for the widespread indifference among discourse analysts to issues of traditional concern in the social sciences. In explaining how chess is played, the author is primarily interested in displaying rules, the patterns they generate, the properties they implicate, and the strategies they call for. Who actually plays the game is a matter of less importance than the requirements for being able to play. (In a certain sense, the community of players is taken to be both open-ended and trivial—it's anyone who knows the rules). Likewise, explaining the frequency of occurrence for particular moves and other behavioral regularities in actual games is going to be a less central concern than explaining what is possible and not possible in generating sensible and orderly patterns of discourse. What people do a lot may be less important than what people *can* do, but don't do very often, or what people mean by what they do, whatever it is. The conditions that lead to particular behaviors is of less interest than the kind of knowledge that makes those behaviors sensible or nonsensical in the first place.[2] And how often the rules are observed by people will be of less interest than what happens if they

---

[2]Of course, regularities in behavior can serve as *evidence* for theoretical claims, but that is not the same as making such regularities a theoretical problem in themselves.

are not. It is within this context of concerns that argument from example finds its place.

ARGUMENT FROM EXAMPLE

Of course, discourse analysts are not simply faced with the task of explicating an already codified system of rules, patterns, strategies, and the like. They must discover what these are and demonstrate the correctness of their formulations. Because most of the work done in discourse analysis outside of linguistics has focused on what are best thought of as conventional patterns rather than rules, I direct my attention to the role of argument from example in justifying characterizations of those patterns.

The problem posed by a pattern is not only to show that it is in some sense "real," but also to explain the logic behind it (i.e., to show how particular structures may satisfy functions that variations cannot and to show how those structures get built up from their component moves). In this research context, examples are used to do more than just illustrate a pattern; they are used to justify a technical description of it. The issues that need to be addressed, then, are the kind of general claims that can be made about patterns of discourse by displaying examples and the kinds of examples that are required to justify such claims. First, what kinds of generalizations can be argued for by the display of examples? Just what kinds of properties can examples show and what must be assumed for them to legitimately do so?

There is a use of examples that, I think, is not very interesting at least as far as its demonstrative power is concerned. A great many analysts use examples in ways that suggest that the display of the examples themselves is somehow a kind of proof that a class of events occurs with some regularity ("frequently," "often," "usually"). Such examples are usually prototypical in appearance and are drawn from an unspecified collection of naturally occurring cases. But the fact that the example is prototypical in appearance in no way justifies the inference that it is typical in occurrence.[3] Nor does the fact that it actually occurred warrant the inference that it occurs with any particular frequency relative to other discursive events. Such arguments would be clear howlers.

What is usually happening in this kind of display of examples is illustration, not demonstration. The properties apparent in the particular example do not warrant the general claims of the analyst. Rather, the authority of the analyst as a sensitive observer, a careful reader, or an otherwise reliable reporter provides the basis for having confidence in the analyst's inductively generated impressions. Although the methods of a micro-analytic version of naturalistic observation may

---

[3]As a case in point, if Jackson and Jacobs' (1980) analysis is correct, the language system actually contains structural pressures to minimize the appearance of prototypical arguments.

provide a legitimate basis for having confidence in the generalization reported, the point to see is that the force of the analyst's argument does not reside in the examples displayed. There are, of course, obvious sorts of regularities in language use that anyone knows about and will recognize once they are pointed out (e.g., that summonses are sometimes repeated if they do not initially receive an answer, Nofsinger, 1975). Examples in this sense might be used to remind readers about such regularities. Although claims about such regularities may be quite unobjectionable, it should be seen that the examples themselves will not prove the existence of the regularity any more than showing a picture of a flying bird will prove the claim that most birds fly.

The strongest use of examples in discourse analysis does not make claims about behavioral regularities at all (though that can always be hypothesized from the claim that is made and may be the reason for interest in the claim). The use of examples I have in mind supports claims about the structural possibilities and coherent configurations generated by the discourse system. Here, discourse analysts use examples of language use and structure together with intuitions about those uses and structures to reflect the abstract system of rules which generates the sense and order found in the examples. The "generalization" that is made is not a prediction to behavioral occurrences, but an abstraction to categorical properties given within the language system (Searle, 1969).

This kind of general claim and the way it is supported with examples finds its parallel in the way prototypical swindles or standard openings are displayed in a chess handbook. How often such an opening or swindle occurs in actual chess matches is irrelevant. The point is to display the structural integrity of the pattern of moves. That is, the point is to show the way in which a sequence of moves performs a function or follows a goal oriented logic that variations are unable to satisfy. This is shown neither by repetition of the same pattern nor by information about the frequency with which the pattern occurs. It is shown through analysis of variations on the pattern. The integrity of such patterns can be demonstrated in a convincing way to the reader without having to go through more than a single case of any particular variation. The reader can verify for him or herself the design features of the pattern by virtue of his or her knowledge of the rules of the game. Several examples may be displayed to clearly articulate the form and logic of the pattern, but each variation need not be repeated several times in order to demonstrate that the pattern will always work the way it does in any particular example.

Generalization in discourse analysis focuses on similar kinds of properties that are intrinsic to the discourse system. Examples are able to serve as evidence for categorical claims about the discourse system because they exhibit a sense and order that is intuitively available to anyone who has mastered the language. Whether the source of the examples is naturally occurring or artificially generated, the "data" in question are not behavioral occurrences per se, but the meanings and commonsense reasoning processes such behaviors manifest for an interpreter.

These intuitions stand as the facts to be accounted for. The properties of any example have a factual character because those properties are necessary consequents of the rules by which people interpret and produce language. The properties are observable because the observer knows the rules; the trick for the analyst is to infer the rules from those observations.

Because examples are assumed to more or less publicly exhibit properties generated by the rules of language, any reader who has mastered those rules can evaluate the prima facie adequacy of any characterization of an example by inspecting that example and comparing the characterization to his own native intuitions. As O'Keefe (1982) explains for the case of conceptual analysis in ordinary language philosophy:

> The ground of my analysis, however, is not any special status I claim for myself alone, but is my appeal to the reader's native sense of the concepts in question: if my intuitions about paradigm cases are idiosyncratic or skewed in some fashion, then my claims will not ring true to the reader's ear, and in that sense the claims advanced here may be said to be intersubjectively confirmable . . . The plausibility of my claim rests on the degree to which my intuitions concretize generally held understandings about the concept. (p. 9)

Likewise, the adequacy of any general claim supported by a series of examples can be evaluated in terms of that claim's overall consistency with the sense and order exhibited by the entire range of examples. This mode of demonstration presupposes a process of analytic induction whereby any claim about the properties of a pattern of discourse must apply to all and just those cases of that pattern (Jackson, this volume; Jacobs & Jackson, 1983). Any reader can evaluate the power of an argument by this method by comparing the "fit" between the technical description offered by the analyst with the intuited details of the examples and by assessing the exhaustiveness of the analysis through the apparent variability among the types of examples presented. Here, argument by counterexample becomes an immensely powerful corrective, and its vigorous exercise by the research community provides a great deal of the security one has in the claims that stand up.[4]

As with any observational technique, the assumptions warranting the use of examples to make arguments about patterns of discourse are corrigible. In any particular circumstance they may become suspect. Where disagreements over the meaning of an example arise, systematic surveying of informants may be needed. Where intuitions seem clouded or their accessibility outside a context of natural use is in doubt, systematic observation of actual behavior may be

---

[4]Argument from example originated in a context of intense falsificationist debate characteristic of linguists and ordinary language philosophers (cf. Soames & Perlmutter, 1979). Where the social norms of a research community tend to suppress criticism generally the absence of counterexamples to any particular study will obviously mean very little.

useful. But this should not be taken as an inherent indictment of the method.[5] There remains a wide range of issues and examples for which obvious, clear-cut intuitions can be reliably gleaned. The progress made by discourse analysts with the method of argument from example makes it reasonable to presume its general validity while questioning any particular case (Labov, 1975).

So, the kinds of claims about discourse patterns for which examples are best suited are not claims about regular occurrences, but claims about what counts as a coherent configuration of moves and why such a pattern works the way it does. And these kinds of claims are warranted by the fact that the pattern and its features are intuitively recognizable in some collection of examples of that pattern.

What kinds of examples, then, are necessary to justify (or to refute) such claims about discourse? The basic way to show that a pattern exists as a coherent configuration in some language game is to display paradigm cases (prototypes) of that pattern. These are the kind of clear-cut, knock-down cases that strongly resonate with the intuitions of any reader. When seen, they elicit an "Aha! I recognize that" reaction. But to show that some particular technical description of that pattern is correct, the analyst needs to go beyond this kind of confirmatory use of examples.

At the very least, a set of clear-cut examples of the pattern with high internal diversity should be displayed. Such diversity allows the analyst to argue for the constitutive quality of the features that do run through the cases and minimizes the chance that any observed resemblance is simply contingent.

Second, just as some instances are clear examples of a pattern, others are less obvious instances. Any adequate description should allow the analyst to show why some cases are fringe cases. (Notice it is possible to see quite clearly a lack of clarity in one's intuitions and to be quite confident in one's lack of confidence about what property is being displayed—and those are facts to be accounted for.) If a technical description is observationally adequate, then the marginal membership of less clear examples should be accountable by finding the relative absence of central features of the pattern (Jacobs & Jackson, 1981).

Third, if a technical description is adequate, it should enable the analyst to explain mistakes or failures by the way such cases deviate from the pattern. How people can fail to produce a pattern is just as important to understanding how that pattern works as are the ways in which people can construct the pattern.

Finally, the characteristics of the pattern in question ought to be relatable to

---

[5]Nor should it be assumed that these "correctives" are somehow intrinsically more objective or less problematic. Fillenbaum and Rapoport (1971), for example, compare the results of their hierarchic cluster analysis and multidimensional scaling of subject ratings of similarity for "verbs of judging" to the componential analysis intuited by Fillmore (1971). They conclude that their own quantificational methods are too clumsy and insensitive to give anything more than a gross representation of most semantic domains.

the characteristics of other types of patterns. Comparisons of different patterns can give insight into the nature of the underlying logic that generates the patterns. Just as a chess player can learn a great deal about the practical properties of a knight and its role in the structure of a standard defense by examining its contributions to a variety of chess patterns, so also the practical contributions of some particular discursive move to a broader pattern can be better understood by examining its functions in a variety of linguistic contexts.

"CONFRONTATION" AS A PATTERN OF ARGUMENT

The discussion so far has been a pretty abstract presentation of the analytic orientation that guides the use of examples to make arguments about the properties of discourse patterns. In this section, I discuss the rationale for argument from example by considering a technical description of a pattern of argument that Bleiberg and Churchill (1975) call *confrontation*. By working through pertinent examples I hope to concretize the role they may play in advancing technical descriptions of discourse patterns.

The Pattern of Confrontation

Bleiberg and Churchill have proposed a model of confrontation which involves a 6-step series of moves. Their paradigm appears in Table 7.1 They claim the pattern works as follows: Confronted makes a declarative statement (rather than a request or question) that opens the opportunity to show that the statement is false by pointing out facts that contradict the statement. The confrontation culminates in a rhetorical question—a "punch line"—that contradicts the declarative

TABLE 7.1
Paradigm of Ideal Confrontation

Step	Actor	Action
1	Confronted	Makes a declarative statement.
2	Confronter	Asks a yes/no question about a particular aspect of the statement
3	Confronted	Picks the answer that shows that the particular aspect under question is an exception to the statement
4	Confronter	Asks a second yes/no question about a particular aspect of the statement
5	Confronted	Picks the answer that shows that the particular aspect under question is another exception to the statement
6	Confronter	Asks a rhetorical question that contradicts the confronted's original declarative statement

statement made earlier by the confronted. The punch line comes after a series of two yes/no questions that are answered by the confronted in a way that establishes support for the contradicting claim expressed in the rhetorical question. Bleiberg and Churchill (1975) illustrate the pattern they have in mind by examples (1) and (2), which come from an initial psychotherapy session between a young female patient and a middle-aged male therapist:

(1) 01 Pt: I don't want them (my parents) to have anything to do with my life, except (pause)//security(?)
     02 Dr: You live at home?
     03 Pt: Yes.
     04 Dr: They pay your bills?
     05 Pt: Yeah.
     06 Dr: How could they not have anything to do with your life?

(2) 01 Pt: I don't—have much faith—in therapy or anything anymore.
     02 Dr: You don't have faith in anything?
     03 Pt: No.
     04 Dr: You want to live? Or you want to die?
     05 Pt: I don't want to die; I'd be dead (very low voice).
     06 Dr: O.K., so there's obviously some evidence that you want to live. Is that right?

An argumentative pattern with some kind of structural integrity should be apparent from these two examples whether or not the reader has had prior acquaintance with such cases. But whereas (1) and (2) provide good reason to think Bleiberg and Churchill have located something that can be dubbed *confrontation,* it is not clear that their model in Table 7.1 is an adequate technical description. By considering further examples of different varieties we see the need for some modification.

Some Preliminary Considerations

Consider examples (3) and (4), which occur between a prisoner and a prison guard (from Recktenwald, 1978) and between me and my 4 1/2-year-old son, Curtis, at the breakfast table.

(3) 01 P: Hey, stupid.
     02 G: (silence)
     03 P: You with the glasses, stupid.
     04 G: What did you call me?

05 P: I called you stupid.

06 G: What are you doing tonight at 11 o'clock?

07 P: (puzzled) I ain't doin' anything. I'm gonna to be right here.

08 G: (pause) Well, while you're locked up here in the joint, I'm going out the front gate and have a couple of beers. And you're calling me stupid?

(4)   01 Me: Hurry up and eat your breakfast.

02 C: But that'll make me sick.

03 Me: Yeah, well, that's O.K. Hurry up and eat it.

04 C: Don't you like me?

05 Me: Yeah, I like you.

06 C: Then why do you want me to get sick?

Intuitively, both (3) and (4) are members of the same class of phenomena as (1) and (2). If anything, they are more clear-cut cases of confrontation than example (2). However, neither example conforms to the technical description supplied in Table 7.1. Consider (3): For one thing, the initiating move in 03 is not a declarative statement; it is a summons of the sort discussed by Schegloff (1968) and Nofsinger (1975). For another thing, the guard's question in 06 is a Wh-question, and not a yes/no question. Nor does the answer in 05 to the question in 04 appear to show "an exception" to anything the prisoner has said in 03 or 01; rather 05 literally confirms what was said in 03. Finally, the "punch line" in 08 contains more than a rhetorical question.

Similar discrepancies can be found in (4). The initiating move in 01 (repeated in 03) is an imperative, not a declarative statement. And the first response by Curtis is a statement that gets confirmed; not a question. Nor does any of the information elicited show in any obvious way "an exception" to what is said in 01.

In fact, similar problems arise upon close inspection of (2)—Bleiberg and Churchill's (1975) own instance. The therapist's question in 04 is not a yes/no question. Nor does the patient's answer in 03 to the question in 02 show "an exception" to anything she said in 01; like (3) the answer confirms what was meant by 01. Finally, the "punch line" in 06 is not a rhetorical question, it is not an obvious contradiction of 01, and the turn contains more than a question. So, by considering a more diverse set of examples we can see the danger of premature formulation. As still further examples will magnify, Bleiberg and Churchill's technical description cannot encompass paradigm cases and cannot accommodate less clear-cut cases.[6]

---

[6]It may be that Bleiberg and Churchill intend only to capture clear-cut paradigm ("ideal") cases. But even so, their analysis fails to account for (3) and (4). Nor does it explain why (2) is, in their words, a more "subtle" case.

Functional Considerations

Bleiberg and Churchill's technical description is too narrow at least in part because it is the wrong kind of description. It is a purely structural description that is not attentive to the functional basis for the design of the pattern. What I want to suggest is that there are certain conditions that are present in patterns of confrontation, and these conditions can be satisfied more or less successfully through a variety of moves—not just through an initiating declarative statement, two yes/no question answer pairs, and a clinching rhetorical question. These elements may do an especially good job of satisfying the functional design, but they are not the only elements that may do so.

To see this, consider some of the commonsense intuitions that any reader has for what transpires in (1)–(4). Among these are the following: The culminating act of confrontation seems to be the establishment of a "proof" in which the confronted is shown to be caught in the grips of a self-contradiction. This self-contradiction results from beliefs the confronter gets the confronted to publicly commit to in leading up to the punch line. In (1) and (2), the contradiction surrounds the propositional content expressed in the initiating move; in (3) and (4) the contradiction surrounds beliefs implied by the initial action.[7] The confronted is thus led into having to back down from his initial position.

As Bleiberg and Churchill (1975) point out, the confrontation seems to have a "sense of inescapable logic" (p. 275). The punch line is recognizably a conclusion implied by the previously established premises. Moreover, the confronted is drawn into building the case against himself by admitting facts he obviously knew all along (Churchill, 1978). As Bleiberg and Churchill state: "The fact that the confronted must cooperate to produce this activity, unlike simple disagreement, is what makes the confronter's view so unassailable" (p. 275). We find, then, an especially powerful version of what Philipsen (1977) calls "enthymematic persuasion" in conversation: The confronter's "proof" is based on premises that the confronted publicly supplies.

Confrontation is more than simply a strong form of proof, however. Catching someone in a self-contradiction creates the sense of a "put-down" (Bleiberg & Churchill, 1975). Confrontation is a particularly aggressive way of doing so. As Churchill (1978) explains, the punch line alone directly denigrates the confronted. But the lead-in questioning adds to the impression that the confronted has been made to look "stupid or slow-witted" by being unable to read what was coming (or, we might add, at least being unable or unwilling to effectively resist the build-up). The aggressive quality is emphasized by the control the confronted exercises over the direction of the sequence and is also reflected in the obvious nature of the information requested or in the high certainty expressed in the

---

[7]Specifically, in (3) calling someone a derogatory label commits the caller to believing that he is not a member of that class of individuals himself. In (4) commanding someone to do something that will make them sick contradicts the implied want to not hurt persons one likes.

phrasing of questions. The lead-in questions are really "loaded," and not genuine at all.

Table 7.2 presents a technical description of confrontation based on these kinds of functional considerations. The model is more abstract and more flexible than that shown in Table 7.1. Although each step must occur in sequence, the steps are not limited to single turns nor are the speech acts defined by any closed class of utterance types. It is assumed that these functional conditions can be accomplished in a variety of ways, and that this is something that will be reflected in the relative fidelity of the pattern's appearance in any given case (as a prototypical or fringe case; as a "misfire" of some sort; or as a related pattern that is not best thought of as confrontation at all). By considering the adequacy of this functional model, the methodological utility of a variety of different example types can be shown.

Step 1 can include any type of speech act, or may not involve an utterance at all. The "arguable" has an open-ended quality that can be located in any belief, want, or intention to which the confronted is mutually known to be committed. Thus, the hypothetical case of (5) exposes a contradiction between B's goal of losing weight and the known consequence of an observed action:[8]

(5) (A observes B eating chocolates)
   01 A: I thought you were on a diet.
   02 B: I am.
   03 A: Then what are you doing eating those chocolates?

Alternatively, Step 1 can occur over a series of turns through repair of an arguable

TABLE 7.2
Functional Model of Confrontation

Step	Conditions
1	Confronted is mutually believed to be committed to some proposition, P, expressing a belief, want, or intention.
2	Confronter requests (or requests confirmation of) information, $I^1 \ldots I^i$, which confronter supplies (or confirms), thereby committing himself to belief in $I^1 \ldots I^i$.
3	Confronter performs a speech act, A, that conveys a proposition, C, where it is mutually understood that: a) C is the contradiction of P, b) C is a necessary implication of $I^1 \ldots I^i$ and other mutually held beliefs, c) confronted is thereby in a self-contradiction, being committed to C and P, d) A counts as an effort to get confronted to backdown from commitment to P.

[8]Thanks to Deborah Rutt for providing this counterexample and pointing out its implications for the analysis of confrontation.

utterance. The commitment of the confronted to P seems to be exactly what is established by the first question–answer pair in (2), (3), and (4).

Step 2 does not determine how much or in what way information is to be elicited. What information is elicited will be a matter of what contradictory conclusion the confronter aims to draw and how much of the information can be taken for granted (for Step 3, C must be a necessary implication of I^1 . . . I^i and other mutually held beliefs). In the previous examples, premises are elicited through a broad class of utterance types: yes/no questions, closed choice questions, Wh-questions with a strongly preferred answer, and even statements that act as confirmation checks. The delicacy of Step 2 can be seen in its need to elicit information that may signal the upcoming punch-line. It is generally assumed that people will try to avoid falling into self-contradictions if they can help it. This intuition is clearly demonstrated in the failure of (6):

(6)   (B and C are Mormon missionaries who have come to A's home. B is explaining that the Mormon church is different from other churches because Mormons believe everyone must be baptized.)

01 B: . . . O.K.? So there's one—one difference. (pause) O.K.?// We believe every—

02 A: My church believes that too.

03 B: (pause) Uh, well what do you believe?

04 A: (pause) I don't believe that.

05 B: You don't believe the Bible?

06 A: (pause) No:—not—(pause) Well I don't believe that uh, uh, uh, put into the context of our times that that's true.

07 C: Wellll, does Jesus Christ change from age to age? Does he change?

08 A: (pause) The world has changed.

09 C: Does Jesus Christ change?

10 A: No, but that doesn't mean that the meaning of his words doesn't.

11 C: *Oh,* but it does.

12 A: Uh—Heh-heh-heh (nervous giggle)

13 C: Mrs. A, I think you need to find out what you believe, first of all. (pause) You've got to find out- reach down inside of yourself and find out what you believe. 'Cause it sounds like you're not even sure of what you believe yourself.

Failures such as (6) serve as evidence for the intuited structural integrity of confrontation not so much by what is done, as by what is not done. Our expectations are violated, and the nature of that violation is brought into bold relief when variations like (6) are juxtaposed with cases like (1)–(5). Moreover, we understand the intentions of the participants on the assumption that they too orient to a potential pattern of confrontation.

Here, the failure to produce a confrontation can be attributed to A continually disrupting the anticipated direction of reasoning by providing dispreferred answers so as not to contradict her statement in 04. In sequences 05–06, 07–08, and 09–10, B and C try to establish mutually agreed facts that would imply that everyone must be baptized to be saved (thus contradicting what A said in 04). In each response, however, A carefully (notice the hesitation markers) avoids supplying simple assent. After several attempts, C aborts the whole effort by issuing a bald disagreement to what A says in 10. Interestingly, 13 appears to be an effort to recoup the force of the projected confrontation: A's avoidance tactics are asserted to be evidence that she is in self-contradiction anyway. (That effort is observable only by seeing how this variation has a function and slot similar to that of the punch line in confrontation.)

The delicacy of Step 2 can be seen in another way in (7), which occurred a few turns after (6):

(7)   01 A: Do you believe that unbaptized babies cannot be saved? //That
              if they die, and they aren't—
      02 C: *Oh nno*! We don't believe in infant baptism. That it's—We
              don't believe it's necessary.
      03 A: Then why are you—why are you telling me that *my* beliefs are
              inconsistent because I say that I don't believe that baptism is
              necessary?

A certain "surprise" value should be evident in the way this punch line came out, a surprise value that comes from our intuitive understanding of what was projected in the first two turns. Given C and B's prior effort to persuade A that everyone must be baptized to be saved, 01 looks to be eliciting an affirmative response to a special case of that general belief, the point being to argue against the general belief by A arguing against the special case. The way in which C amplifies his denial reinforces the sense that this line of argument has been stopped before it ever got off the ground. It is the unanticipated relevance of a denial that makes 03 into a turnaround.

Not only does (7) show the delicacy of the way in which information must be elicited in Step 2, together with (5) it shows that how much information is elicited will depend on the demands for proof. Where other beliefs necessary to logically imply C in Step 3 can be safely taken for granted, only one question–answer sequence may be necessary to build an unassailable case in which the confronted has cooperated. In fact, more recently Churchill (1978) has suggested that his original paradigm of confrontation is "an expanded form" of a "three-liner" like (5) and (7).

By considering a pattern of indirect argument through questioning that is related to confrontation (though missing the aggressive quality that makes the term *confrontation* apt) we can also see that the amount of questioning may be indefinitely large depending on the requirements for proof. Example (8), reported by Levinson (1979), illustrates the value of examining the way a move functions in a related pattern in order to appreciate the contribution it makes to the pattern under analysis. In (8) a rape vicitim (V) is being cross-examined by a defense attorney (A) in an English court of law.

(8) 01 A: Your aim that evening was to go to the discoteque?
     02 V: Yes.
     03 A: Presumably you had dressed up for that, had you?
     04 V: Yes.
     05 A: And you were wearing make-up?
     06 V: Yes.
     07 A: Eye-shadow?
     08 V: Yes.
     09 A: Lipstick?
     10 V: No I was not wearing lipstick.
     11 A: You weren't wearing lipstick?
     12 V: No.
     13 A: Just eye-shadow, eye make-up?
     14 V: Yes.
     15 A: And powder presumably?
     16 V: Foundation cream, yes.
     17 A: You had bronchitis, had you not?
     18 V: Yes.
     19 A: You mentioned in the course of your evidence about wearing a coat?
     20 V: Yes.
     21 A: It was not really a coat at all, was it?
     22 V: Well, it is sort of a coat-dress and I bought it with trousers, as a trouser suit.
     23 A: That is it down there, isn't it, the red one?
     24 V: Yes.
     25 A: If we call that a dress, if we call that a dress you had no coat on at all had you?
     26 V: No.
     27 A: And this is January. It was quite a cold night?
     28 V: Yes it was cold actually.

What is going on in the questioning is very similar to Step 2 in the pattern of confrontation. As Levinson (1979) points out, "the functions of the questions here are to extract from the witness answers that build up to form a 'natural' argument for the jury" (p. 381). Presumably, it is an argument that contradicts the witness' claim that she had been raped, going something like this: The victim was dressed up like a painted lady. Despite the fact that she had bronchitis she was wearing no coat on a cold winter's night. The facts imply that the girl was looking for sexual adventures. Although the information elicited builds to something less than an "inescapable logic," the possibility for such elaborated questioning in confrontation should be intuitively apparent once seen in cases like (8).

Step 3 of the model, like the other steps, does not correspond to any single utterance. Nor does C need to be expressed through any particular utterance-type—although rhetorical questions do seem to be particularly well-suited to expressing the obviousness of the contradiction and to forcing a backdown. However, we can imagine other types of "punch lines" that are more or less effective. Consider the following alternatives to 03 in (5):

03a I sure don't see how you can eat those chocolates then.
03b Well it sure doesn't look like it.
03c Then quit eating those chocolates.
03d You're sure not going to lose weight if you eat stuff like that.
03e Well, don't bother eating those. It's quicker to just rub them on your thighs.

None of these carry the full force of a direct, unmitigated challenge that holds the confronted answerable for having done, wanted, or believed something that has been publicly contradicted. A rhetorical question has the advantage of directly expressing the contradiction and baldly making the challenge. It is probably for this reason that Bleiberg and Churchill describe (2) as a "subtle" case of confrontation. The move in 06 calls for acceptance of a positively formulated claim by the therapist rather than for a backdown from the patient's original claim. Likewise in (8), no punch line is ever delivered—it is only implied (as is the exact nature of what, precisely, the attorney's argument contradicts). The degree to which a final move by the confronter can be seen intuitively to satisfy the requirements of Step 3 determines how close to a paradigm case an exampjle is—or if it is seen as an example of a pattern at all.

But not only must the punch line clearly express a self-contradiction by the confronted and make a challenge, the punch line must be based on a necessary logic accepted by the parties. Here, premises other than those publicly expressed must be mutually believed or else the punch line will not carry its force as an unassailable contradiction of P. Consider another confrontation between me and my son, this time at the dinner table:

(9) 01 Me: Curtis, eat your broccoli.
     02 C: All of it?
     03 Me: Yes, all of it.
     04 C: Do you like me?

05 Me: Yes, of course I like you.
06 C: Then why do you want me dead?
07 Me: *Huh?*
08 C: Well, if I eat all my broccoli my stomach will be so full that it'll blow up and I'll die.

Notice that although the structural form of (9) closely follows prior examples it "misfires" because the punch line is based on more than what is obvious to both parties, specifically Curtis' leap from eating all his broccoli to dying is based on a belief that only Curtis understood and accepted. Clearly, there is a functional requirement that the punch line not go beyond premises mutually accepted by the parties. This requirement is part of what makes a contradiction apparent in the punch line at all.

This requirement can also be seen at work in avoidance tactics like those in (6). Any conclusion is defeasible, becoming invalid by inserting additional premises of the right sort. It is this fact that accounts for the disruptive power of "yes, but" and "no, but" answers (Churchill, 1978).

CONCLUSION

In this chapter I have tried to articulate a rationale behind the use of examples that shows this discourse analytic method to be more than a micro-analytic version of naturalistic observation or speculative philosophy. Examples can do more than illustrate claims. There is a genuine sense in which examples have a demonstrative power within the framework of discourse analytic argumentation. That demonstrative power is grounded in the idea of an institutional fact and in the claim that intuitions are social facts to be accounted for. From within this analytic stance the problem of the communicative power and meaning of language can be approached in a rigorous and methodical fashion.

In comparing and contrasting examples of language structure and language use, the discourse analyst is involved in finding out how our social knowledge makes language appear. By selecting for analysis examples of a variety of types, the analyst can (1) bring those intuitions into bold relief, showing that we in fact have them, and (2) argue for the correctness of technical descriptions based on those intuitions, justifying the description by the way in which the described features are required for having the intuitions we do. By clearly understanding the argumentative potential and requirements of using examples, solid progress can be made in developing models that remain true to the intricacy, subtlety, and nuance of meaning that we all hear spoken in language.

REFERENCES

Bach, K., & Harnish, R. M. (1979). *Linguistic communication and speech acts.* Cambridge, MA: MIT Press.

Bleiberg, S., & Churchill, L. (1975). Notes on confrontation in conversation. *Journal of Psycholinguistic Research, 4,* 273–278.

Chomsky, N. (1965). *Aspects of the theory of syntax.* Cambridge, MA: MIT Press.

Churchill, L. (1978). *Questioning strategies in sociolinguistics.* Rowley, MA: Newbury House.

Fillenbaum, S., & Rapoport, A. (1971). *Structures in the subjective lexicon.* New York: Academic Press.

Fillmore, C. J. (1971). Verbs of judging: An exercise in semantic description. In C. J. Fillmore & D. T. Langendoen (Eds.), *Studies in linguistic semantics* (pp. 273–296). New York: Holt, Rinehart & Winston.

Hymes, D. (1971). *On communicative competence.* Philadelphia: University of Pennsylvania Press.

Jackson, S., & Jacobs, S. (1980). Structure of conversational argument: Pragmatic bases for the enthymeme. *Quarterly Journal of Speech, 66,* 251–265.

Jacobs, S., & Jackson, S. (1981). Argument as a natural category: The routine grounds for arguing in conversation. *Western Journal of Speech Communication, 45,* 118–132.

Jacobs, S., & Jackson, S. (1982). Conversational argument: A discourse analytic approach. In J. R. Cox & C. A. Willard (Eds.), *Advances in argumentation theory and research* (pp. 205–237). Carbondale and Edwardsville: Southern Illinois University Press.

Jefferson, G., & Schenkein, J. (1978). Some sequential negotiations in conversation: Unexpanded and expanded versions of projected action sequences. In J. Schenkein (Ed.), *Studies in the organization of conversational interaction* (pp. 155–172). New York: Academic Press.

Labov, W. (1975). *What is a linguistic fact?* Lisse, The Netherlands: Peter de Ridder Press.

Levinson, S. (1979). Activity types and language. *Linguistics, 17,* 365–399.

McLaughlin, M. L. (1984). *Conversation: How talk is organized.* Beverly Hills: Sage.

Nofsinger, R. E. (1975). The demand ticket: A conversational device for getting the floor. *Speech Monographs, 42,* 1–9.

Nofsinger, R. E. (1977). A peek at conversational analysis. *Communication Quarterly, 25*(3), 12–20.

O'Keefe, D. J. (1982). The concepts of argument and arguing. In J. R. Cox & C. A. Willard (Eds.), *Advances in argumentation theory and research* (pp. 3–23). Carbondale and Edwardsville: Southern Illinois University Press.

Philipsen, G. (1977). *Enthymematic persuasion in conversation.* Paper presented at the Speech Communication Association meeting, Washington, DC.

Recktenwald, W. (1978, October 30). Working the cells where three died. *Chicago Tribune,* p. 11.

Schegloff, E. A. (1968). Sequencing in conversational openings. *American Anthropologist, 70,* 1075–1095.

Searle, J. R. (1969). *Speech acts.* London: Cambridge University Press.

Shimanoff, S. B. (1980). *Communication rules: Theory and research.* Beverly Hills: Sage.

Soames, S., & Perlmutter, D. M. (1979). *Syntactic argumentation and the structure of English.* Berkeley and Los Angeles: University of California Press.

Wittgenstein, L. (1953). *Philosophical investigations* (G. E. M. Anscombe, Trans.). New York: MacMillan.

8 Conversation Analysis Methods

Robert Hopper
Susan Koch
Jennifer Mandelbaum
University of Texas at Austin

This chapter describes conversation analysis (CA) as a research method in communication studies. We begin with a brief characterization of CA, then describe four tasks: recording, transcribing, analysis, and reporting results. Each of these is illustrated with examples from scholarship. We hope to provide guidance for beginners and bases for dialogue with colleagues.

WHAT IS CONVERSATION ANALYSIS?

Conversation is "that familiar predominant kind of talk in which two or more participants freely alternate in speaking," (Levinson, 1983, p. 284). Conversation analysis rests on repeated listenings to audio and video recordings of natural talk (Sacks, Schegloff, & Jefferson, 1974). CA is a search for patterns in the mode of natural science. As paleontology describes fossils to understand geological history, CA describes recordings to understand structures of conversational action and members' practices for conversing. Levinson (1983) praises CA's emphasis on descriptive detail, and calls CA "the outstanding empirical tradition in pragmatics" (p. 285).

We cannot claim to describe all CA research, nor to speak for others besides ourselves. We describe CA as it appears in our own experiences and the scholarly literature. Some subjects treated in current conversational analysis research are:

(1) How do participants in conversation achieve turn-taking?
(2) How do partners accomplish utterance sequences across turns?
(3) How do speakers coordinate talk with gaze, movement, and other action?

169

(4) How do partners identify and repair problems in interaction?

(5) How does conversation function in particular settings, such as interviews, court hearings, or card games?

Each of these questions focuses on how participants in conversation encounter and deal with certain recurring problems. We consider these questions briefly at the outset, less to summarize findings than to indicate areas of present concern.

Turns.   A fundamental problem faced by conversational parties is: How does one figure out when to begin talking and when to stop talking. A somewhat universal solution to this problem is that one participant speaks at a time, with one speaker's turn beginning as the other's ends. Sacks, Schegloff, and Jefferson (1974) display evidence that parties take turns quite efficiently, with only brief utterance overlaps and few gaps between parties' alternating turns. Sacks et al. propose that parties allocate conversation turns as scarce resources and in regular ways. Because turns at talk vary in length, parties must monitor each others' utterances for points of possible completion—moments at which speaker change is possible. These moments at which speaker change is possible are called *transition relevance places* (TRPs). Parties may indicate TRPs by such features as falling intonation, the drawing out of a final word's penultimate syllable, or various features of surface structure grammar (Levinson, 1983, p. 287; Sacks, Schegloff, & Jefferson, 1974, pp. 705–709). At each transition relevance place, the current speaker may continue talking, or the next speaker may self-select.

These observations, none of which is startling in itself, provide a framework for describing how speakers accomplish transitions between their speaking turns. This framework posits conversational constraints that provide organizational structure for interaction—a structure within which parties display message details.

Sequences.   An examination of transitions between speaker turns reveals that some adjacent turns bear close relationships to each other. For instance, a greeting is often followed by a return greeting, and a question is frequently succeeded by an answer. Such two-part sequences are sometimes called *adjacency pairs* (Schegloff & Sacks, 1973). The first turn in such a sequence seems to project that the next utterance will be heard as "in response" to it. The second turn is then fashioned to show orientation to the first. Consider example (1)

(1) H:S:11, Pomerantz, 1978, p. 84.
   A: It's very pretty.
   B: Thank you.

Speaker A's utterance is hearable as a compliment, which provides some constraint to speaker B to fashion an utterance that can be taken as "in response to" a compliment. In example (1) B immediately responds by saying, "Thank you."

indicating that A's utterance has been interpreted as a compliment and displaying appreciation in response to the compliment. Taken together, the two utterances constitute a compliment sequence. Two-turn sequences may be expanded into longer sequences, either by inserting some adjacency pairs within others, or by chaining together interlocking pairs. For instance, Jackson and Jacobs (1980) describe arguments as expanded adjacency sequences; and Schegloff (1980) describes how the utterance "Can I ask you a question?" can serve as preliminaries to certain kinds of sequences (see also Beach & Dunning, 1982). Consider example (2):

(2)Terasaki, 1976, p. 29 (Cited in Levinson, 1983, p. 356).
01 D: I-I-I had something terrible t'tell you.
02 So uh
03 R: How terrible is it.
04 D: Uh, the- as worse it could be.
05 (0.8)
06 R: W- y'mean Edna?
07 D: Uh yah
08 R: Whad she do, die?
09 D: Mm:hm,

Example (2) shows a chaining of paired utterances. The second utterance is fitted to the first, and also constrains the third. Each utterance in the sequence coheres in topic with previous ones, and each moves the parties toward collaboratively constructing an announcement of news. There is a "pre-announcement" at 01. this indication that an announcement is coming precedes a set of inquiries about the news. Finally, in 08, R suggests a formulation of the announcement. The questioning intonation of this utterance indicates that 08 is a candidate announcement that D may confirm or reject. At 09, D offers confirmation that this was indeed the announcement hinted at in 01.

To summarize, parties' turns are constructed in relationship to previous and subsequent turns, and speakers use the details of their communicative action to display their monitoring and interpretation of unfolding interaction. Conversational analyses frequently display microfine details of interactional understanding. The claim is not that speakers are explicitly aware of how details are used, only that the details occur in orderly ways.

Coordination of Utterances With Other Actions. Many details of communicative action that speakers display to each other involve precise coordination of speech with gaze, gesture, rhythm, and the like. Goodwin (1981) has investigated the role of gaze in turn-taking, as well as the uses of rhythmic dysfluencies in securing attention. Consider example (3):

(3) (G.26: (T)8:50), Goodwin, 1981, p. 98.
   JOHN: I gave, I gave up smoking cigarettes::. =
   DON: = Yea:h,
            (0.4)
   JOHN: I-uh: one-one week ago t'day. acshilly,

John's talk in (3) is littered with *false starts* and *dysfluencies,* which are terms indicating the common belief that such features are errors or signs of flawed speaker performance. Goodwin, however, argues that false starts such as "I gave, I gave" in (3) can operate in close coordination with mutual gaze to help speakers get attention and select the next speaker. (See further discussion of this example on p. .)

Repairs.   A ubiquitous family of conversational practices are used to identify problems and repair them. Repairs may be used to ask for or offer clarification, correct mistakes, and for other reasons. Consider example (4):

(4) 5(28), Zahn, 1984.
   01   FS: Oh um hum-just out of idle curiosity ah in terms of my interest
   02   in political science um um hum what what party are you ah,
   03
   04   F1: Liberal.
   05   F2: Liberal?
   06   F1: Um, Democrat.

In example (3) the repeat of the word *liberal* (with questioning intonation) initiates a repair by identifying the trouble source, or word to be repaired. The repair is accomplished in the next turn by F1 offering the word *democrat* to replace the word *liberal*. Both the initiation of repair and the correction itself may be done by either speaker though self-initiation and self-correction seem conversationally preferred (Schegloff, Jefferson, & Sacks, 1977).

    Several communication researchers have attempted analyses of repair and related concepts, such as *alignment* (Morris & Hopper, 1980); and *account sequences* (McLaughlin, Cody, & O'Hair, 1983). Zahn (1984) argues that certain differences in repair practices that are correlated with relational history. For instance, Zahn found more instances of other-initiation among previously acquainted parties than in initial interactions.

CA in Particular Settings.   Some projects have focused on how communicators accomplish practical tasks in specific social situations. Situations studied include job interviews (Ragan, 1983); judicial hearings (Atkinson & Drew, 1979); therapy sessions (Turner, 1972); and medical interviews (Frankel, 1983). This research is of interest to teachers of communication whose goals are to improve the quality and efficiency of such interactions. Studies of romance, family communication, and play are also emerging (e.g., Fishman, 1978).

CA and DA.   Levinson (1983) distinguishes CA from discourse analysis (DA). Both approaches use tape recordings and both seek to understand sequential structures of talk. However, DA involves coding utterance segments into categories of function or illocutionary force. A DA researcher, for instance, might code the first utterance in example (2) as "giving information," and code each utterance in a conversation into such categories. The discourse analyst then searches for statistical relationships among these categorical data.

CA, in contrast with DA, resists finalized categorization in favor of continuing to add details to description. The conversation analyst seeks to preserve nuances of interaction that would be lost in coding operations. CA and DA may eventually complement one another, but at present these perspectives seem separated by goals as well as concerns of method.

Universality.   Most CA to date has been performed by English speakers on recordings of American and British English speech. This may limit the universality of findings, although cross-cultural studies to date show promising confirmations of CA in such far-flung language communities as Lue, Mayan, Tzoltzil, and Tamil (see for instance, Moerman, in Sudnow, 1972). More such studies should be undertaken in years to come. They will offer opportunities for scholars studying intercultural communication, and may refine some questions regarding universals of conversation.

Conversation researchers in communicaton have been eclectic, mingling CA insight with presuppositions of DA, notions from speech act philosophy and other traditions (e.g., Jacobs & Jackson, 1984; McLaughlin, 1984; Nofsinger, 1975). These mingled perspectives produce diverse fruit. (Note, for instance, the variety of perspectives argued by various authors in Craig & Tracy, 1983.)

Our goal in this chapter is to describe some ways that CA proceeds. Reading this chapter will not qualify anyone as a conversation analyst. CA, like most research methods, is best learned in tutorials, collaborations, and small groups. Interacting with other researchers one learns gradually to adopt some CA perspective and terminology.

FOUR CA ACTIVITIES

We describe four sets of activities routinely encountered in CA: making tape recordings, transcribing, analyzing, and writing research reports. We bypass theoretical issues in favor of procedural ones.

Recording

How do you select an event to record? If you are beginning to learn CA, and have no particular project requirements, then many kinds of conversations might be suitable: telephone recordings are among the easiest to obtain, and two-party conversations are less complicated to transcribe than multi-party ones.

Perhaps the research setting is already fixed—job interviews, initial interactions, or courtroom cross-examinations—and you are looking at CA as a candidate research method. Whatever your choice of events to record, adhere to the criterion of naturalness: Record interactions that would have occurred whether or not you had recorded them. Unfortunately, the very presence of recording devices may initially disturb the scene. Minimize the intrusiveness of recording equipment. Do not give instructions to the parties about how to interact.

How does one minimize the impact of recording while protecting individuals' rights to privacy? The most natural conversational sampling might be obtained by eavesdropping, which we do not recommend on ethical grounds. Some researchers have recorded conversations covertly, obtained approval of the subjects immediately afterward, and offered to destroy the recording should objections arise. Others have tapped telephones or recorded interviews with permission of one party only, which raises questions about the rights of the second party.

It is preferable to obtain permission of all parties in a natural setting. Parties can record conversations during such events as supper, a walk, a phone conversation, or at a business meeting (e.g., Fishman, 1978). Sometimes subjects show self-consciousness, or address asides to the recorder, but these usually become quite infrequent after subjects get used to being recorded.

You may legally record self-consciously public talk, but not private conversations in public places. You may record political discussions, debates, or talk shows. Mass-mediated texts vary in their similarity to co-present conversation, but frequently their social impact makes them important.

Finally, conversations may be recorded in artificial situations, as when researchers ask subjects to role-play situations or just to "get acquainted" on tape. Although these are certainly not natural situations, they may offer useful data. For example, Brenneis and Lein (1977) asked children to role-play arguments, and recorded these conversations.

Reconstructions.   Some analyses have used remembered speech or made-up examples for analysis (Beach & Dunning, 1982; Garfinkel, 1967; Lakoff, 1975; Nofsinger, 1975), but CA relies on the details provided by audio/video recordings. Even recordings, although considerably factual and detailed, are less than perfect copies. How much of reality does a recording capture? Recordings evoke a confidence that they provide a complete record of conversation, though they are actually incomplete representations—flat copies. One must remain alert to interactive practices absent from recordings, especially recordings on audiotape.

We recommend video recording whenever possible. However, audio recordings of telephone conversations do provide most of the details that are available to telephone participants.

Technical Quality.   No analysis can overcome flawed recordings. Conversation analysts may play a recording hundreds of times, so technical quality is essential. Simply lending people a tape recorder and disregarding fidelity may yield useless recordings. We offer the following suggestions.

Audiotaping may be less intrusive and less expensive than videotaping. Still, if resources and location permit, video-recording provides a richer record, and audio-tapes may be dubbed from video.

Two-party conversations are easier to transcribe than multi-party conversations. With more than three speakers, it becomes difficult to tell who is talking, especially in audio recordings. Try using two recorders, and place them to increase the likelihood that every utterance will be recorded clearly on at least one. Experiment with lavalier microphones and remote-transmitting systems.

Maximize the signal and minimize noise. Use the best available recording equipment. Inexpensive high-fidelity cassette recorders are available. We use automatic volume control, which gives increased word-recognition but flattens, variation in loudness and pitch. Use high-fidelity durable tape, because the repeated listening in CA wears out inexpensive tape. If you obtain an interesting recording, copy it at once, saving the original as an archive. Use the copy to transcribe because repeated playings may damage recordings.

Reduce background noise in the recording environment when this is practical. Consider turning off fans and other nearby motors. Make test recordings ahead of time in the setting to identify these noise sources. However, it is sometimes difficult to tell what sounds in the environment may be useful in CA. The chatter of a television or a business machine may affect conversation. We anticipate, for instance, studies of family television viewing that show interactiveness between family members' speech and the televised messages.

Transcription

The detailed transcripts developed by CA researchers are striking to many readers. Essays contain transcripts that offer opportunities to clarify and verify the analyses. Transcribing conventions have been refined by Gail Jefferson (See Sacks, Schegloff, & Jefferson, 1974; Schenkein, 1978; and out Appendix).

Transcribing involves repeated listening to recordings. If you were to listen to a tape without transcribing, this might be like flying a helicopter over the conversation. Transcribing is more like crawling across the countryside. Wherever you start with CA, you must soon commit to the transcribing trenches. If you are a beginner, start transcribing at the beginning, or at the first interesting place you find.

A skillfully crafted transcript can be an immense aid to analysis. Both the product (the transcript) and the process (transcribing) aid researchers in locating finding intricacies of conversation. Transcribing forces you to listen for the precise sounds that were said, rather than just noting the sense of what you thought you heard. Don't hire a transcriber; roll up your sleeves.

CA transcripts display information about pitch and loudness, as illustrated in example (5):

(5)
> Ah can't belie:ve I ate the WHO::LE thing!

Example (5) is our attempt to transcribe a popular advertising slogan. Most readers will be familiar with the sound of the slogan, and hence be able to interpret our use of Jefferson's symbols. Underlining in transcripts shows stress of the underlined sounds, capital letters indicate loudness, and the colons denote "stretched" sounds. Irregular spellings (e.g., "ah" for "I") denote noticeable variations in pronunciation. These conventions are designed to display on the transcript precisely those features that would be noticeable to the participants.

CA transcripts differ from drama scripts in their emphasis on the precise moments that utterances begin and end. The timing with which speakers take turns, interrupt one another, or speak in overlap is transcribed with care. The importance of timing can be shown by one of Jefferson's (1979) examples of laughter in conversation.

(6) Jefferson, 1979, p. 89.
    ROGER: *You*:: are what dey refer to in rougher circles as a chick'n
              shit. =
    ROGER: = hhh hhehh
    KEN: [
                      heh:heh heh

In example (6) Roger follows up an insult with a noise that could be interpreted as laughter, indicating that the insult may be taken as a joke. As Ken joins the incipient laughter, Roger's laughter becomes more obvious. According to Jefferson, had Ken not chosen to laugh at this point, Roger could have turned out to be clearing his throat or making an audible exhalation. This illustrates the precision of speakers' timing in conversation, and demonstrates the importance of close transcription. Stenographic pedals, earphones, and variable speed playback devices may be useful in deciphering the precise beginnings and endings of overlaps in recorded speech.

Alternate Styles of Transcribing.   Jefferson's transcription conventions do not approach complete prosodic representation. Transcribers sometimes vary transcript format in order to emphasize conversational objects of interest to them.

We advise beginners to imitate the form of Jefferson's published transcripts, however. The Jefferson system uses symbols available on standard typewriters and word processors. It is precise in showing the sequence of turns and the timing of overlaps.

Several scholars describe transcribing innovations. Moerman (1972) provides a phonetic rendering of a Lue conversation, alongside translation and other materials. Goodwin (1981; and in Psathas, 1979) displays shifts in eye gaze in relation to shifts in conversation. Kendon (1977) and Condon and Ogston (1967) attempt to transcribe rhythmic patterns in interaction. Labov and Fanshell (1977) display graphs of intonation patterns. Koch (1983) has used musical notation to describe conversations of video arcade players:

The transcript in Fig. 8.1 pictures simultaneous events by human communicators and by machines. It offers a representation of some musical features in the machine's noises, and helps to recreate on the page some of the experience of the participants. You may notice, however, that this transcript de-emphasizes speaker alternation of turns in order to emphasize the embeddedness of human utterances in the total noise environment. The point here is that adaptation of transcription to any purpose is likely to underemphasize other features.

Students encountering CA for the first time sometimes ask how much transcribing suffices for a particular project. Given that transcribing is an ongoing process, how does the novice decide to put aside transcribing for a time and move to other CA activities? There is no satisfactory answer to this question, though we've heard these suggested: (a) transcribe until things come into clear focus; and (b) transcribe until you see things begin to recur over and over (analogous to Glaser & Strauss' 1967 concept of "saturation of categories").

Transcripts develop throughout analysis and should never be regarded as final. Keep records of what has been transcribed, and the location of transcribed materials in tape recordings.

Electronic word processing can simplify transcription by allowing you to work over a draft again and again without time-consuming retyping. Computerization may also help researchers share transcripts.

Transcription blends into analysis. As you transcribe, write down your observations; these will begin to accumulate toward making and testing claims.

Analysis

Analysis, the word that best stands for the whole of CA, occurs in multiple listening to recordings (often with aid of transcripts) in order to reason about how people accomplish conversational actions. You simply must experience these parts of the process for yourself. There is simply no describing it.

We focus the present discussion on two issues: multiple listening to recordings, and reasoning from recorded evidence.

Listen to recordings over and over, with the aid of transcripts. Do not practice analysis with just transcripts; use transcripts with recordings. Focus your attention

video:  (BEEP)
player: Bad bonus thoughman   This is a really
observer:

---

video: (BEEP)   (BEEP)
player: fast game does it seem that way to you?
observer:

---

video:
player: Seems to me it's set
observer: ⌐Mm no, I (took a

---

video:
player:
observer: licking) pretty fast, that happens

---

video: / / / / / / THUD / / / THUD / / /
player: ⌐twenty one hundred is a re:al low
observer: ⌐occasionally

---

video: THUD / / / / / / / / / / / / / /
player: bonus. it seems to me. (1.8)
observer:

VIDEO GAME: Donkey Kong   First four lines of
                                 video are transition
   / / / Moves of man up ladder to next game pattern.

on very brief segments, perhaps 5 seconds long, and listen to a single segment 20 or more times, making notes frequently. Number each line of the transcript for easy reference. There is no "correct" way to begin the multiple-listening process, in fact the best procedure may be to stay as "unmotivated" as you can. Remain open to being surprised by what you hear. To keep your mind on the task, you might write down line-by-line notations of how speakers take turns, make repairs, interrupt each other, and so on.

Maintain a mental set open to observing obvious things. Consider what a speaker "might have said but didn't," or "seemed to start saying, then changed it." Consider what words or noises speakers have used before in the conversation. If you feel "stuck" you may attempt to "expand" the text by specifying materials that are not explicit in the conversation but seem to be shared-in-common by the participants (see Garfinkel, 1967; Labov & Fanshell, 1977, for instances of expansions; also take care to remain centered upon the text).

State your intuitions about what a speaker is doing in a particular utterance. Then try to develop a text-basted demonstration of how they are accomplishing it.

Listen in groups to transcribed recordings. This activity can help with knotty problems of transcriptions, and provides an environment for testing of preliminary observations and claims. CA benefits from informed and candid group work.

Listed here are some procedures for a 2-hour group listening exercise. (It is also informative to perform this exercise as an individual.)

1. Up to seven members listen to a segment of a recording, perhaps 2 minutes, with a transcript.

2. After about the fourth listening, members select a brief segment, perhaps 2 to 5 seconds, for more detailed listening.

3. The brief segment is played repeatedly until members are satisfied (perhaps a dozen repetitions).

4. Members write their observations for 15 minutes, with replayings if needed.

5. Members present their descriptions to the group, proceeding clockwise from the first volunteer, until everyone has spoken. Interruptions and questions of clarification are kept brief.

6. Members formulate points of disagreement and agreement, argue, attempt collaboration to build analyses, and so on.

Reasoning from Recordings. Any claim should be grounded in details observed in recordings. You may begin by describing what you observe or believe to be happening in a recording, even though you are unsure of the basis for the claim. For example, you may suggest that a given speaker seems "hesitant" as she or he begins to speak. Focus your observation to a single line of transcript where the "hesitancy" occurs. Ask how the speaker displays hesitancy. Try to specify the precise moment when the event happened allowing intuitions to work in tandem with specifying detail.

To illustrate these considerations, we return to example (3):

(3) (G.26:(T)8:50), Goodwin, 1979, p. 98.
    01 JOHN: I gave, I gave up smoking <u>ci</u>garettes::. =
    02 DON: = Yea:h,
    03   (0.4)
    04 JOHN: I-uh: one-<u>one</u> week ago t'<u>da</u>:y. acshilly,

This sentence is part of a video-taped conversation of two young couples: John and Beth, and Ann and Don. Goodwin (1979) uses the segment to demonstrate how the emerging structures of sentences are modified by speakers and hearers as they interactively construct turns at talk. We use a portion of Goodwin's analysis of example (3) to demonstrate how preliminary or intuitive observations about a conversation segment may be developed into conversation-analytic claims.

The first thing you may notice about example (3) is that John is the main speaker. He utters every word but one in this segment. Second, you may notice that Don's single word "yeah" does not really interrupt John's turn, but rather encourages John to continue (Schegloff, 1981, p. 91, footnote 16). John's utterances in this segment are essentially a single turn. Third, you may observe that John's turn is marked by restarts in line 01 and at the beginning of 04, and by a pause at line 03, suggesting that John might be shifting directions as his turn develops.

Examine and describe details of conversation in order to sharpen preliminary observations into questions about how John accomplishes the shifting of directions in mid-turn. Goodwin argues that John systematically changes the nature of his utterance several times during this turn, because of his interaction with other participants, and therefore that even a single turn at talk can be an interactional construction of the parties to the conversation.

Goodwin's analysis rests on three kinds of features in this segment: (a) restarts at line 01 and 04; (b) use of gaze of the parties as captured by video recording and preserved through a transcribing innovation, and (c) the nature of the "news" that John communicates throughout his turn. Through his analysis, Goodwin shows how John's restarts at lines 01 and 04 may "request the gaze" of his recipient. Goodwin (1979) explains, "After such a phrasal break nongazing recipients regularly bring their gaze to the speaker" (p. 106).

Goodwin devised a transcribing system that tracks gaze direction and movement. The speaker's gaze is marked above each utterance; a line indicates the speaker is gazing at a particular object, and commas and periods indicate that the gaze is moving toward or away from an object:

(7) Goodwin, p. 99

JOHN: . . , ...   [$\underline{\text{Don,,}}$ [$\underline{\text{Don}}$
          I gave, I gave u p smoking $\underline{\text{ci}}$ garettes::. =

DON: = Yea:h,

JOHN: ... [$\underline{\text{Beth}}$ ...[$\underline{\text{Ann}}$
          I-uh: one-$\underline{\text{one}}$ week ago t'$\underline{\text{da}}$: y. acshilly

John begins to reveal the news about his quitting as his eyes come to rest on Don. According to Goodwin, only Don or Ann would be appropriate recipients of this utterance, in keeping with a conversational rule that one should not tell one's conversational partners something they already know. Thus Don and Ann are unknowing recipients, whereas Beth, his wife, can be assumed to be a knowing recipient. Once Don acknowledges the news, John's gaze shifts to Beth. Because Beth already knows about his quitting, he transforms his news into a report of an anniversary, which makes it news for her as well.

Goodwin describes John's use of *acshilly* by considering the eye gaze of the listeners, which is noted in example 7. As John relays his news to Beth, she does not look at him. He then looks at Ann, who is looking at Beth. At the word *today*, John reaches a transition relevance place. No other speaker self-selects at this moment, and John finds himself unable to pass the turn because no one is looking at him. Ann, however, is beginning to shift her gaze to him. John adds the word *acshilly*, giving Ann time to meet his gaze and again reframing the function of this turn back to announcing the news of quitting smoking. Ann then takes the next turn.

To summarize, John restructures his utterance during the course of its production. He makes the content of his message relevant to each of his interlocutors individually, and coordinates eye gaze and message to successfully pass the turn to Ann.

The description has now been stated in formal terms. A formal description may incorporate numerous details to answer "how" questions about a segment. If the description can be applied to more than a single case, it may have some status as a conversational phenomenon (e.g., "passing a turn").

Having formulated a provisional conversational phenomenon, the analyst may begin to collect other instances of this phenomenon. Through a process akin to "analytic induction," (Znaniecki, 1934), each instance is tested against the formalization that must account for each newly located instance case. Every exception to the explanation must be considered. Records of your analysis can be kept in the form of transcript-fragments plus notes. This collection provides illustrations of the analysis, and becomes useful as you formulate findings into a research report.

To summarize, analysis happens as investigators, singly and in groups, listen many times to brief segments and test claims against recordings. A description of a general conversational phenomenon must stand empirical test—other investigators should be able to validate your claim by listening to the recordings, studying transcripts and reading your written report. Also, your claims can be tested against other recordings. As you begin to write for other scholars, you move from analysis toward presentation of findings.

Presenting Findings

As you report findings to other scholars you must state your claims clearly and present evidence. Be careful to account for exceptions and reservations. Do not hurry to answer questions of sweeping theoretical importance.

CA findings have been presented in a variety of formats. Some CA essays examine a single conversation or even a single conversational fragment (Sacks, 1979). Other reports describe a particular feature, such as responses to compliments (Pomerantz, 1978). Still others describe interactive sequences such as conversation-closings (Schegloff & Sacks, 1973). Other researchers describe conversations within institutional settings such as classrooms (Mehan & Griffin, 1980); traffic courts (Pollner in Psathas, 1979), and those mentioned in the introduction to this essay.

Whatever the domain of the analysis, research reports to date have de-emphasized the publication of precise counts of features and statistical tests of significance. Some resistance to numbers in CA stems from the analytic goal of accounting for every case, rather than just a percentage of cases. Like ethology, CA describes events in detail rather than insisting upon quantification of observations.

CONCLUSION

In sum, conversation analysis is a flexible research method offering: (a) closeness to factual data; (b) focus upon conversation itself; (c) techniques for achieving detailed description of features noticeable to and used by participants; and (d) attachment to a well-reasoned paradigm.

Problems emergent in the present treatment include: (a) the method is difficult to learn except in tutorial; and (b). The absence of rigid step-by-step counting-and-coding operations makes the process difficult or unsettling for some researchers.

In considering future prospects, communication researchers must deal with a now-familiar problem of the "transplanted paradigm." What modifications are necessary to adapt a sociological paradigm to communication studies? We have already noted the interests of communication research in issues of applied communication and communication instruction.

How is conversation analysis best adapted to fit with communication theory? Here one must be careful, for some adaptations violate CA's goals and assumptions. It remains to be seen how CA approaches will affect such areas as relational communication cross-cultural communication.

To open dialogue on standards for CA research in communication, we suggest the following guidelines, organized in the subdivisions of this chapter.

Recording:

1. Describe the sample of recordings upon which the analysis is based—the number of hours of conversation, and the number of parties involved. Describe criteria used in sample selection.

2. Describe the circumstances of recording, in terms of subjects, situational constraints, and equipment used in recordings. Credit the researchers who collected recordings.

3. Seek avenues to make full recordings available to other researchers. (We are beginning a library for tapes and transcripts at the University of Texas.)

Transcribing:

1. Give credit to transcribers.

2. Describe your transcription procedures in ways that make it possible to check your transcripts against recordings.

3. Include your transcripts in your essays; urge editors to publish complete transcripts if possible (see Craig & Tracy, 1983).

Analysis:

1. Specify research questions.

2. Specify presumptions and procedures of your analysis.

3. If you isolate certain segments for analysis (e.g. account sequences), state the criteria you used to identify the set of segments.

Reporting:

1. State your claims clearly, and discuss their generalizability.

2. Identify the source and location of all transcribed examples.

3. Include reviews of relevant literature. Relate your results back to this literature.

4. Separate rigorous results from speculative material.

ACKNOWLEDGMENTS

We are grateful to a number of colleagues who commented on drafts of the present work, including J. Maxwell Atkinson, Janet Alberts, Richard Frankel, Christopher Zahn, and especially Anita Pomerantz.

APPENDIX: TRANSCRIBING SYMBOLS*

Speaker identification is justified with left margin, and the conversation progresses chronologically from the top of the page to the bottom.

[ ]   Brackets are used to indicate overlapping utterances. Left brackets note beginning of the overlap, and right brackets "close" or end the overlap.

> MOM: Who wants <u>gum</u>! =
> TED: = I do!
>
>   [   ]
> ANN: <u>I</u> do!

=   The equals sign indicates that two utterances are immediately contiguous but not overlapping.

___   <u>Underlining</u> indicates stress/emphasis.

^   (in mother/daughter) precedes an upward shift in pitch.

?   Question mark indicates rising inflection, not necessarily a question.

> JOHNBOY: Goodnight? Grandma,
> GRANDMA: Good<u>night</u>, Johnboy.

.   Period indicates falling inflection, not necessarily at the end of an utterance or sentence.

,   Comma indicates a continuing intonation, that is a slight stretching of sound with a very small upward or downward intonation-contour.

(1.6)   Single parentheses enclosing numbers indicate pause lengths in seconds and tenths-of-seconds. Very short pauses shown by (.)

> JAN: It's o<u>kay</u>, don't <u>worry</u>, ((sniffle))
>   (1.6)
> I- I'll be fi::ne.

:   Colon indicates the extension (stretching) of the sound it follows.

-    Hyphen following a sound indicates a cut-off, a definite stopping of the sound.

(( ))   Double parentheses enclose transcribers' descriptive remarks.

hhh   h's indicate audible out-breaths, sighing, hearable as unvoiced laughter.

(h)   h in parentheses indicates explosive aspiration, sometimes laughter.

> BEE: <u>They</u> always are(hh)hhh

'h   (in "chicken dinner") or .h (in "mother/daughter") indicates audible in-breath.

pt   lip-smack sound

°   A degree sign preceding and following an utterance indicates that it is said more quietly than surrounding talk.

( )   Single parentheses indicate hearings which are in doubt.

*These transcribing notations were developed by Gail Jefferson. Sources: J. Schenkein (Ed.), *Studies in the Organization of Conversational Interaction,* Academic Press, 1978, pp. xi–xvi; J. M. Atkinson and J. Heritage (Eds.), *Structures of Social Action,* Cambridge, 1984, pp. ix–xvi.

REFERENCES

Atkinson, J. M., & Drew, P. (1979). *Order in court.* London: Macmillan.

Atkinson, J. M., & Heritage, J. (1984). *Structures of social action.* Cambridge and New York: Cambridge University Press.

Beach, W., & Dunning, D. (1982). Pre-indexing and conversational organization. *Quarterly Journal of Speech, 68,* 170–185.

Brenneis, D., & Lein, L. (1977). You fruithead: A sociolinguistic approach to children's dispute settlement. In S. Ervin-Tripp & C. Mitchell-Kernan (Eds.), *Child discourse* (pp. 49–66). New York: Academic Press.

Condon, W., & Ogston, W. (1967). A segmentation of behavior. *Journal of Psychiatric Research, 5,* 221–235.

Craig, R., & Tracy, K. (1983). *Conversational coherence: Studies of form and strategy.* Beverly Hills, CA: Sage.

Fishman, P. (1978). Interaction: The work women do. *Social Problems,* 397–406.

Frankel, R. (1983). The laying on of hands: Aspects of the organization of gaze, touch, and talk in a medical encounter. In S. Fisher & A. Todd (Eds.), *The social organization of doctor-patient communication.* Washington, DC: Center for Applied Linguistics.

Garfinkel, H. (1967). *Studies in ethnomethodology.* Englewood Cliffs, NJ: Prentice-Hall.

Glaser, G., & Strauss, A. (1967). *The discovery of grounded theory: Strategies for qualitative research.* Chicago: Aldine.

Goodwin, C. (1981). *Conversational organization.* New York: Academic Press.

Jackson, S., & Jacobs, S. (1980). Structure of conversational argument: Pragmatic bases for the enthymeme. *Quarterly Journal of Speech, 66,* 251–265.

Jacobs, S., & Jackson, J. (1984). Structure and strategy in conversational influence attempts. *Communication Monographs,* 285–304.

Jefferson, G. (1979). A technique for inviting laughter and its subsequent acceptance declination: In G. Psathas (Ed.), *Everyday Language* (pp. 79–95). New York: Irvington.

Kendon, A., (Ed.). (1977). *Studies in the behavior of social interaction.* Indiana University and Lisse: Peter DeRidder Press.

Koch, S. (1983). Video game talk. International Communication Association, Dallas.

Labov, W., & Fanshell, D. (1977). *Therapeutic discourse.* New York: Academic Press.

Lakoff, R. (1975). *Language and woman's place.* New York: Harper & Row.

Levinson, S. (1983). *Pragmatics.* Cambridge: Cambridge University Press.

McLaughlin, M. (1984). *Conversation: How talk is organized.* Beverly Hills: Sage.

McLaughlin, M. L., Cody, M. J., & O'Hair, H. D. (1983). The management of failure events: some contextual determinants of accounting behavior. *Human Communication Research, 9,* 208–224.

Mehan, H., & Griffin, P. (1980). Socialization: the view from classroom interaction. In D. D. Zimmerman & C. West (Eds.), Language and social interaction; special issue of *Sociological Inquiry,* 357–392.

Moerman, M. (1972). Analysis of Lue conversation: Providing accounts, finding breaches, and taking sides: In D. Sudnow, (Ed.), *Studies in social interaction* (pp. 170–220). New York: Free Press.

Morris, G., & Hopper, R. (1980). Remediation and legislation in everyday talk: How communicators achieve consensus. *Quarterly Journal of Speech, 66*, 266–274.

Nofsinger, R. (1975). The demand ticket: A conversational device for getting the floor. *Speech Monographs, 42*, 1–9.

Pomerantz, A. (1978). Compliment responses: Notes on the cooperation of multiple constraints. In J. Schenkein (Ed.), *Studies in the organization of conversational interaction* (pp. 79–112). New York: Academic Press.

Psathas, G. (Ed.). (1979). *Everyday language*. New York: Irvington.

Ragan, S. (1983). A conversational analysis of alignment talk in job interviews. *Communication Yearbook, 7*, 502–516.

Ragan, S. L., & Hopper, R. (1984). Ways to leave your lover. *Communication Quarterly, 32*, 310–317.

Sacks, H. (1979). Hotrodder, a revolutionary category. In G. Psathas (Ed.), *Everyday Language* (pp. 7–14). New York: Irvington.

Sacks, H., Schegloff, E. A., & Jefferson, G. (1974). A simplest systematics for the organization of turn taking for conversation. *Language, 50*, 696–735.

Schenkein, J. (Ed.). (1978). *Studies in the organization of conversational interaction*. New York: Academic Press.

Schegloff, E. A. (1980). Preliminaries to preliminaries: "Can I ask you a question?" in D. D. Zimmerman & C. West (Eds.), Language and social interaction; special issue of *Sociological Inquiry*, 104–152.

Schegloff, E. A. (1981). Discourse as an interactional achievement: Some uses of "uh huh" and other things that come between sentences. In D. Tannen (Ed.), *Analyzing discourse: Text and talk* (pp. 71–93). Georgetown University Roundtable on Languages and Linguistics. Washington, DC: Georgetown University Press.

Schegloff, E. A., Jefferson, G., & Sacks, H. (1977). The preference for self-correction in the organization of repair in conversation. *Language, 53*, 361–382.

Schegloff, E. A., & Sacks, H. (1973). Opening up closings. *Semiotica, 8*, 289–327.

Sudnow, D. (Ed.). (1972). *Studies in social interaction*. New York: Free Press.

Turner, R. (1972). Some formal properties of therapy talk. In D. Sudnow (Ed.), *Studies in social interaction* (pp. 367–397). New York: Free Press.

Zahn, C. (1984). A re-examination of conversational repair. *Communication Monographs, 51*, 56–66.

Zimmerman, D. H., & West, C. (Eds.). (1980). Language and social inquiry; special double issue of *Sociological Inquiry*.

Znaniecki, F. (1934). *The method of sociology*. New York: Farrar & Rinehart.

9 The Analysis of Action Sequences in Conversation: Some Comments on Method

Margaret L. McLaughlin
University of Southern California

Recent years have seen an increased interest in *strategic behavior* as it is man-ifested in conversational interaction; that is, in the way in which people *plan* and *implement* sequences of action whose intended outcome is the attainment of some desired *goal* (Cohen & Perrault, 1979; Hayes-Roth & Hayes-Roth, 1979; Hobbs & Agar, 1981; Hobbs & Evans, 1980). I address myself here to some of the problems that traditional empiricists like myself are likely to face when trying to reduce the complexities of strategic action in conversation to sets of categories that are susceptible of statistical analysis. To do so, I draw upon a recently collected set of data on the production of self-serving utterances, or, in the vernacular, *bragging*. The points developed are, I believe, applicable to the study of any of a variety of goal-oriented action sequences that an actor might imbed in an otherwise casual conversational encounter, including information-seeking (Berger & Kellerman, 1983; Kellermann & Berger, 1984); compliance-gaining (Clark, 1979; Cody, McLaughlin, & Schneider, 1980; McLaughlin, Cody, & Robey, 1980); accounting (Cody & McLaughlin, 1985; McLaughlin, Cody, & O'Hair, 1983; McLaughlin, Cody, & Rosenstein, 1983), and a variety of other actions, both transparent and covert.

The study from which the examples were drawn (McLaughlin, Altendorf, Baaske, Cashion, Louden, & Smith, in press) was designed to answer a number of questions about the realization of self-serving goals in conversational inter-action, including (a) how are macrorules (van Dijk, 1980, 1981) used to manip-ulate global topic structures; (b) what are the specific kinds of local coherence devices that are exploited to "occasion" self-serving utterances; and (c) how do "top-down" as opposed to "opportunistic" planning styles affect the cohesiveness in context of self-serving utterances—that is, can self-serving utterances be made nonobviously without active manipulation of topical and functional structures in conversation?

Subjects in the study were run in groups of two. One member of the pair was naive throughout, whereas the other was led to believe that she or he was to be a confederate of the experimenter. The "confederate," upon arrival at the waiting area, was asked to list three boasts about him or herself that she or he might be reluctant simply to announce to the stranger with whom she or he was about to be paired, but was nonetheless proud of. The boasts obtained included statements like "My grandfather was Mr. America," I was a model for the "Lookin' Good Calendar," "I come from a distinguished family in Beverly Hills," and so forth. One of the confederate's boasts was selected at random, and she or he was instructed to communicate the information to his or her partner during the course of a 15-minute videotaped conversation. The only instruction given was that the self-flattering information was to be imparted in such a way that the naive partner not become suspicious of the confederate. After the 15-minute session with the naive partner, confederates were interviewed about their plans and strategies. Videotapes of the conversations were coded on a variety of features, including the nature of the coherence relation between the confederate's "brag" and the immediate local context, the cohesiveness of the self-serving utterance, the presence or absence of topic control strategies such as extinguishing unproductive topics, and so on. Although the substantive findings from the project are reported elsewhere (McLaughlin et al., in press), I examine here some methodological issues that bear on the study of action sequences generally, using examples from the study for illustration.

Decisions about unitizing sequences of action can have a significant impact on the kinds of strategies that get "discovered." In preparing a transcript for coding, one of the first tasks is to determine the unit of analysis, and then to estimate the reliability with which the discourse can be "chunked" in that particular way. (Although Jackson, this volume, proposes that "people" rather than "units of discourse" are the cases for study in traditional social scientific approaches to discourse, this is clearly false. See for example McLaughlin and Cody, 1982, in which conversational "gaps" were the analytic unit, and McLaughlin, Cody, and Rosenstein, 1983, in which the unit of analysis was the account sequence.) When our units of analysis are defined according to syntactic or paralinguistic characteristics, as with the sentence, the utterance, or the turn (Auld & White, 1956; Stiles, 1978), we have problems enough in obtaining agreement on how the stream of behavior ought to be punctuated. When we want to unitize at the level of action, for example, when we want to mark off storytellings (McLaughlin, Cody, Kane, & Robey, 1981) or arguments (Jackson & Jacobs, 1981), we are confronted with the problem that it's not always easy to tell when or where the action begins (although we probably will be able to tell when it's over). Disagreement among coders as to the point at which a particular sequence of actions begins can have a significant effect on the quality and number of actions that are observed.

In some cases, coders might appear to have little trouble agreeing as to the onset of some particular action in conversation. In the following example, it seems to be clear that the actor's (C_1's) strategy for accomplishing his boast about his abilities as a sailor begins at line 11:

1	N:	So. That's weird. So do you ever see this girl
2		anymore? or was this a long time ago?
3	C_1:	Couple of years back, you know, high school, three
4		years ago, whatever.
5	N:	Is your girlfriend here? or is she in Long Beach?
6	C_1:	No, actually she ah she goes to Northridge State. I
7		met her over summer when I was home =
8	N:	Oh.
9	C_1:	= with my parents you know.
10	N:	Oh. That's nice.
11	C_1:	Yeah, well, *my big thing is sailing.* I
12	N:	Oh, I love to sail!
13	C_1:	*I uh right now I'm trying really hard to uh working hard toward the '88 Olympics in sailing.*

That C_1's strategy seems so clearly to begin at line 11 is due entirely to the fact that his transition is abrupt; C_1 is not long on subtlety, and makes no effort to make the topic shift appear to be occasioned by anything in the previous talk. Because the boundaries of the event of interest seem to be so readily apparent (lines 11–13), coders ought to be able to agree as to the nature and number of actions that took place within it; for example, that the bragging statement was not cohesive with the immediately prior context, that the brag was not elicited by the partner, and so forth. However, if one goes back a few lines to lines 3–4, there is clear evidence of strategic activity at a much earlier point. Specifically, C_1 is attempting to extinguish the "girlfriend" topic, an unproductive one from the point of view of accomplishing his boast:

1	N:	So. That's weird. So do you ever see this girl
2		anymore? or was this a long time ago?
3	C_1:	Couple of years back, you know, high school, three
4		years ago, *whatever.*

The unitizer could probably find evidence suggesting that C_1, from the very onset of the conversation, worked systematically to extinguish all of N's topics that seemed unlikely pathways to the brag.

In other cases it is not easy to pinpoint even the *apparent* onset of strategic action. In the following example, in which it was C_2's plan to boast that her father was President of his own computer company, C_2 and N have just discovered that they both spend summers in the South of France.

```
 1  N:   This is really too much.
 2  C₂:  That is hysterical. Did you go to the Cave every
 3       night? We went to the Cave every night til three
 4       o'clock in the morning, four o'clock in the morning.
 5  N:   Yeah.
 6  C₂:  What beach did you go to?
 7  N:   Fifty-five?
 8  C₂:  Quinze-quinze. Ha ha ha.
 9  N:                          (
                Quinze-quinze. Ha ha ha. That's the best (?)
10  C₂:  I can't BELIEVE that! This is too funny. Ha ha ha.
11  N:   I know. Ha ha ha.
12  C₂:  We do this every summer. We've done this five summers
12       in a row.
13  N:   This is our second summer in a row.
14  C₂:  We go every summer. My dad HAS to go.
15  N:   Or what happens?
16  C₂:  Oh! He goes nuts! My dad started his own computer
17       company, and so he's really into his computers and
18       when he gets out he goes crazy!
```

Although it is clearly C₂'s design locally to link the brag about father's computer company to the South of France topic by invoking an *occasion* relation (Hobbs, 1978) between the pressures of the computer business and the annual visits there, what is less clear from the discourse itself is when it occurred to C₂ that she might use such a strategy.

One possible solution to the problems inherent in studying action sequences in discourse is to *ask the actors* when the action began. Unfortunately, actors are not always forthcoming with the necessary assistance (Meichenbaum & Cameron, 1981; Nisbett & Ross, 1980; White, 1980). Although the brags by C₁ and C₂ were accomplished in quite different ways, their accounts of what they did, and when they did it, were equally unrevealing. For example, C₂ was shown a tape of her conversation with N and asked at what point she initiated her strategy:

C₂: Well, I was thinking about it the whole time. The whole con-
         versation it was in my head—I gotta talk about . . . my father.
         I didn't want to make it too obvious. I just tried to end "Europe"
         and go on to "the father."

I: Was there a specific point in the conversation that you started
         to
                (
C₂: No, the whole time I was thinking I gotta end this conversation
         and get on to the other topic. So, I just cut it there.

In C_2's version of events she was in a strategic mode from the onset of the conversation, but at some point she "cut" the old topic and "got on" to the new topic (father's computer company); that is, she waited for an opportunity and then acted in an abrupt and precipitate fashion. This account of events does not, of course, begin to correspond to the observer's impression.

C_1 also fixed the onset of his strategy as the beginning of the conversation ("it was always in the back of my head"), but confuses the issue further by claiming that he had tried to prompt his partner into eliciting the brag from him:

> C_1: I was waiting for her to say "Well, what do you do?" I asked her I think about what do you do? or what's your thing? or whatever and she said it's aerobics and you know I didn't wanta talk out of turn and I was in turn almost waiting for her to say, "Well, Jim, what do you do in your spare time?"—something like that, and I was going to bring it up then.

C_1 describes a strategy here that is considerably earlier, and considerably more subtle, than the one we observed immediately prior to his brag.

What these examples suggest, then, is that in trying to use actors' accounts merely to establish the *boundaries* on an action sequence, that is, to know when it begins and when it ends, we may find that the actor attributes to him or herself, retrospectively, a degree of premeditation that simply wasn't present; or, conversely, the actor may deny having had a strategy when its traces are readily apparent in the discourse. The actor may also be unable to disentangle doing something about a conversational goal from merely thinking about it. My own experience suggests that most people are not particularly adept at reconstructing a sequence of actions they have undertaken in conversation, even though to the observer those actions appear to evidence a considerable degree of structure and premeditation.

There does not seem to be any really satisfactory, uniform method of establishing the boundaries of an action sequence. Even if one could obtain from actors at least *plausible* accounts of when strategic action was undertaken, it will often be the case that what one actor thinks she or he accomplished in a single turn, another will claim to have taken several or even many turns to accomplish. For example, some actors might not regard a "pre" like "Could I ask you a favor?" as part of the action undertaken to gain compliance, whereas others would include it. The problem then becomes that the chunks of discourse that constitute the unit of analysis are of unequal length. In the longer chunks there is a higher probability that there will be multiple strategies, or that non-goal oriented behaviors by the actor will be interpreted as strategic.

One solution that has proved expedient, although not fully satisfactory, has been to work backward for some fixed number of utterances (turns, sentences) from the point at which the sequence seems to be completed (i.e., the boast has been uttered, the compliance-gaining request has been granted, the information sought has been obtained, and so forth). This method was used in a study of the interaction patterns that led to "awkward silences" (gaps in conversation of three or more seconds) (McLaughlin & Cody, 1982), and in the analysis of the data set described in this essay. The drawback of such a procedure, of course, is that the width of the analytic unit may not be sufficient to capture the deep structure underlying the discourse (van Dijk, 1980, 1981).

It is important that schemes for coding action sequences be sensitive to topical as well as functional structures in conversation. Many of the coding schemes that have been developed in recent years have been directed strictly to the functional content of an utterance: is it a command? a suggestion? a retreat? an agreement? an instruction? a question? In short, how, as a speech act, is the utterance to be recognized? What does it do? It seems clear to me that students of conversation have been woefully indifferent to the importance of topical constraints on what persons can do in (with) conversation. Although we are of course free within certain limits to talk about whatever we like, we are powerfully constrained by the propositional structure of prior talk when we are, so to speak, in the midst of interaction, so much so that we may be unable to accomplish certain kinds of acts because the right topical context in which to imbed them is not available to us when we need it (Foster & Sabsay, 1982). Consider the boast. Because open promotion of one's own cause is generally regarded as inappropriate, a clever boaster may try to induce her or his partner to "elicit" the boast from her or him. One strategy that we encountered frequently, which we called *reciprocal question*, exploited functional constraints as well as the norm of reciprocity. It was described perfectly by one of our subjects in the post-experimental interview:

> If you want someone to ask you about what you do then you ask them first, and you just kind of go, "Well, what do you do on campus?" and they'll say, "Well, I do this and that" and then they'll—just to keep the conversation flowing they'll come back to you and just say, "What is it that you do?" and then you—and I'm—and I'm able to go from there.

Although such a technique has the advantage of making the boaster appear "compelled," by virtue of the sequential implicativeness of the question, to supply the brag, the technique will be transparent if the *propositional* content of the initiating question is not pertinent to the prior context. It is therefore as appropriate to note the exploitation and manipulation of topical structures as it is of functional ones, particularly if down the line there is to be some attempt to connect strategies to outcomes.

One strategy that seemed to be particularly effective (effective in the sense that the subject did not appear to be bragging) was to supply the boast as an answer to a question the impetus for which came from the other party. In the following example, the confederate's boast was to be that he restores and shows antique cars:

1	N:	Yeah, my grandmother's up there. Yeah. (2.0) Well.
2		(.8) Why'd you start (school) late?
3	C_3:	I didn't start late, I transferred from another school.
4	N:	Oh.
5	C_3:	*I got involved with restoring a car. It took me three*
6		*years to restore that,* so that took time off.
7	N:	Ha ha ha.
8	C_3:	*I've been showing that for the past couple of years,*
9		so I took time off to do that.

Here the confederate has achieved a (non-transparent) boast by implying that there is a *strong temporal relation* (Hobbs, 1978) between his late start in school and his interest in antique cars; the former *occasioned* the latter. The boast is non-obvious because the alleged propositional link between it and the immediately prior context is plausible. (In fact, C_3 told us in an interview following the taping session that he had lied, and that his interest in cars had nothing to do with his purported late matriculation.)

What I'm proposing is that a good coding scheme for strategies in conversation should include a set of topical categories to capture the kinds of propositional links actor exploit (or fail to exploit) in moving conversation in a desired direction. One observation I have made with respect to the examples of boasting is that many persons whose strategies were complex and highly organized seemed to prefer to link their brags to prior talk by alleging a temporal relation of some kind; that is, that some element in an earlier proposition had been *occasioned, enabled,* or *caused* by some element mentioned in the brag. For example:

1	C_4:	Yeah, I like it, you know. My dad's a pilot for
2		American Airlines, so I've-I've always been able to
3		fly for free and, yeah, ha ha=
4	N:	Ha ha.
5	C_4:	=really like it.
6	N:	Do they ever let you (?)
7	C_4:	I can, but I haven't gone a lot, especially since
		college. You're at the age when it would be really
9		fun to go traveling off by yourself but=
10	N:	Uh huh.
11	C_4:	=then you have college and you're all busy with that
12		and you can't really leave for the summers to go off,
13		'cause you have to work to save for the next year. But

13   'cause you have to work to save for the next year. But
14   I've gone some places, like—not through my dad but when
15   I was in—well right after I graduated from high school
16   *in '80 I won, you know, the Miss McIver contest?* ha ha
17   N: Oh, how fun!
18   C_4:   and uh I was Mis McIver and—and one of the prizes was
19   my mom and I got to go to the Bahamas.

Here C_4 supplies the brag as one of the *enabling* factors in her extensive travelling.

Less successful (obvious; non-cohesive) boasts tended to be linked less immediately to the prior talk; that is, it might take several propositions to connect the topic of the partner's previous turn to the brag; further, the propositional links were usually weak assertions of an *expansion* relation (Hobbs, 1978) such as parallelism or exemplification. In the following example, C_5, whose plan ostensibly was to boast about his belonging to ROTC, makes an abortive effort to draw a parallel between his current conversation about the Super Bowl with N, and a similar discussion during an ROTC meeting:

1   N: Uh-who do you pick in the Super Bowl?
2   C_5: Um, I like the Raiders. I think, un, I think the Raiders.
3   N: Is that a biased view, living in L.A.?
4   C_5:   (
                                  Oh, definitely. And yourself?
5   N: Uh, yeah, I kind of go for the Raiders. I- I don't
6   have any favorites in football but it seems that, uh, uh,
7   choose the Raiders just because, you know, we're in
8   L.A. and they're the home team.
9   C_5: Y'know, um, we were talking about that like during ROTC,
10   and you know, uh, *ROTC, in itself, for me, y'know,*
11   *promotes a pretty good attitude and feeling.* I- I
12   don't know, if you know, y'know, you can see I'm in
13   uniform.
14   Yeah, well I kind of figured that wasn't a facade.

In the previous example functional structures are useless in helping C_5 to accomplish his boast; he could, however, have achieved his goal through the right sort of topical manipulations. For example, he might have claimed that he was so busy with ROTC that he hadn't had much time to follow football this year (a *temporal* relation), which would have given him a less patently labored pathway to the brag. The reader might find it instructive to supply C_5 with other sentences at line 9, and see where they might lead him.

Topical cohesion is an aspect of conversational interaction that most people interested in message strategies simply overlook. The argument being made here is that our coding schemes must be adapted to reflect the fact that actors have to accomplish their goals within the constraints imposed by the need to maintain coherence at the propositional as well as the functional level.

Coding schemes must be sensitive to changes and adjustments in the actor's strategy. One factor that is clearly related to outcomes of strategic conversational behavior is the ability of the actor to make immediate adjustments to her plan of action should situational contingencies require that she shift ground. In the following example, a really useful coding scheme would have to be able to register not only that a reciprocal questioning strategy has been initiated by C_6, but that it is *particularized* (from "do this summer" to "go to school this summer"), *adjusted* for topical pathway (from "school" to "visit"), and then finally *abandoned* when the reciprocity norm fails to operate on the partner's behavior.

1	C_6:	What'd you do this summer?
2	N:	I stayed here.
3	C_6:	Oh, really?
4	N:	Uh huh.
5	C_6:	Did you go to school?
6	N:	No, I didn't go to school. Probably I should've.
7		I had a pretty good summer.
8	C_6:	Did you go visit anywhere?
10	N:	No. I did go to the beach, though. First we'd go to
11		the beach, and then out to dinner.
12	C_6:	*I went to China this summer.*

Hopper, Koch, and Mandelbaum (this volume), advise that in listening to conversation the analyst consider what a speaker might have said but didn't or seemed to start saying then changed it. Indeed, a consistent theme in our post-experimental interviews was the actor's need to make continuous adaptations to the behavior of the partner in order to achieve the goals that had been established. The extent to which a particular strategy is effective is not just a function of the actor's own analysis and planning, but is also to a large extent influenced by the competing goals and plans of the partner. The particular topical or functional pathway down which the actor hopes to lead her or his partner may in fact be incompatible with the partner's own plans for the conversation. One of our subjects, for example, was to boast that he was graduating from the university with a 3.0, even though he had been at the bottom of his high school class.

Interviewer:	Were there any places in the conversation where you started to talk about that and did not?
Confederate:	O.K. When I started telling her about my aerobics instructor here and I started to explain to my aerobics instructor that I didn't want a grade for the class—I just wanted it

pass/fail, which would afford me more absences if I couldn't— if I got tied up on the freeway which happens sometimes, and you know, so I just explained to her—I'm, I'm not a scholar—and it was at that point that I wanted to follow through maybe, or I saw it as a natural delivery to go into talking about not being a scholar all the way through my high school years when I graduated from the bottom of my class. So—but I wasn't able to do it because she came back at me with a couple of questions . . . So rather than just talk all—you know, maintain complete control of the conversation and just not pay any attention to her questions, I followed her questions at that point and put it off for a while.

The point to be made here is that a good analyst will attend not only to what the actor actually did, but also to what she tried to do, and perhaps to what she was "unable" to do, by virtue of politeness constraints, reciprocity norms, and so forth (at least to the extent that the traces of such efforts and obstacles are manifest in the conversational text).

Much can be learned from the aberrant cases. In a typical pencil-and-paper study, data from subjects who fail to perform as instructed are usually excluded from analysis. If a subject makes Xs in the neutral category on every single item of every single page of her or his questionnaire, we would probably regard the subject's "Mach" scores or "locus of control" as suspect, and toss her or him out of the sample without asking why the subject had behaved in that way. When a subject fails at a specifically conversational task, however, there may be a great deal to be learned from the defective performance. Jacobs (this volume) put it very well:

> If a technical description is adequate, it should enable the analyst to explain mistakes or failures by the way cases deviate from the pattern. How people can fail to produce a pattern is just as important to understanding how that pattern works as are the ways in which people can construct the pattern.

Having observed a number of subjects fail at a task which others seemed to carry out so effortlessly, it seems obvious to me that there are factors that affect a person's ability to effect a goal in conversation beyond the obstacles presented by the competing plans and goals of the partner (although subjects who fail will tend to attribute that failure to the partner's not behaving in the conventionally appropriate manner).

One of our subjects who failed to accomplish her boast ("I am athletic") in the course of a 15-minute conversation claimed that her partner controlled the conversation too much, and that he did not seem to be subject to reciprocity norms:

Interviewer: But that was the first point that you were trying to bring it up.

Confederate: Yeah, It took me that long to get him to stop talking.

. . . .

Interviewer: At that point when you started to plan what did you decide to do?

Confederate: First I decided to talk about high school, 'cause I know a lot of guys—like high school—in high school they play football or basketball, or they're in some type of athletics—sports.

. . . .

So I tried to get the conversation—um—about high school sports. And I think I mentioned that I did a few things and he said that he played a little baseball and a little ball but he quickly after that was over went on to something else.

. . . .

Interviewer: O.K. And was there any particular reason for the fact that you couldn't get it in?

Confederate: He was—I don't think he was interested in that. He was more interested in his—he's into a law program, he wants to go to law school, he's going to be going to London. He was more interested in his, I guess, uh, studies more so than—than athletics. He tried to dominate the conversation.

We asked the confederate to identify for us on the videotape a place or places in the conversation where she had tried, but failed, to give her boast. The following was a sample failed attempt:

```
 1   C₇:      What was your big sport in high school?
 2   N:       My high school was so pathetically weak in all sports =
 3   C₇                                                    ( Ha ha ha
 4   N:       = we uh, our neighbor high school, Burbank, I don't know,
 5            ( )rivals with Laguna Beach ( ) Burbank got the
 6            championship in football, got the championship in
 7            basketball, and we came in like the last place in football,
 8            the last place in basketball. We were—our good sport
 9            was basketball.
10   C₇:      Did you play any sports there?
11   N:       I was tennis—and I played football for a couple of
12            seasons.
13   C₇:      That's good.
```

It is most instructive to compare what C_7 does at line 13 ("That's good"), when her partner fails to cooperate with her reciprocal question strategy, to what C_6 does (line 12 of the previous example) when her partner shows a similar lack of interest in reciprocating. What are the factors that on the one hand induce C_6 to believe that it would be appropriate simply to announce "I went to school in China this summer," but on the other hand lead C_7 to conclude that adding, "I am athletic, too" following "That's good" would be unacceptable, when both utterances would appear to the observer to be equally cohesive in context.

A comparative analysis of the two texts doesn't shed much further light on the question. In C_6's case, she had made three successive formulations of the to-be-reciprocated question, none of which elicited a response in kind. C_7 had made two formulations of the initiating question, and had used this same strategy several times earlier to no avail. Only if we examine the propositional content of the two boasts do any real differences seem to emerge. C_6's task is to brag about something she had *done* (that is, something objectively verifiable), C_7's to brag about something she *is, according to her own self-evaluation*. In all of the other cases that we have observed of failure to perform the assigned task, or of extreme procrastination (the 14th minute of the 15-minute session) in performing the task, the boasts were similar with respect to this doing versus being construct: "I have pretty eyes," "I am a warm and friendly person," and so on. Although this is not to suggest that such boasts weren't carried out effectively by others in the study, what it does imply is that for boasts and many other kinds of potentially face-threatening acts (Brown & Levinson, 1978) that get done in conversation (requests, questions, explanations, digs, etc.), the *degree of threat to face* may be a significant determinant of outcomes regardless of the kinds of strategies that are employed. If one tries to establish links between choice of strategy and effectiveness, without controlling for the level of threat to face associated with the action to be undertaken, the expected relationships between strategy type and outcomes simply may not emerge.

All of the foregoing has served to make (or re-make) some simple but fundamental points: (a) how we punctuate the stream of discourse is a significant determinant of the kinds of action we observe; (b) we have to pay attention to what actors are saying as well as what they are doing; (c) we must take note of the kinds of adjustments actors make as communicative action unfolds; and (d) we shouldn't disregard data from subjects who don't behave the way we want them to. Following these suggestions may serve to move us marginally closer to understanding what happens when people talk to each other.

REFERENCES

Auld, F., Jr., & White, A. M. (1956). Rules for dividing interviews into sentences. *Journal of Psychology, 42,* 273–281.

Berger, C. R., & Kellermann, K. A. (1983). To ask or not to ask: Is that a question? In R. N. Bostrom (Ed.), *Communication Yearbook 7* (pp. 342–368). Beverly Hills, CA: Sage.

Clark, R. A. (1979). The impact of selection of persuasive strategies on self-interest and desired liking. *Communication Monographs, 46,* 257–273.

Cody, M. J., & McLaughlin, M. L. (1985). Models for the sequential construction of accounting episodes: Situational and interactional constraints on message selection and evaluation. In J. Cappella & R. Street (Eds.), *Sequential social interaction: A functional approach* (pp. 50–69). London: Edward Arnold.

Cody, M. J., McLaughlin, M. L., & Schneider, M. J. (1980). The impact of relational consequences and intimacy on the selection of interpersonal persuasion strategies: A reanalysis. *Communication Quarterly, 29,* 91–106.

Cohen, P. R., & Perrault, C. R. (1979). A plan-based theory of speech acts. *Cognitive Science, 3,* 213–230.

van Dijk, T. A. (1980). *Macrostructures: An interdisciplinary study of global structures in discourse, interaction, and cognition.* Hillsdale, NJ: Lawrence Erlbaum Associates.

van Dijk, T. A. (1981). *Studies in the pragmatics of discourse.* The Hague: Mouton.

Brown, P. R., & Levinson, S. L. (1978). Universals in language usage: Politeness phenomena. In E. N. Goody (Ed.), *Questions and Politeness: Strategies in social interaction* (pp. 56–289). New York: Cambridge University Press.

Foster, S., & Sabsay, S. (1982). *What's a topic?* Unpublished manuscript, University of Southern California, Los Angeles.

Hayes-Roth, B., & Hayes-Roth, F. (1979). A cognitive model of planning. *Cognitive Science, 3,* 275–310.

Hobbs, J. R. (1978). *Why is discourse coherent?* Menlo Park, CA: SRI International.

Hobbs, J. R., & Agar, M. H. (1981). *Planning and local coherence in the formal analysis of ethnographic interviews.* Unpublished manuscript, Menlo Park, CA: SRI International.

Hobbs, J. R., & Evans, D. A. (1980). Conversation as a planned behavior. *Cognitive Science, 4,* 349–377.

Jackson, S., & Jacobs, S. (1981). The collaborative production of proposals in conversational argument and persuasion: A study of disagreement regulation. *Journal of the American Forensic Association, 18,* 77–90.

Kellermann, K. A., & Berger, C. R. (1984). Affect and social information acquisition: Sit back, relax, and tell me about yourself. In R. N. Bostrom (Ed.), *Communication Yearbook, 8,* (pp. 412–445). Beverly Hills, CA: Sage.

McLaughlin, M. L., Altendorf, D., Baaske, K., Cashion, J., Louden, A., & Smith, S. (in press). Topical and functional constraints on the production of self-serving utterances in dyadic conversations. *Journal of Language and Social Psychology.*

McLaughlin, M. L., & Cody, M. J. (1982). Awkward silences: Behavioral antecedents and consequences of the conversational lapse. *Human Communication Research, 8,* 299–316.

McLaughlin, M. L., Cody, M. J., Kane, M. L., & Robey, C. S. (1981). Sex differences in story receipt and story sequencing behaviors in dyadic conversation. *Human Communication Research, 7,* 99–116.

McLaughlin, M. L., Cody, M. J., & O'Hair, H. D. (1983). The management of failure events: Some contextual determinants of accounting behavior. *Human Communication Research, 9,* 208–224.

McLaughlin, M. L., Cody, M. J., & Robey, C. S. (1980). Situational influences on the selection of strategies to resist compliance-gaining attempts. *Human Communication Research, 7,* 14–36.

McLaughlin, M. L., Cody, M. J., & Rosenstein, N. E. (1983). Account sequences in conversation between strangers. *Communication Monographs, 50,* 102–125.

Meichenbaum, D., & Cameron, R. (1981). Issues in cognitive assessment: An overview. In R. M. Merluzzi, C. R. Glass, & M. Genest (Eds.), *Cognitive Assessment.* New York: Guilford Press.

Nisbett, R., & Ross, L. (1980). *Human inference: Strategies and shortcomings of social judgment.* Englewood Cliffs, NJ: Prentice-Hall.

Stiles, W. B. (1978). *Manual for a taxonomy of verbal response modes.* Chapel Hill, NC: University of North Carolina Press.

White, P. (1980). Theoretic note: Limitations on verbal reports of internal events. A refutation of Nisbett and Wilson and Bem. *Psychological Review, 87,* 105–112.

III INTERACTION STRATEGIES AND DISCOURSE

10 Interacting Plans in the Accomplishment of a Practical Activity

Julie A. Burke
University of Iowa

Explaining why speakers say what they do and how hearers understand what is meant from what is said are two foci that have engaged the interest of scholars from diverse fields. To assess the contemporary theories of discourse production and comprehension yielded by such interest, the research reported in this chapter adopted what might be called an empirical approach. A corpus of data was gathered for the purpose of assessing and revising such theories. In other words, contemporary theories of discourse production were judged in terms of their adequacy in accounting for the discourse produced by a group of subjects, and theories of comprehension were judged in terms of their ability to account for another group of subjects' interpretations of that discourse. The data set produced by these two groups of subjects is described in the next section. Then two theories of discourse production are critically reviewed and their adequacy in accounting for the data is assessed. Several theoretical inadequacies were identified when these theories were relied on to explain the corpus of data because the discourse actually produced by the subjects differed from the discourse one would expect based on these theories. These discrepancies served as the basis for suggesting revisions in theories of discourse production. In a similar fashion, theoretical works on discourse comprehension are critically reviewed, assessed, and revised when they prove inadequate to account for the subjects' comprehension.

THE PUMP ASSEMBLY TASK

Videotapes were made of 20 dyads assembling and testing a toy water pump. The water pump, an educational toy produced by Educational Designs, consisted of 12 components that, when assembled, function as a water cannon. Twenty subjects were randomly assigned to the role of experts, 20 to the role of apprentice. Experts and apprentices were randomly paired. Each expert, having been trained to assemble the pump at an initial session, later produced instructions for an apprentice who was unfamiliar with the water pump but responsible for assembling and testing it.

Each expert–apprentice pair was randomly assigned to work in one of four contexts: face-to-face, telephone, audiotape, and written. This resulted in five dyads in each context except the audiotape context, for which one pair was discarded because an expert chose not to complete the task.

Discourse processes in the pump assembly task are worthy of analysis, not because anyone particularly cares about this task and its accomplishment, but because focusing on the particulars of the discourse in this task may lead to a more complete understanding of discourse processes in general when the data generated by such a task are used to assess and revise current theories.

EXPLAINING DISCOURSE PRODUCTION

Two contemporary bodies of work provided starting points for constructing an account of discourse production. One approach is articulated in Austin's (1962) and Searle's (1969, 1974, 1975, 1977) work in the philosophy of language. The other reflects the cognitive scientists' emerging interest in the role background knowledge plays in discourse production.

Austin (1962) originally advanced the distinction between performative and constative utterances to cope with the philosophical problems posed by the recognition that many utterances could not be appropriately judged true or false. In addressing this problem, Austin realized that speakers use language to perform actions as well as to describe the world. This made intentions central to language use. In his continuing concern with speech acts, Searle (1969, 1974, 1975, 1977) also accorded intentions a central role. For example, in his 1974 critique of Chomsky, Searle noted that utterances are not abstract objects produced and understood independently of their role in performing speech acts. Despite some problems with the approach, it assured communicative intentions a central role in subsequent theories of discourse production.

Having accorded intentions a central role, Searle focused on the rules constraining the utterances that might be produced by an ideal speaker to realize a single intention. This yielded the systematic identification of felicity conditions for different speech acts. Searle's analysis of the rules for translating communicative intentions into expressions, though quite elegant, offers limited help in the analysis of utterances produced by real speakers, because it assumes that researchers already know speakers' communicative intentions. Analysts actually require some means for determining communicative intentions when dealing with real, as opposed to ideal, speakers.

A corollary problem resulting from Searle's approach is that it encourages the analysis of isolated communicative intentions. An analysis of the following hypothetical dialogue between two co-authors illustrates why this is inadequate.

P: I've got my part done. Have you finished revising your part of the theoretical section?
B: Not quite.
P: How 'bout your section of the analyses? Have you written that yet?
B: Nooo
P: Have you run your analyses yet?
B: No, I was gonna get to that this week.

An analysis of the connection between isolated communicative intentions and utterances might allow one to describe P's first utterance as an assertion, her second as a request for information and so forth. Yet this analysis of isolated communicative intentions, if it could in fact be done on real interactions as easily as on hypothetical dialogues, misses the point of P's actions. She produced, not a single utterance, but a series of utterances to chide B for lack of industry, thereby prompting B to work harder. Her goal and plan shaped the communicative intentions realized in these utterances. Ignoring the complexity of intentions directing action and focusing only on each communicative intention in isolation yields an incomplete analysis.

Recent work in cognitive science provides a partial remedy for these limitations in speech act theory. Whereas Searle presupposed knowledge of speakers' communicative intentions in his analyses of ideal speakers and their utterances, cognitive scientists are concerned with plans and goals as generative sources of intentions (Miller, Galanter, & Pribram, 1960). Plans, as cognitive representations of the various lines of action and their relationship to various goals (Schank & Abelson, 1977a, 1977b), represent the information individuals have available for selecting strategies or lines of action to be implemented in behavior in order to realize goals.

When individuals have pragmatic goals requiring coordination and cooperation from others, they must plan their *communicative* action to secure such cooperation. Indeed, Cohen and Perrault's (1979) formalization of the plans underlying various speech acts revealed that a speaker must plan different speech acts to accomplish different pragmatic goals. Because speakers' plans and goals shape their communicative action, knowledge of these helps analysts to determine speakers' communicative intentions. Plans and goals also supply links among communicative intentions. Therefore, knowledge of speakers' plans and goals dissuades analysts from focusing on isolated communicative intentions and encourages them to recognize the complexity of intentions directing and organizing speakers' actions.

Discourse Production in the Pump Assembly Task.   Based on these theoretical accounts of discourse production, a preliminary analysis of the discourse produced by the experts in the pump assembly task is now possible. A practical activity such as the pump assembly task was selected for studying communication because in such activities analysts can circumvent some problems with the tacit and diffuse nature of intentions in everyday interaction by concentrating on task-relevant communicative intentions. Although individuals may employ communication to accomplish multiple goals, these analyses focus only on the way communication is designed to accomplish the instrumental goal.

First, experts' goals and plans must be examined. The experts' goal was to get another person, an apprentice, to assemble and test a water pump. Experts needed a plan for getting someone else to perform the actions because they were not allowed to touch any of the components or perform any of the actions themselves. Clark and Clark (1977) suggest that either goal-oriented or means-oriented instructions might be employed to accomplish this goal. Goal-oriented instructions merely identify the end product and depend on the listener to determine the necessary actions to achieve it (i.e., "Build a water pump with these components"). Means-oriented instructions describe in greater detail the actions required to produce the end product. Experts did not plan goal-oriented instructions presumably because they believed that a novice would need means-oriented instructions detailing the order in which the actions should be performed with the various components.

The water pump itself structured experts' plans for means-oriented instructions. With 12 components to be connected, the task naturally subdivided into 11 steps. Each step required the identification of two components and the performance of an action to connect them. Intrinsic constraints on the order of the 11 steps were minimal. Experts' most difficult problem was determining the amount of detail necessary to insure that apprentices could identify the correct components and perform the appropriate actions. To achieve maximum clarity, experts' instructions had to be neither more nor less informative than required at each step given the purpose of the exchange, because giving either more or less information than required might result in misunderstanding (Grice, 1975). Based on their assumptions about the ignorance of apprentices *qua* apprentices and the non-obvious nature of the task, experts initially planned elaborate step-by-step instructions describing the components involved in each step and specifying the precise manner in which these components should be connected.

An examination of the discourse produced by experts revealed that this plan was executed without modification in the *non-interactive* contexts. In these contexts, experts produced instructions for all 11 steps, usually following the sequence of steps they had learned in the training session.[1] For each step, they identified

---

[1]Spearman rank order correlations were calculated to assess the relationship between the order of steps in the original training session and the order of steps the experts used when instructing apprentices. Of the 19 possible correlations (ranging from 0.48 to 1.00), 18 were significant.

the two components necessary for completing the step and described the action to be performed with them.

In the *interactive* context, on the other hand, experts did not always include all this information. Sometimes they did not identify a component involved in a step. Other times they failed to describe the action to be performed with the components. Occasionally no instruction at all was produced for a particular step. The fact that information was not supplied, should not necessarily be treated as an error because the occurrence of such omissions is quite systematic. If they were simply errors, such omissions could have occurred in any context. Yet they did not occur in non-interactive contexts. It is also important to note that even though experts omitted information, apprentices succeeded in assembling and testing the pump. So, these differences in instructions did not result in differential success in accomplishing the task as one might have expected if they were simply errors.

DISCOURSE PRODUCTION IN INTERACTIVE CONTEXTS

The initial account offered by cognitive scientists yielded some expectations about the discourse experts would produce. Their account proved satisfactory for explaining characteristics of the discourse produced in non-interactive contexts. Yet the expectations generated by their theory are inconsistent with features of the discourse actually produced in interactive contexts. The cause for this theoretical inadequacy can be traced, in part, to the simplifications adopted by cognitive scientists when using the computer as an analogue for a speaker or hearer.

To produce a machine capable of simulating human performance, cognitive scientists must translate their theories of cognitive representations and cognitive processes into a computer program. The computer program then serves as a concrete instantiation of their theory. The computer's uncooperative literal mindedness forces theorists to be explicit and precise; all relevant background knowledge, all cognitive processes, and all assumptions must be specified in the program. To achieve the necessary precision and rigor, theorists often simplify their task in various ways. For example, they can reduce the amount of background knowledge that must be represented in a computer program, if they focus on natural language processes in microworlds as Winograd's (1972) SHRDLU program has done. Alternatively, they can make their task more tractable by restricting the scope of the explanation. For example, Schank's MARGIE program (1973) ignores context when paraphrasing and drawing inferences from sentences, and Riesbeck's (1980) McMAP program ignores goals when judging the clarity of a set of linguistic directions to a location.

Accepting simplifications or restrictions may be necessary, in principle, when programming computers to simulate human performance, but, in practice, only some simplifications are acceptable whereas others are theoretically misleading. For example, Rommetveit (1974) would argue that the exclusion of context in the MARGIE program is an unacceptable restriction because he believes that the acceptability of paraphrases and inferences depends on context. Riesbeck himself noted that excluding knowledge of the goal might be problematic, because knowing where you are going can be important for understanding a set of instructions. Following is Riesbeck's illustration of a problem that could result from excluding goals when following the rules in the McMAP program:

> One rule that was given said:
>   IF the present location is equated with a distant location
>   THEN infer motion to the distant location
> This rule converts things like "The Midway Drive intersection is about two blocks away" into "Go about two blocks to the Midway Drive intersection." But suppose the direction giver said, "At this point you will be about two blocks away from the restaurant we went to with George." We do not want to interpret this as "Go to the restaurant we went to with George." We have to know that the restaurant is *not* the goal of the directions. (Riesbeck, 1980, p. 30)

In most computer programs, the necessary precision is achieved by adopting some restrictions. Introducing these artificial restrictions to simplify the task is a good research strategy when what is included is relatively autonomous from that which is excluded. When this is not the case, theoretical inadequacies are bound to result from such simplifications. Judging which simplifications are acceptable and which are misleading is an empirical question (Miller, Polson, & Kintsch, 1984). The poor fit between the theory and data in the pump assembly task suggests that simplifications adopted by some cognitive scientists in their accounts of discourse production may be misleading. In any case, some theoretical revision is necessary to account for discourse production in interactive contexts.

As cognitive scientists have suggested, interactants' plans and goals probably do organize their communicative intentions and the discourse they produce to realize those intentions even in interactive contexts. But divorcing the study of discourse production from the situations in which it would naturally occur has resulted in the formulation of an overly rigid, formalized, and static conception of plans and goals. Contemporary theories could be improved by identifying factors that may influence speakers' plans and goals and by indicating when and how these factors might operate. For example, because interactants' pragmatic goals and communicative intentions and the discourse they produce to actualize those intentions always occur in concrete situations, their plans and goals are not immutable. They are often influenced by the situation as well as their interactional partners' actions, plans, and goals as these become apparent in the unfolding situation. A situation may block some goals or render some plans ineffectual. Any shifts in interactants' goals and plans as a result of the unfolding situation will necessarily affect the specific communicative intentions they have and consequently the discourse they produce for actualizing those intentions. So, in interactive contexts, the plans and goals of each interactant may be modified in the course of interaction by the need to secure cooperation from others (Bruce & Newman, 1978).

Interacting Plans in the Pump Assembly Task. In the water pump task, the experts' goals and plans may be influenced by the apprentices' goals and plans when these are made available in the unfolding situation. To determine what changes to expect in the experts' plans in interactive contexts, an analysis of the apprentices' goals and plans is necessary. Only then can potential interactions between experts' and apprentices' goals and plans be considered.

Apprentices were told by the experimenter that they would be expected to follow a set of instructions to complete a task described therein. Although apprentices' initial plan had been simply to follow the instructions, as they proceeded with the task they realized that they did not need much of the detail supplied in experts' instructions. Neither technical expertise nor elaborate instructions were required to figure out how to connect most components, because they would fit and stay together in very few ways.[2] Realizing that they did not really need all the detailed instructions supplied by experts, apprentices relegated the experts' discourse to a subsidiary rather than a central role in planning and producing their own task actions.

An examination of potential interactions between experts' and apprentices' goals and plans is now possible. This study was designed to insure that experts and apprentices shared a goal. Consequently, no analyses of goal alignment are required, although it is important to recognize that in many interactions, interactants must negotiate conflicting goals to insure that individual goals are brought into alignment. In such cases, an analysis of each interactant's goals and their potential fit would be necessary.

Although apprentices and experts shared a goal, their plans for accomplishing that goal do not mesh without some adjustments. If experts recognized apprentices' plans and adjusted their own plans to accommodate apprentices' plans, in

---

[2]To assess subjects' ability to assemble the pump without linguistic instructions, some subjects were given all the components and instructed to build one thing using as many of the components as they could. Subjects working without linguistic instructions correctly connected each of the 11 component pairs from 62% to 90% of the time. They correctly connected the slide valve, a component that does not fit and stay on its own, to the main tube least often. They correctly connected the plunger plug and plunger most often. Overall, subjects produced a pump in accord with the manufacturer's specifications 38% of the time when working without linguistic instructions compared to 89% with linguistic instructions. Subjects produced a functioning pump (though not necessarily in accord with the manufacturer's specifications) 67% of the time when working without linguistic instructions compared to 94% of the time with linguistic instruction.

general, they should have produced less detailed and complete instructions as the task unfolded.

To detect differences in the completeness of experts' instructions in the four contexts as the task unfolded, each expert's instructions were segmented into 11 steps, each step consisting of an instruction to perform some action for connecting two components. A crude coding system was developed for assessing the completeness of the instructions for each step (see Table 10.1). Each step received a single score. An independent coder scored four sets of instructions (one from each context). Exact agreement for each step was achieved 75% of the time. When disagreements occurred, the two scores were from adjacent levels in the system. The two coders resolved all disagreements by discussion.

To assess the influence of context and step on the completeness of experts' instructions, a 4 (context) x 11 (step) ANOVA with repeated measures on the second factor was calculated. Main effects for both context ($F = 5.90$, $df = 3$, 15, $p < .007$) and step ($F = 2.95$, $df = 10$, 150, $p < .002$) were significant.[3] The interaction between context and step was also significant ($F = 2.63$, $df = 30$, 150, $p < .00006$). Mean levels of completeness by context and step are reported in Table 10.2.

TABLE 10.1
Coding System for Assessing the Completeness of Instructions

4. *Confirm/disconfirm apprentice's move.* The expert never even issues an instruction for the step. The apprentice initiates an action (either physical or linguistic) and the expert merely confirms or disconfirms. (e.g., The apprentice says, "Don't tell me, this goes here?" The expert responds, "Yeah.")

3. *Partial instruction.* The expert only partially describes the action and components required for completing the step. Since any step involves at least two components and one action, for this level, the expert only indicates two of these three. With this partial information the apprentice executes the step. (e.g., for connecting the plunger and main tube: "Take this plunger and insert it Yeah.")

2. *Complete instruction.* The expert identifies both components involved and indicates the action to be performed with them but provides no elaboration beyond that. (e.g., for connecting the plunger and main tube: "Okay, take the piece with the wire on it and place it inside the long tube.")

1. *Elaborate instruction.* Experts include all the information provided in a level 2 instruction, but they provide additional elaboration such as indicating not only the components but also some feature of one component that the apprentice should attend to for connecting the two components correctly. (e.g., for connecting the plunger and main tube: "Place the plunger into the top of the cylinder, green end first, pushing it down until the green cap is securely in.")

---

[3]Some assembly actions required more elaborate instructions than others. Ideally the analysis would have assessed the influence of (a) the particular assembly action and (b) the particular step in the sequence, because both might influence the completeness of the instructions. In this set of data, sorting out these two factors is not possible. Thus, the analysis of the influence of the step in the sequence on the completeness of an instructions is clouded by differences in the elaboration required for the particular assembly action being described.

TABLE 10.2
Mean Completeness of Instruction By Modality and Step

	Face-to-face	Telephone	Audiotape	Written	Overall
Step 1	1.00	1.00	1.00	1.00	1.00
Step 2	1.00	1.20	1.00	1.20	1.11
Step 3	1.40	1.00	1.00	1.40	1.21
Step 4	1.00	1.40	1.00	1.00	1.11
Step 5	1.00	1.00	1.25	1.00	1.05
Step 6	1.40	1.40	1.00	1.00	1.21
Step 7	1.40	1.00	1.00	1.00	1.11
Step 8	1.00	1.00	1.00	1.00	1.00
Step 9	1.60	1.00	1.00	1.20	1.21
Step 10	1.80	1.00	1.25	1.40	1.36
Step 11	2.60	1.00	1.25	1.00	1.47
Overall	1.38	1.09	1.07	1.11	1.17

As this data suggests, experts in all contexts began with very elaborate and complete instructions. As expected, experts in non-interactive contexts (audiotape, written) provided detailed instructions throughout the task. Again, as expected, experts in the face-to-face context adjusted their plan and produced much less complete and detailed instructions as the task progressed. The experts did not produce any less detailed instructions when supplying instruction by telephone, though it, too, is an interactive context.

Differences in the discourse produced by experts in the two interactive contexts were not expected on the basis of the theories of discourse production examined thus far. Each interactive context provided interactants an opportunity to influence the plans of their partners. There is no reason to believe that apprentices' plans differed in these two contexts. Nor is there any reason to expect experts to be more willing to cooperate in one context than the other. Yet experts only adjusted their plans to accommodate the apprentices' plans in the face-to-face context. If the lack of interaction between the experts' and apprentices' plans in the telephone contexts is not the result of a failure to secure cooperation, perhaps it results from problems with understanding. Clearly, inferring another's communicative intentions, plans, or goals is prerequisite to accommodations.

Unfortunately, the theories examined thus far have attempted to deal with the process of production in isolation. They have offered theories for the situated production of discourse in interactive contexts without taking into account the process of comprehension and the way such a process might influence production. If comprehension indeed influences production, then differences in the meshing of plans would be expected if the two interactive contexts differed in ways that systematically affected discourse comprehension or plan recognition. Assessing the plausibility of this suggestion requires an examination of explanations for discourse comprehension and its relationship to discourse production in the different contexts.

EXPLAINING DISCOURSE COMPREHENSION AND ITS RELATIONSHIP TO DISCOURSE PRODUCTION

Speech act theorists and cognitive scientists have also developed theories of discourse comprehension. These are reviewed and then used to analyze discourse comprehension and its relation to discourse production in the pump assembly task. Searle (1975) was interested in explaining how hearers understand what is meant from what is said. His primary contribution was to assure intentions a central role in theories of discourse comprehension by formulating the problem as one of explaining how hearers recognize speakers' communicative intentions from the linguistic meaning expressed by their utterances.

Arguing that speaker's intentions may be expressed more or less straightforwardly in linguistic expressions, Searle (1975) distinguished direct and indirect speech acts. For Searle, direct speech acts unequivocally express intentions through function indicating devices such as word order, stress, intonational contour, the inclusion of performative verbs, and the like. In contrast, the comprehension of indirect speech acts, he argued, depends on inferences because speakers' utterances literally mean something less than what they intend. For Searle, that which assures expressibility also assures comprehensibility, even with indirect acts. Thus, he suggested that with indirect speech acts hearers rely on felicity conditions to infer or calculate speakers' intentions from the literal meaning of their utterances.

Searle's account of discourse comprehension has been criticized on a number of grounds. Fish (1980) challenged Searle's distinction between direct and indirect speech acts arguing that it depends on the flawed assumption that literal meaning in direct acts is a product of an acontextual language. As the following example borrowed from Searle (1969) shows, even the use of an illocutionary verb does not obviate the necessity for inference because the illocutionary verb may be used in the performance of an indirect act. Suppose A accused B of stealing some money. A said, "You stole that money, didn't you?" and B replied, "No, I didn't, I promise you I didn't." The phrase "I promise" could be an illocutionary force indicating device (IFID) unequivocally expressing the intention to issue a promise. In this case, however, the intention seems less like a promise than an emphatic denial, as Searle himself noted. The use of the phrase "I promise" in fact, functioned more to add emphasis and commitment to the denial rather than making clear the intention to promise. If A had assumed that the phrase was an IFID literally corresponding to B's intention, A would have misunderstood. Yet how was A to know in this particular case that, despite B's use of the phrase "I promise" this was not a direct act unequivocally expressing the speaker's intention, but an indirect act requiring inferences.

Even though Searle acknowledged, in his explanation for the comprehension of indirect speech acts, that comprehension of indirect acts depends on inferences, his explanation has been criticized on other grounds. For example, Levinson (1981) argued that Searle's formulation of indirect acts suggests that an utterance serves a single function and hence encourages analysts to find the single action performed by an utterance when it might be more profitable to acknowledge that utterances are multifunctional.

Kreckel (1981) and Jackson (1983), have questioned, for different reasons, whether felicity conditions can serve as the basis for calculating the intention expressed by an indirect act. If these conditions are to serve as the basis for coordinating inferences, individuals must have similar beliefs about the particular conditions underpinning each speech act. Yet Kreckel (1981) questioned whether Searle's felicity conditions are conventional rules shared by language users because she found, in her research, that individuals disagreed on the felicity conditions for the act of warning. Even if language users have similar beliefs about the conditions necessary for the performance of a speech act, Jackson (1983) has argued that such felicity conditions would be inadequate for the interpretation of indirect acts because of the similarities among felicity conditions for different speech acts. As a consequence, two hearers could infer quite different intentions from the same utterance even though each used the felicity conditions to arrive at his or her interpretation.

Cognitive scientists, believing that discourse comprehension is always an inferential process, have dispensed with Searle's notion of direct acts. In their explanations of discourse comprehension, they have explored how beliefs concerning plans and goals serve as interpretive resources. Clark (1979) suggested that hearers may rely on beliefs about speakers' goals or plans to infer their communicative intentions. Perrault and Allen (1980) have argued that hearers' cooperative actions may often be the result of their responding directly to speakers' goals and plans instead of relying on these to infer speakers' communicative intentions. Tyler (1978) provided an illustration of this when he said "If I should say, 'Bring me the telephone book,' and a waitress brings me a child's booster seat, then why should I accept it with thanks as if that was what I asked for?" (p. 386). In this case, the waitress, recognizing Tyler's goal of elevating the child, responded to his goal rather than to the propositional content of the utterance. According to cognitive scientists then, hearers' beliefs concerning a speakers' plans and goals may serve as resources for coordinating meaning and actions.

Although utterances are one form of action used by speakers to make their communicative intentions publicly available, individuals are also capable of planning and employing physical actions as a means of conveying intentions to accomplish goals (Cohen & Perrault, 1979). For example, if my goal is to let you know I am angry, I may plan physical actions (e.g., I may exit abruptly and slam the door) and/or linguistic actions (e.g., I may yell, "I'm so mad."). This suggests that analysts must attend to interactants' physical actions as well as to the discourse they produce.

In summary, cognitive scientists have recognized that discourse comprehension is an inferential process. Utterances and nonlinguistic actions serve only as indices of communicative intentions. Hearers must infer intentions from actions. To do so, they rely on their background knowledge concerning plans and goals as well as on the discourse and nonlinguistic actions produced by speakers.

Discourse Comprehension in the Pump Assembly Task.   For experts to adapt their plans to those of the apprentices they had to be able to infer apprentices' communicative intentions or their plans and goals. Because differences in the reciprocal coordination of communicative intentions and the meshing of individual plans in the two interactive contexts may have resulted from differences in the resources available to experts for inferring apprentices' communicative intentions, I turn to a description of the means available to apprentices for forwarding their intentions, plans, and goals in each interactive context.

Apprentices did not want to dispense with experts' instructions altogether; they simply wanted to reduce the amount of needless detail at some points during the task. They had at least two discourse strategies available to indicate their competence to plan some of their task actions without experts' detailed instructions. They could indicate successful identification of a component or completion of an action with an affirmation such as saying "Okay" (Grosz, 1977) or repeating the final portion of an instruction (Goldberg, 1975). An alternative discourse strategy involved producing a *transformed repeat* (Goldberg, 1975). In a transformed repeat, rather than producing a verbatim repetition, some content from a previous instruction is upgraded to display knowledge in the task domain. For example, apprentices could refer to a component with a technical label when such terminology had not been previously supplied by an expert. Following is an example of such a transformed repeat.

38 E: And attach the pink thing so it covers the hole in the middle.
39 A: Got it. One-way valve. We're all set.

The apprentice's use of the technical label, "one-way valve," to refer to the pink thing suggests considerable knowledge concerning the task. Apprentices could also upgrade the experts' descriptions of the actions to be performed by supplying a functional explanation for the action.

These two discourse strategies, affirmations and transformed repeats, differed in availability because they differed in the degree of task expertise required for their performance. Because an affirmation required no technical expertise, it was available to all apprentices whenever they wanted to convey their competence to plan their own actions. A transformed repeat, on the other hand, required greater technical expertise concerning pumps. To produce a transformed repeat, apprentices had to have a technical vocabulary if they were to upgrade component labels or they had to understand the functioning of pumps if they were to upgrade action descriptions.

Although the discourse strategy of simple affirmation was generally available to all apprentices, it was not very effective in conveying apprentices' ability to plan their own actions without the experts' elaborate instructions. Affirmations could be interpreted in a number of different ways including:

1. I heard you.
2. I heard you and I understand.
3. I heard you, I understand, and I am now doing or will do what you said.
4. I'm finished (Okay, what next?) (Grosz, 1977, p. 30)

Each of these interpretations should have different consequences for experts' subsequent actions.

Without visual monitoring, experts had few resources for selecting from among these interpretations. Not surprisingly, given their initial plan, many experts selected the most conservative interpretation and continued with elaborate instructions though that was often inappropriate given the apprentices' intentions. The following excerpt from a telephone interaction shows the way experts systematically misinterpreted apprentices' affirmations. For all examples, experts are referred to as E and apprentices as A. The actions of apprentices are reported in brackets as they occurred.

1 E:	Okay, I want you to take the largest tube. Or actually it's the largest piece of anything, that has two openings
2	[A picks up the main tube.]
3 E:	on the side//
4 A:	//Yeah.
5 E:	and threads on the bottom.
6 A:	Yeah.
7 E:	Do you see it?
8 A:	Yeah.
9 E:	Okay. Take that. Now there's a thing called a plunger. It has a red handle
10	[A picks up the plunger.]
11 E:	on it, a green bottom//
12 A:	Okay.
13 E:	and its got a blue lid. Take that, and starting—insert the green end
14	[A inserts the plunger in the main tube.]
15 E:	into the top of that large piece that//

16 A: //Okay.
17 E: you have in your hand and push the green thing down until it comes
        to the threaded end.

In turns 4 and 6, the apprentice attempted to indicate with affirmations that he
had identified the component in question. The expert treated these affirmations
as if they meant "I heard you." and continued to describe the component. The
same thing happened again in turn 12. In turn 16, the apprentice *interrupted* the
expert to indicate that he had performed the action, but again the expert misunderstood and continued to describe the action. As this interaction displays,
apprentices who relied on affirmations to influence experts' plans had little
impact. Experts, failing to grasp apprentices' communicative intentions, continued to execute their initial plan of providing elaborate instructions.

Although a transformed repeat might have been a more effective strategy for
influencing experts' plans, few apprentices evidenced such technical knowledge
by producing transformed repeats. Due to their infrequency, no analyses of
transformed repeats and their effectiveness were possible.

These two discourse strategies are not the only means available to apprentices,
because they could also physically display the limited role experts' instructions
played in their plan for completing the task. For example, they could pick up
components before experts finished describing them or they could connect components before experts indicated how they should be connected. Although apprentices anticipated experts' instructions in all four contexts, their actions were
unavailable to experts in any but the face-to-face context. In the telephone
context, apprentices had to rely on discourse alone to convey their intentions
and plans. In the face-to-face context, apprentices could employ linguistic and/
or nonlinguistic action to forward their intentions, plans, and goals. With these
additional resources for conveying their intentions and plans, they had greater
success influencing experts' plans; they were able to get experts to supply less
detailed instructions in this context. In fact, in this context, experts usually
truncated their instruction for a particular step as soon as apprentices had selected
the correct component or started to perform the correct action.

The following excerpts illustrate such differences in the completeness of
experts' instructions in the two interactive contexts. The first occurred in the
face-to-face context, the second on the telephone.

106 E: Right. And now, place the base in the bottom
107   [A picks up the feed tube.]
108 E: of the
109   [A puts the feed tube in the tube base.]
110 A: Okay.

In line 108, the expert truncated her instruction because the apprentice had performed the correct action. She never even identified the second component involved in this step. In the telephone context, such truncations did not occur because apprentices were unable to use their physical actions for communicative purposes.

99 E: Now I want you to screw that cap
100   [A picks up the tube base and the main tube and begins to connect them.]
101 E: onto that big air tube that had the threads on it
102 A: Okay.
103 E: that you put the plunger in
104 A: Okay.

The expert could have terminated this instruction at line 99 because the two components had been correctly identified and the correct action had been initiated by the apprentice. The expert, not knowing this, continued to describe one of the components in turns 101 and 103, despite the apprentice's production of an affirmation in turn 102.

In the telephone context, apprentices generally had fewer resources for demonstrating their competence to plan their own task actions. Most had only one discourse strategy, the affirmation, available for influencing experts' plans. Unfortunately, experts frequently misunderstood these affirmations, given their limited resources for making inferences about apprentices' plans and intentions. The greater difficulty experts and apprentices had coordinating intentions and plans in the telephone context is, therefore, not surprising. Experts had to make inferences concerning the apprentices' communicative intentions and plans, but they had only the apprentices' discourse for drawing those inferences. They did not have the additional resource of apprentices' actions. In the face-to-face context, apprentices' plans and goals were manifest in their discourse and their physical actions. Having these multiple resources increased the likelihood that experts would recognize apprentices' intentions and plans and would adjust their own discourse to accommodate these.

CONCLUSION

Almost 3 decades ago, Austin (1962) identified the goal when he said, "The total speech act in the total speech situation is the *only actual* phenomenon which, in the last resort, we are engaged in elucidating" (p. 148). In the time that has elapsed since, much work has been done though only modest progress has been made. Explaining human communication in all its complexity is a formidable theoretical task. The sheer complexity of the phenomenon has the potential to overwhelm or immobilize scholars. Because one cannot explain everything at once, a sensible course of action, in the face of such complexity, is to focus on a limited problem and forge ahead with any methods that will allow one to develop explanations of such smaller problems or individual processes.

This is precisely what speech act theorists and cognitive scientists have done. Neither approach purports to explain all of human communication, but rather each sets out with a more modest goal of explaining only some of the processes involved. And each approach has made important contributions to the explanation of language and discourse processes. In fact, as long as one remains within the limited domain each has carved out for itself (e.g., expressing a single intention in a linguistic expression or actualizing a goal and plan in discourse), one would judge these theories to be wholly adequate. It is only when one expands the limits of the domain (e.g., to situated interaction) that their theoretical inade- quacies become apparent. Adopting Austin's goal, however, would suggest the need to expand the limits in just this way. Speech act theory should not be judged only in terms of its ability to explain processes of discourse production and comprehension in hypothetical examples, but also in terms of its ability to explain these processes in real interactions. Cognitive scientists' theories must also be held responsible for explaining real interaction, not just, for example, the output generated by computers programmed to simulate natural language processes. In other words, these theories of discourse production and compre- hension must be evaluated as general theories of language and discourse processes in situated interaction and they must be criticized if they only work in restricted domains.

Inadequacies in contemporary theories of discourse production and compre- hension are largely the result of isolating and tackling limited and manageable problems. Although this may be necessary given the current state of knowledge and the complexity of the phenomenon of interest, it often yields theories of limited generality. So, although asserting that contemporary theories of discourse production and comprehension are completely wrong would be a mistake because they are quite adequate within some limited domains, accepting these theories without determining the limits of their generality would also be a mistake. To evaluate and further develop these theories, this research began with a corpus of interactional data and assessed the adequacy of current theories in terms of their ability to account for characteristics of this data. This approach for eval- uating and generating theory was useful for establishing the limits of the domains within which the explanations offered by speech act theorists and cognitive scientists worked and for determining what theoretical revisions would extend the domain their theories were capable of explaining.

I do not mean to suggest that the methods by which cognitive scientists and speech act theorists have generated their theories are inherently flawed. Theories of language and discourse processes may be generated by a variety of methods including: constructing and analyzing hypothetical examples as Searle and Austin have done, programming computers to simulate natural language processes and analyzing the protocols generated by these computer programs as some cognitive scientists have done, and analyzing natural or experimentally structured interactions that occur between human interactants in concrete situations as the research reported here and as some cognitive scientists have done (e.g., Clark, 1979; Hobbs & Evans, 1980; Levy, 1979). None of these strategies for generating theoretical claims and insights is, in principle, defective, and, in fact, each has strengths to recommend it. What I mean to suggest is that, however theories of language and discourse processes are *generated,* they must be *evaluated* in terms of their ability to account for actual occurrences of human communication.

From the approach employed in this research we learn that to account for the discourse speakers produce, analysts must attend to speakers' plans and goals as well as to their communicative intentions. Because Searle was not concerned with the generative source of communicative intentions, he overlooked the role plans and goals play in utterance production. This oversight was unproblematic as long as analyses were confined to ideal speakers producing single utterances to realize single predetermined communicative intentions. But because the discourse produced by real speakers often requires analysts to account for multiple utterances, they need some means of determining the complex intentions generating and linking speakers' utterances. Cognitive scientists offered plans and goals as a partial solution to this problem. When analysts attend to plans and goals, they are not limited to an analysis of ideal speakers or isolated communicative intentions, because communicative intentions are generated and linked by plans and goals. With this theoretical advance, cognitive scientists are able to account for series of utterances produced by individual speakers in non-interactive contexts. Consequently, in the pump assembly task, this framework was adequate for characterizing the experts' instructions in *non-interactive* contexts.

Unfortunately, divorcing the study of each interactants' plans and goals and communicative intentions from the contexts in which they occurred yielded a theory incapable of explaining the process of discourse production in interactive contexts. To provide a more complete account, the role the context or situation played in the emergence of individuals' goals, plans, and communicative intentions had to be considered. In interactive contexts, each interactant's plans and goals could be modified to secure the cooperation of others. Plans and goals would, therefore, necessarily emerge as the alignment of individual goals and the meshing of individual plans were tacitly negotiated in the on-going course of action. Consequently, to explain the discourse produced by an individual interactant in interactive contexts, interrelations among the goals and plans of all interactants had to be considered. In the pump assembly task, for example, an analysis of the possible interactions between experts' and apprentices' plans served as the basis for the expectation that experts, in general, should adjust their plans to produce less complete instructions as the task progressed. Because aligning goals and meshing plans in interactive contexts requires the reciprocal coordination of communicative intentions, discourse production cannot be explained independently of discourse comprehension. Coordinating with others depends, not simply on willingness, but also on the ability of each interactant to infer others' communicative intentions, plans, and goals. As a consequence, it was necessary to integrate explanations for discourse comprehension with theories of discourse production to account for the differences in the situated unfolding and meshing of interactants' plans in the two interactive contexts.

Discourse is one means used by speakers to make their communicative intentions, plans, and goals publicly available to secure the cooperation of others. Unfortunately, utterances serve only as indices of communicative intentions. Because there is an indeterminate relationship between intention and action, hearers must infer intentions from actions. If hearers had to rely only on speakers' linguistic expression to infer their intentions, hearers' task would be a good deal more difficult. Fortunately, communication is an overdetermined system, so that many different inferential routes can all lead to the same interpretation. For example, beliefs concerning plans and goals, the social situation, relational history, and so forth can all serve as interpretive resources. These resources usually support one another. Therefore, the more interpretive resources available to interactants, the more likely they are to understand one another.

In the water pump assembly task, experts in the telephone context had fewer resources for interpreting apprentices' discourse; they did not have access to apprentices' task actions. With fewer resources, they had greater difficulty understanding apprentices' intentions and plans. Consequently, they were less successful in adjusting their plans to those of the apprentices. In the face-to-face context, experts had the additional resource of apprentices' task actions. The way in which this additional resource enhanced experts' understanding of apprentices' communicative intentions and plans is reflected in their instructions; they adjusted the amount of detail to fit apprentices' needs. In principle, if apprentices had required more, rather than less, detailed instructions at any point, they should have had the greatest success in eliciting this additional detail in the face-to-face context as well.

Whether context and the process of discourse comprehension could safely be ignored when developing a theory of discourse production was an empirical question. Speech act theory and work in cognitive science ignored them and made advances toward the goal of explaining language and discourse processes. Although the explanations each offered in more limited domains laid a foundation for successive approximations, the interactional data from the pump assembly task indicates that contemporary theories of discourse production, which ignore context and the way context influences the relationship between processes of discourse production and comprehension, have limited explanatory power. The research reported here suggested modifications to expand the generality of these theories, though it, too, accepted restrictions, the most limiting of which must be noted.

If communication is indeed multifunctional, analyzing discourse production and comprehension in terms of the way it is designed to accomplish a single task-relevant goal is a serious limitation. This restriction was accepted because of the difficulty, given our current level of understanding, in analyzing communication in terms of the multiple goals that might be pursued in less structured tasks. In general, these goals are less accessible to analysts, because interactants themselves are often less reflective about them. Conceptual work on the identification of these more diffuse and tacit goals and the means for pursuing them in situated interaction is necessary first, though Clark and Delia (1979) and Brown and Levinson (1978) offer some promising beginnings. Clark and Delia have suggested that researchers focus on three classes of goals: instrumental, relational, and identity. Brown and Levinson have identified general strategies available for reconciling speakers' and hearers' competing face wants and instrumental goals. Obviously, more work on the types of goals and the means for reconciling, pursuing, and recognizing them in less structured interaction is necessary if a more complete account of discourse production and comprehension is to be provided.

ACKNOWLEDGMENT

The collection of data for this study was supported by a contract (US–NIE–C–400–76–0016) from the National Institute of Education to the Center for the Study of Reading, University of Illinois at Urbana–Champaign.

REFERENCES

Austin, J. L. (1962). *How to do things with words*. Cambridge: Harvard University Press.

Brown, P., & Levinson, S. (1978). Universals in language usage: Politeness phenomena. In E. Goody (Ed.), *Questions and politeness* (pp. 56–311). New York: Cambridge University Press.

Bruce, B., & Newman, D. (1978). Interacting plans. *Cognitive Science, 2*, 195–233.

Clark, H. H. (1979). Responding to indirect speech acts. *Cognitive Psychology, 11*, 430–477.

Clark, H. H., & Clark, E. V. (1977). *Psychology and language*. New York: Harcourt Brace Jovanovich.

Clark, R. A., & Delia, J. G. (1979). *Topoi* and rhetorical competence. *Quarterly Journal of Speech, 65*, 187–206.

Cohen, P. R., & Perrault, C. R. (1979). Elements of a plan-based theory of speech acts. *Cognitive Science, 3*, 177–212.

Fish, S. (1980). *Is there a text in this class? The authority of interpretive communities*. Cambridge: Harvard University Press.

Goldberg, J. A. (1975). A system for the transfer of instructions in natural settings. *Semiotica, 14*, 269–296.

Grice, H. P. (1975). Logic and conversation. In P. Cole & J. L. Morgan (Eds.), *Syntax and semantics, Vol. 3: Speech acts* (pp. 41–58). New York: Academic Press.

Grosz, B. J. (1977, July). *The representation and use of focus in dialogue understanding*. Note 151. Stanford Research Institute.

Hobbs, J. R., & Evans, D. A. (1980). Conversations as planned behavior. *Cognitive Science, 4,* 349–377.

Jackson, S. (1983). *Contributions of rule knowledge and world knowledge to inferences about beliefs and intentions*. Paper presented at the University of Kansas Conference on Social Cognition and Interpersonal Behavior, Lawrence, Kansas.

Kreckel, M. (1981). *Communicative acts and shared knowledge in natural discourse*. London: Academic Press.

Levinson, S. E. (1981). The essential inadequacies of speech act models of dialogue. In H. Parret, M. Sbisa, & J. Verschueren (Eds.), *Possibilities and limitations of pragmatics* (pp. 473–492). Amsterdam: John Benjamins, B. V.

Levy, D. M. (1979). Communicative goals and strategies: Between discourse and syntax. In T. Givon (Ed.), *Syntax and semantics, Vol. 12: Discourse and syntax* (pp. 183–210). New York: Academic Press.

Miller, G. A., Galanter, E., & Pribram, K. H. (1960). *Plans and the structure of behavior*. New York: Holt.

Miller, J. R., Polson, P. G., & Kintsch, W. (1984). Problems of methodology in cognitive science. In W. Kintsch, J. R. Miller, & P. G. Polson (Eds.), *Methods and tactics in cognitive science* (pp. 1–20). Hillsdale, NJ: Lawrence Erlbaum Associates.

Perrault, C. R., & Allen, J. G. (1980). A plan-based analysis of indirect speech acts. *American Journal of Computational Linguistics, 6,* 167–182.

Riesbeck, D. K. (1980). "You can't miss it!": Judging the clarity of directions. *Cognitive Science, 4,* 285–303.

Rommetveit, R. (1974). *On message structure*. London: Wiley.

Schank, R. C. (1973). Using knowledge to understand. In R. Schank & B. L. Nash-Webber (Eds.), *Computer models of language and thought* (pp. 131–135). San Francisco: Freeman.

Schank, R. C., & Abelson, R. P. (1977a). Scripts, plans and knowledge. In P. N. Johnson-Laird & P. C. Wason (Eds.), *Thinking: Readings in cognitive science* (pp. 421–432). Cambridge: Cambridge University Press.

Schank, R. C., & Abelson, R. P. (1977b). *Scripts, plans, goals, and understanding*. Hillsdale, NJ: Lawrence Erlbaum Associates.

Searle, J. R. (1969). *Speech acts: An essay in the philosophy of language*. Cambridge: Cambridge University Press.

Searle, J. R. (1974). Chomsky's revolution in linguistics. In G. Harmon (Ed.), *On Noam Chomsky: Critical essays* (pp. 2–33). Garden City, New York: Anchor.

Searle, J. R. (1975). Indirect speech acts. In P. Cole & J. L. Morgan (Eds.), *Syntax and semantics, Vol. 3: Speech acts* (pp. 59–82). New York: Academic Press.

Searle, J. R. (1977). A classification of illocutionary acts. In A. Rogers, B. Wall, & J. P. Murphy (Eds.), *Proceedings of the Texas conference on performatives, presuppositions, and implications* (pp. 27–45). Arlington, VA: Center for Applied Linguistics.

Tyler, S. A. (1978). *The said and the unsaid*. New York: Academic Press.

Winograd, T. (1972). *Understanding natural language*. New York: Academic Press.

11

Negotiation Competence: A Conceptualization of the Rules of Negotiation Interaction

Mary E. Diez
Alverno College

Despite its obvious relationship to communication, negotiation research has been pursued almost exclusively in the disciplines of social psychology, economics, sociology, and marketing for over 2 decades (see reviews by Putnam & Jones, 1982; Roth & Malouf, 1979; Rubin & Brown, 1975; Strauss, 1978). Only recently have communication scholars begun to focus on the area, pointing to the need to examine interaction patterns in negotiation, and noting that communication too often has been controlled or even eliminated in mainstream negotiation literature (Donohue, 1978; Putnam & Jones, 1982).

Much communication research in negotiation, however, still shows the influence of a social-psychological view, treating communication as an independent variable, for example, by looking at the effect of mode or amount of communication on outcomes (Miller, Brehmer, & Hammond, 1970; Turnbull, Strickland, & Shaver, 1974, 1976; Wichman, 1970), or by examining the effects of manipulation of message strategies on outcome (Michelini, 1971; Tedeschi & Rosenfeld, 1980; Tedeschi, Schlenker, & Bonoma, 1973). Other work, growing out of interaction-based approaches, has treated communication more functionally, by identifying phases of negotiation interaction (Druckman, 1977; Theye & Seiler, 1979), or by categorizing tactics and strategies (Anglemar & Stern, 1978; Donohue, 1978, 1981 or 1981b; Donohue, Diez, & Hamilton, 1984; Putnam, 1982), but this approach has proceeded at a fairly macroscopic, generalized level.

None of these approaches has drawn upon important, current strains in communication theory that could explicate the mechanisms allowing individuals to understand how various types of negotiation proceed, or, indeed, to conduct negotiation competently. They do not address the question of how adult speakers of American English conduct interaction so that it becomes negotiation of one sort or another. To begin to answer that question requires a focus on the structuring of communication as negotiation.

How is communication structured as one type of interaction rather than another? Notions of communicative competence (Hymes, 1972) suggest that we "carry around" a tacit awareness of appropriate conventions of our society for different situations—much like we have a tacit awareness of the rules of our language's grammar. We know, for example, that our speech differs when we talk to our neighbor across the fence about our gardens and when we talk to a judge across his bench about a traffic violation. The two are different *situations*.

The elements and their relationships integrated in the notion of situation as commonly employed include the *setting* (literally the place or type of place) or the *type* of interaction. Both follow Schutz's (1973) notion of "typification," the taken-for-granted, implicit expectations that speakers have for the commonsense world, as generated out of a social structure. These expectations imply, according to Argyle (1980), a repertoire of moves available to interactants or a set of limits on what may transpire. The typification of situation also includes the participants and their role relationships within the situation. Role relationship features, e.g., social distance, social status, power differential, are not (as is sometimes assumed) stable attributes of either the persons or of their relationships. Rather, these features may and do shift depending on the activity and setting (Brown & Fraser, 1979; Ervin-Tripp, 1980).

Perhaps most important, however, is the "built in" sense of goal or purpose that is part of the typification included in the definition of *situation*. As Brown and Fraser (1979) note, "Purpose is the motor which sets the chassis of setting and participants going" (p. 35). Observers faced with any situation define it by asking what the participants are trying to do (Gregory & Carroll, 1978); and Goffman (1959) refers to this goal-centeredness as the interactants' understanding of their task, a "working consensus" of what they are about.

Discourse analysts have argued that situation is important to the study of situated interaction because the purposes inherent in the definition of situation are crucial determiners of linguistic behavior (Brown & Fraser, 1979; Graham, Argyle, Clarke, & Maxwell, 1981; Hall & Cole, 1978) and because meaning itself depends on the elements of the situation (Argyle, Furnham, & Graham, 1981). But this is not to imply that the sense of situation provides a rigid framework—for researchers or interactants. Some situations are defined fairly clearly within a culture (e.g., for middle-class America, a classroom lesson, a job interview), but they may be "portable" (e.g., a class visiting a supermarket, cf. Hall & Cole, 1978) or "adjustable" (cf. Miller & Steinberg's 1975 notion of the movement from extrinsic to intrinsic rules in interpersonal communication). Thus, the discourse analytic view is that the "shared stock of knowledge" is at once made available to members of the culture and subtly redefined by them in an ongoing way. As Mehan, Fisher, and Maroules (1976) explain (emphasis added): "Ultimately, social contexts consist of *mutually shared and ratified* definitions of situation and *in the social actions persons take* on the basis of those definitions" (p. 463).

The Situation Called Negotiation

The focus of this chapter is a conceptualization of what native speakers of American English need to know to structure interaction as negotiation; it places that knowledge within the larger framework of communicative competence— the generally tacit knowledge used by speakers to produce and interpret situated discourse. Because the idea of situation is central to this framework, the development of a conceptualization of negotiation competence begins with a review of previous research in negotiation as one way of tapping the "shared knowledge" of both the social science community and, by inference, the broader community of speakers.

The varied conceptions of negotiation tend to be focused on specific aspects of the "event" being labeled. For example, some are concerned with conflict (Chertkoff & Esser, 1976; Swingle, 1970), others with more competitive versus more cooperative exchanges (Bartos, 1974; Hagburg & Levine, 1978; King & Glidewell, 1980; Zartman, 1977), or even mixed motivated interaction (Beisecker, 1970; Schelling, 1960; Walton & McKersie, 1965). Some focus on outcome exclusively (Benton, Kelley, & Liebling, 1972; England, 1979), distinguishing between zero-sum and non-zero-sum "games" (Roth & Malouf, 1979; Schelling, 1960). Others have been concerned with settings, e.g., intra-organizational (Walton & McKersie, 1965), inter-organizational (Druckman, 1977; Hagburg & Levine, 1976; Spector, 1977; Walton & McKersie, 1965), international politics (Schelling, 1960), and even interpersonal problem solving (Fisher & Ury, 1981). The common elements appear to be that the interactants create or affirm relationships that fall (or move) along a continuum from high conflict orientation (e.g., "distributive" or "confrontational" or "competitive") to low conflict orientation (e.g., "integrative" or "cooperative" or "collaborative") and that they arrive at decisions as mutual outcomes.

Combining this composite definition of *negotiation* as a range of outcome-determining behavior along a continuum from relatively more competitive to relatively more cooperative goal orientation, with Hymes's (1972) notion of communicative competence, a definition of *negotiation competence* is proposed: the ability of adult speakers to draw upon a continuum of linguistic choices in order to create or affirm both the relationships between interactants and the limits of their mutual decision-making process. Such a conceptualization allows us to clarify more specifically what is involved in that ability by examining naturally occurring negotiation interaction and by using the body of literature about the meanings of linguistic choices across situations in social interaction. This will provide a means to draw up a list of rules that will capture the sense of a native speaker's tacit knowledge of the structuring of interaction as negotiation.

A Study of Naturally Occurring Interaction

Consistent with discourse analytic philosophy and practice, the conceptualization of the interaction work of negotiation and the proposed set of rules grew out of the examination of naturally occurring interaction, representing both ends of the continuum from competitive to cooperative. Clearly, what was needed were situations where the goals of the interaction were explicit and commonly agreed upon. The interactions studied were situations in which the goals were *assigned*, in training sessions for the Michigan Education Association bargaining teams. Participants, all teachers' union bargainers, were given information about con- tract issues between a school board and the teachers' union and were told to act out the negotiations, breaking at certain points for caucuses within the separate teams. Thus, the data can be considered as paradigm examples of negotiation behavior, one competitive (participants were told to fight for the most favorable solution for their side), and the other cooperative (participants were told to work together to produce effective strategy decisions).

The transcripts and tapes (approximately 80 pages, representing nearly 6 hours of negotiation and caucus interaction) were examined by a team of two under- graduate students in an organizational communication class and the researcher. Meeting weekly over a 3-month period, the students were instructed to listen to the tapes and to read the transcripts, taking notes on what features of discourse stood out consistently in the two types of interaction. They were instructed to look particularly for behaviors that appeared to provide contrasts between the two types of interaction in the linguistic choices made by speakers.

Emerging from this examination of naturally occurring negotiation interaction were three kinds of discourse "work" that appeared to require different choices in the two situations: coherence making, distance setting, and structuring. Each is developed more fully later, both in terms of the general patterns observed in the data and in relationship to findings in other discourse research. Specific rules related to each type of work are proposed.

Coherence Work

The first kind of discourse work relates to the need to make connections, both within the flow of discourse and between the discourse and elements outside it. Within discourse, coherence work fulfills the need to clearly tie references and referents. Ambiguities result from unclear links, so coherence work is disam- biguating work. This aspect of coherence is generally defined as the correspon- dence between elements in a sequence of parts, whether words and clauses or sentences and paragraphs. It is the sense-making work that allows discourse to be heard as connected (Clarke, 1975; Ellis, Hamilton, & Aho, 1983).

Another aspect of coherence work, however, is the linking of new information to old, or as Clark and Haviland (1977) term it "the given-new contract." These researchers have identified the various means by which speakers refer to some information in an utterance as assumed to be already in the other's awareness and the means by which speakers highlight that information not assumed to be known.

In the interactions examined, there appeared to be differences in the need to specify what is "given" and what is "new." Competitive negotiation sessions produced exchanges with very clearly spelled out content; speakers would give, for example, an introductory statement on a topic, a rationale for the proposal, and implications for the other side's accepting or rejecting the proposal. Subsequent utterances were tied specifically to these context-setting utterances. Cooperative negotiations, or caucus sessions, in contrast, often used shorthand references to common understandings (at times such that, although the "observers" could tell that there was such a reference, they weren't able to identify what the exact referent was!).

In competitive negotiation, there appeared to be reason to be even more attentive to marking the given information, emphasizing what one wants to assume as shared. For one reason, negotiators may want to be able to use past agreements or shared assumptions as the basis for making their proposal stronger (e.g., in the data, both sides appeal to the common concern for "the education of our children" as a basis for promoting their position). The fact that "given" information receives more stress may be part of the overall persuasive strategy of the negotiator in a competitive situation.

Another reason may be the need to control equivocality. If meanings are not clearly tied to other meanings (the business of coherence, after all), then utterances may be interpreted in various ways. There is more danger in being equivocal if one's opponent might thus be able to reinterpret one's utterance to their advantage. As a result, competitive negotiators appeared to choose to connect ideas tightly, preventing ambiguity.

The impact on linguistic choices was fairly clear. Competitive negotiators appeared to be careful about specifying the "given" and the "new" in their use of referents (more likely to be anaphoric or cataphoric than exophoric). As a result, their sentence structure was often complex, with dependent clauses and subordinating conjunctions used to link ideas. The overall result was the production of longer utterances.

In cooperative interaction, neither of the reasons to specify the givens appeared to function. Past agreements among team members could be assumed because they were shared along with the goal. As a result, references were less tightly constructed and were often exophoric or implicit. Utterances could be equivocal, not only because there was no fear of exploitation of ambiguity, but also because positions were open to change within the group as it worked out a strategy.

The following rule-sets contrast how coherence work appears to be accomplished through the linguistic choices of interactants in the two types of negotiation. For the competitive negotiation interaction, if P (one negotiator or side) cannot assume knowledge on the part of 0 (the other negotiator or side) or if P does not want to allow 0 to redefine equivocal statements: (a) P will specify clearly what is "given" and what is "new" by structuring utterances with clear referents and explicit relationships; (b) P will use anaphoric and cataphoric referents, avoiding exophoric referents; (c) P will tend to encode longer utterances; and (d) P's sentence structure will be, grammatically, both complex and complete.

In contrast, for the cooperative caucus interactions, if P (one speaker on a given side) can assume both shared goals and shared frameworks for processing information on the part of Q (another speaker on the same side), then: (a) P will tend to leave connections implicit; (b) P will use exophoric referents; (c) P will tend to encode shorter utterances; and (d) P's sentence structure will often be elliptical or incomplete.

Distance Work

The second kind of discourse work relates to the ongoing definition of relational control within the interaction. Ervin-Tripp (1980) has pointed out that language "*does* social acts, and systematically relies on social features to do so" (p. 395). Scotton (1983) has argued that code choice, or the form of the message, creates conversational implicatures that allow interactants to interpret relational messages (i.e., indications of the rights and obligations speakers want to be in force relative to one another). Donohue and Diez (1983) have extended Scotton's idea of "negotiating identities" through code choice to include negotiation of a broader range of rights and obligations relative to the distributive bargaining situation.

People "code their social world" (Ervin-Tripp, 1980) and establish rights and obligations through *distance work*. Distance work involves linguistic choices that signal psychological distance (immediacy), social distance (relative formality) and role distance (power/solidarity). In the two paradigm examples of negotiation interaction examined, there appeared to be differences in all three aspects of distance work.

Psychological distance is signalled by what Wiener and Mehrabian (1968) call immediacy, or "the degree of directness and intensity of interaction between the communicator and his referents." They explain that the use of encoding differences in the verbal content of the communication implies varying orientations about the psychological relationships between the speaker, the addressee, and the topic.

The two sets of interactions were examined for signals of directness. In referring to their own team in the negotiation sessions, for example, speakers could choose to say "we" or "our team" or "the teachers' union"/"the school board." Similarly, in referring to the other side, obvious variations from "you" to "the school board"/"the teachers' union" were possible. When a teachers' union representative began a statement made to the board by saying "It is incumbent upon the board to re-examine . . . ," the linguistic choice was doubly distancing; "you" was replaced by the third person "the board" and the subject of the clearly imperative-in-intent statement was moved, through use of a passive transformation, out of the subject position.

There were more examples of distancing through referent use and sentence construction in the negotiation interactions; few, if any, marked the caucus exchanges. In the cooperative frame, speakers referred to themselves as "we" and "us," calling the opposing team "they" and "them." The caucus interaction, thus, appeared more direct, more immediate.

Social distance, or formality, is indicated by overall "register" (see Gregory & Carroll, 1978; Joos, 1962), a collection of linguistic indicators tied to situations. Brown and Fraser (1979) have noted the correlation between interactants' sense of "formality" and the extensive use of nominal constructions, nouns, adjectives, and prepositions. Similarly, they have pointed to the predominance of verbs, pronouns, and adverbs in more "informal" situations. It is commonly observed that elaborated vocabulary and careful pronunciation is more formal than simple vocabulary and slurred speech; contractions are less formal than full forms (Gregory & Carroll, 1978). Goffman (1959) noted that "front region" (formal) behavior is likely to be marked by the use of titles and the avoidance of vulgarity or humor, in contrast to "back region" (informal) behavior, where personal reference, slang, humor, and vulgarity are commonly acceptable.

In the two sets of interactions, there were concrete indications of "more formal" and "less formal" exchanges. In proposing more talk on a topic, for example, a formal statement like "Let's submit it to discussion" would be more likely in the negotiation setting. In caucus, interactants would be more likely to say "Let's talk about it." Note that the more formal variation is also a nominalized form, underlining the "nouny" nature of formal interaction. Difficult vocabulary was also characteristic of the competitive negotiation setting. Besides using technical terms required for the contract discussion, interactants' use of "difficult" vocabulary included "ameliorate," "allude," "abdicate," "advisement," "behooves," "incumbent," and "expunged." There was little or no humor, and no vulgarity in these negotiation sessions.

In spite of the fact that the same speakers were involved in the caucus sessions, their language showed marked differences. None of the aforementioned difficult vocabulary was used. When technical terms were used, they were tied to the caucus task of drafting specific contract language proposals. And, although the teams were generally task-oriented in the caucus sessions, there was some evidence of humor and minor vulgarities.

Role distance is cued by the dimensions of power and solidarity encoded in linguistic choice. In their classic discussion of "tu" and "vous" as signals of power and solidarity, Brown and Gilman (1960) explored how reciprocal and nonreciprocal relationships are signalled by the use of pronouns in a number of languages. Nonreciprocal use of pronouns—the superior says "tu" and receives "vous"—indicates a power relationship, encoding the sets of rights and obligations in effect. Reciprocal use signals solidarity.

Although modern English avoids such pronoun use distinctions, we are not without means of signalling such relational messages linguistically. One way is the use of indirect forms (replacing "you" with "the board"); another is the optional use of backchannels or other supportive cues. In Ervin-Tripp's (1976) research on directives, the social distribution of illocutionary acts by which speakers attempt to constrain the actions of others indicates the operation of relational signals of power and solidarity in choice of directive form.

In the competitive negotiation interactions, more indirect forms of address were used, as previously noted. There were few backchannels, and any support statements were generally directed at content rather than toward persons. The most common directive forms used—need statements, embedded imperatives, and question imperatives—represent those most common in a superior–subordinate relationship. Although negotiation is not necessarily a superior-subordinate situation, the zero-sum game of competitive negotiation involves parallel attempts to establish power, making these choices meaningful signals.

In the cooperative caucus interactions, very different signals were given. The use of the pronoun "we" was a particular cue of the solidarity being established. Backchanneling (both "uh huh" and repetitions of the other's idea) was common, and support was given both for ideas and to persons. There also appeared to be more socio-centric language (i.e., language focusing on the group and its mutual goal rather than on the individuals within the group). Participants in the caucuses used many direct imperatives, a form in which the speaker assumes the right to make a bald request of another. Ervin-Tripp (1976) notes that these are most common among equals and coworkers, and are "marked" between superiors and subordinates. Although embedded imperatives were used in both caucus and negotiation interactions, the "sense" of their use appeared to differ—a politeness message inferrable in the negotiations contrasted with a tentativeness, or planning, signal in the caucuses.

The following rule-sets illustrate the differences in distance work in the two contrasting situations. For the competitive negotiation interaction, if P wants to establish a differential power relationship with O: (a) P will use linguistic forms that impose obligations on O while maintaining P's rights; (b) P will use less supportive language in the exchange (e.g., fewer backchannels); (c) P will use more technical and formal vocabulary in the exchange; (d) P will use indirect references to both P and O as teams; and (e) P will use little socio-centric speech.

In contrast, for the cooperative caucus interactions, if solidarity and shared goals are salient for P and Q in the situation: (a) P and Q will use linguistic forms that emphasize co-action and co-responsibility; (b) P and Q will use supportive language and frequent backchannels; (c) P and Q will use informal vocabulary, including humor and vulgarity as acceptable choices; (d) P and Q will use more direct references to each other and about O; and (e) P and Q will use more socio-centric speech.

Structuring Work

The third kind of discourse work relates to the organization of the interaction, both in the management of "the floor," usually studied as turn-taking, and in the management of the flow of information, a question of processing techniques. The management of turn-taking and information processing appeared to create different forms of talk at either end of the continuum. Specifically, more cooperative interaction, focused toward an explicitly common goal, appeared to require less attention to overt structuring than did the more competitive interaction. The differences seemed to impact the length of individual utterances, the types of turn exchange, and the form of illocutionary acts employed.

The length of utterances has already been addressed as a function of the relative need to make explicit the links between ideas in the interaction (i.e., in coherence work). But length could also be related to the factors involved in turn management, as will be explained later.

More competitive interactions appeared to have what Edelsky (1981) has called "a singly developed floor." That is, although the situation is a multi-party interaction, the flow of turns is parallel to what Sacks, Schegloff, and Jefferson (1974) describe for dyadic interaction. In the more competitive setting, turn exchanges were relatively smooth, with interruptions occurring rarely. In fact, interruptions were generally not attempts to take over the floor, but requests to facilitate the attention of the other side to the turn itself (e.g., a request to slow down so that the other side could get the specific contract language down in writing). Length was thus affected, because few turns were cut off by interruption. For the most part, the exchanges could be charted in an alternating pattern:

$$P \text{ - - - } \rightarrow O \text{ - - - } \rightarrow P \text{ - - - } \rightarrow O \text{ - - - } \rightarrow P \text{ - - - } \rightarrow O \text{ (etc.)}.$$

The more cooperative interactions functioned much differently, with frequent talkovers, break-ins, or multiple speaker segments. These appeared to be like Edelsky's (1981:383) "shared floor" interactions: "A collaborative venture where several people seemed to be either operating on the same wavelength or engaging in a free-for-all." The alternating pattern seen in the negotiation interactions was replaced by several interactants speaking at once, or in such quick, overlapping succession that the turn appeared to be shared. The focus, and its manifestation, is caught in this diagram:

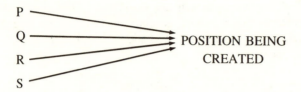

showing that the "shared floor" acted not to have the speakers respond in turn to each other's questions or statements, but to have them mutually engage in what Goffman (1959) called "building a common front." Thus, speakers not only accepted interruptions and talkovers, but appeared to *invite* participation through the formulation of their own talk.

Of course, not all of the interaction in caucus sessions displayed the same intensity of "shared floor" exchanges. As the group moved toward agreement on what their position on a given issue would be, there tended to be a more ordered approach to solidifying or specifying the wording or strategy. However, there were no instances of this kind of "free-for-all" floor in the more competitive interactions.

The structuring of the interactions differed in another way as well: the relative firmness of statements, indicated by the form of speech acts used. Differences in illocutionary force encoded within the two types of interaction distinguished the situations, as did the use of forms that prevented or invited specific types of responses by the other.

The competitive negotiations were marked by four primary types of utterances: proposals, directives, questions, and clarifications. Proposals generally stated the "offer" being made by one team, or restated a previous offer that had been adjusted in the course of the interaction. Directives included "need statements," statements attempting to gain compliance with a proposed way of operating or statements attempting to establish the relative importance of a given aspect of the discussion. Other directives (e.g., embedded imperatives and question directives) served as information requests; more often, interactants used questions to request information. Responses to information requests from the other side resulted in clarifications; speakers often coupled clarifications with a repetition of the proposal (maintaining an attention to coherence).

The pattern observed in the use of the types of utterances was similar to that reported more extensively by Donohue and Diez (1983). They found that competitive negotiators control patterns of interaction by using a series of questions to maintain their right to uncover the information needed to move toward a favorable decision. Alternatively, they noted that the series of questions may be over-turned when negotiators respond to a question and then, in the same utterance, pose a question of their own. Both patterns of attempt to control the flow of information were observed in the competitive interactions in this study. Moreover, the directives and questions were marked by the "firmness" of their tone and construction. Even though proposals were not the "bottom line" discussed in the caucus, they were presented as firm and clear, as exemplified by this statement of the teachers union speaker: "We expect to have complete retroactivity to July of 1980."

The cooperative caucus sessions, in contrast, were marked by a greater variety of utterance forms, with a general patterns of identifying the areas to be focused, discussing and clarifying various options for approach to the area, suggesting a specific focus, and coming to agreement on a position. Participation tended to be the free-for-all characteristic of "shared floor" multi-party groups. The utterances were often partial, elliptical, or otherwise incomplete. When directives were used, they tended not to be elaborated (as need statements or embedded imperatives); rather, they were most often direct imperatives. At times, they appeared to be addressed to the group as a whole, rather than to another specific member (e.g., "Give them this as our last offer!").

During the phase of discussing and clarifying options, caucus utterances were marked by their tentativeness and by the use of "sympathetic circularity" (see Bernstein, 1962). Interactants used tentative expressions like "I think" or "What do you think about . . .?" to signal that they were suggesting possible positions rather than proposing a plan they had fully worked out and were committed to. They invited feedback through the use of tag questions ("isn't it?" or "can't we?"), a particular form of sympathetic circularity. They invited "shared floor" responses by leaving the ends of sentences unfinished for others to pick up and fill in.

The following rule-sets indicate the patterns that appeared to mark the two types of negotiation interaction related to structuring work. For the competitive negotiation interaction, if P wants to manage information in the exchange such that maximum information is elicited from O: (a) P will use multiple question forms; (b) P will follow answers to O's questions with their own questions; and (c) P will maintain clear turn sequences with O. In this same interaction situation, if P's purpose is to win as many arguments for proposed actions/statements as possible and to accept as few of O's proposals as possible: (a) P will avoid tentative expressions; (b) P will conclude utterances firmly; and (c) P will not accept interruptions from O.

In contrast, for the cooperative caucus interaction, if P and Q are focused on planning their joint strategy with relationship to Q: (a) P and Q will use directives addressed to the group as a whole; (b) P and Q will use brief and varied utterance types; and (c) P and Q's talk will be characterized by talk-overs and interruptions. In this same situation, if P is open to Q's modification of proposed actions or statements: (a) P will encode utterances with tentative expressions and expressions of sympathetic circularity; (b) P will leave utterances unfinished to invite completion by Q; and (c) P will allow Q to interrupt.

Rule Sets as Explanations of Negotiation Interaction

Two initial comments need to be made regarding these sets of rules guiding interactants' choices of linguistic forms in negotiation settings. First, these proposed rules are "constitutive" rules; that is, they function to make an interaction competitive rather than cooperative in the same way that the rules of chess or football define the game by demarcating it from other games. They are not rules for which there are sanctions imposed if the rules are not followed. To follow constitutive rules simply means that interactants are structuring that which the rules describe as the game being played.

Unlike the rules of chess, however, these particular rules define the *extremes* along a continuum of negotiation settings. Within a range of negotiation situations, there are subtle shifts from highly competitive all the way across to highly cooperative. To the degree that interactants structure negotiation following either rule set, they are creating that "type" of negotiation interaction. Of course, as they make adjustments moving toward the middle points of the continuum, they create slightly different senses of negotiation, including what researchers call "mixed-motive" bargaining (Beisecker, 1970). Because both competitive and cooperative goals are involved in such a situation, aspects of both rule sets may be employed in its structuring. The concept of the rule-governed nature of the interaction implies that interactants produce and interpret linguistic choices using the rule sets as *guides* to the changes they are signalling.

Because the features identified in the sets of rules cluster behaviorally in an extreme situation, speakers respond to a "collection" of behaviors in interpreting the relative position of an ongoing interaction on the competitive-cooperative continuum. As Owsley and Scotton (1982) suggest, communicative competence "includes a component which can sum incidences of related features and evaluate them as percentages in relation to some probability framework." The rules sets outlined here are an attempt to spell out aspects of that "probability framework" for negotiation interaction.

The usefulness of such a notion is that it helps explain how communicative competence functions in experienced speakers. The rule sets attempt to spell out what is the "taken-for-granted" knowledge included in typifications that speakers develop for the range of negotiation situations. By bracketing these examples of competitive and cooperative interaction performed by the same interactants, it is possible to examine the patterns of linguistic choices to see how the speakers make specific types of adjustments in order to create the coherence, distance, and structuring effects appropriate to those situations.

It is these adjustments that specify *how* communication becomes structured as one kind of negotiation interaction rather than another. The rule sets, then, describe for the particular situation of mutual group decision making what it means to be communicatively competence (i.e., to produce and interpret appropriate interaction for these situations).

REFERENCES

Angelmar, R., & Stern, L. W. (1978). Development of a content analytic system for analysis of bargaining communication in marketing. *Journal of Marketing Research, 15,* 93–102.

Argyle, M. (1980). Language and social interaction. In H. Giles, W. P. Robinson, & P. M. Smith (Eds.), *Language: Social psychological perspectives* (pp. 397–407). New York: Pergamon Press.

Argyle, M., Furnham, A., & Graham, J. A. (1981). *Social situations.* Cambridge: Cambridge University Press.

Bartos, O. J. (1974). *Process and outcome of negotiation.* New York: Columbia University Press.

Beisecker, T. (1970). Verbal persuasive strategies in mixed-motive interactions. *Quarterly Journal of Speech, 56,* 149–160.

Benton, A. A., Kelley, H. H., & Liebling, B. (1972). Effects of extremity of offers and concession rate on the outcome of bargaining. *Journal of Personality and Social Psychology, 1,* 73–83.

Bernstein, B. (1962). Social class, linguistic codes and grammatical elements. *Language and Speech, 5,* 221–240.

Brown, P., & Fraser, C. (1979). Speech as a marker of situation. In K. Scherer & H. Giles (Eds.), *Social markers in speech* (pp. 33–62). Cambridge: Cambridge University Press.

Brown, R., & Gilman, A. (1960). The pronouns of power and solidarity. In T. A. Sebeok (Ed.), *Style in language* (pp. 253–76). Cambridge: Cambridge University Press.

Chertkoff, J. M., & Esser, J. K. (1976). A review of experiments in explicit bargaining. *Journal of Experimental and Social Psychology, 12,* 464–486.

Clark, H. H., & Haviland, S. E. (1977). Comprehension and the given-new contract. In R. O. Freedle (Ed.), *Discourse production and comprehension* (pp. 1–40). Norwood, NJ: Ablex.

Clarke, D. D. (1975). The use and recognition of sequential structure in dialogue. *British Journal of Social and Clinical Psychology, 14,* 333–339.

Donohue, W. A. (1978). An empirical framework for examining negotiation processes and outcomes. *Communication Monographs, 45,* 247–256.

Donohue, W. A. (1981a). Analyzing negotiation tactics: Development of a negotiation interact system. *Human Communication Research, 7,* 273–387.

Donohue, W. A. (1981b). Development of a model of rule use in negotiation interaction. *Communication Monographs, 48,* 106–120.

Donohue, W. A., & Diez, M. E. (1983, May). *Information management in negotiation.* Paper presented at the annual meeting of the International Communication Association, Dallas, Texas.

Donohue, W. A., Diez, M. E., & Hamilton, M. (1984). An expanded model of communication rule use in negotiation. *Human Communication Research, 10,* 403–425.

Druckman, D. (1977). *Negotiation: Social-psychological perspectives.* Beverly Hills: Sage.

Edelsky, C. (1981). Who's got the floor? *Language and Society, 10,* 383–421.

Ellis, D. G., Hamilton, M., & Aho, L. (1983). Studies in discourse coherence: Conversational reconstruction. *Human Communication Research, 9,* 267–282.

England, J. L. (1969). Two bargaining automata. *Journal of Conflict Resolution, 23,* 296–325.

Ervin-Tripp, S. (1976). Is Sybil there? The structure of some American English directives. *Language in Society, 5,* 25–66.

Ervin-Tripp, S. (1980). Speech acts, social meaning and social learning. In H. Giles, W. P. Robinson, & P. M. Smith (Eds.), *Language: Social psychological perspectives* (pp. 389–396). New York: Pergamon Press.

Fisher, R., & Ury, W. (1981). *Getting to yes*. Boston: Houghton Mifflin.

Goffman, E. (1959). *The presentation of self in everyday life*. Garden City, NY: Doubleday Anchor Books.

Graham, J. A., Argyle, M., Clarke, D. D., & Maxwell, G. (1981). The salience, equivalence and sequential structure of behavioral elements in different social situations. *Semiotica, 35,* 1–27.

Gregory, M., & Carroll, S. (1978). *Language and situation*. London: Routledge & Kegan Paul.

Hagburg, E. C., & Levine, M. J. (1978). *Labor relations: An integrated perspective*. St. Paul: West Publishing.

Hall, W. S., & Cole, M. (1978). On participant shaping of discourse through their understanding of the talk. In K. E. Nelson (Ed.), *Children's language* (Vol. 1, pp. 445–465). New York: Gardner Press.

Hymes, D. (1972). On communicative competence. In J. Pride & J. Holmes (Eds.), *Sociolinguistics* (pp. 269–293). London: Penguin.

Joos, M. (1962). The five clocks. Supplement 22 to the *International Journal of American Linguistics*.

King, D. C., & Glidewell, J. C. (1980). Dyadic bargaining outcomes under individualistic and competitive orientations. *Human Relations, 33,* 781–803.

Mehan, H., Fisher, S., & Maroules, N. (1976). *The social organization of classroom lessons*. Technical Report, Ford Foundation.

Michelini, R. L. (1971). Effects of prior interaction, contact, strategy, and expectation of meeting on game behaviors and sentiment. *Journal of Conflict Resolution, 15,* 97–103.

Miller, G. R., & Steinberg, M. (1975). *Between people*. Chicago: Science Research Associates.

Miller, M. J., Brehmer, B., & Hammond, K. R. (1970). Communication and conflict resolution: A cross-cultural study. *International Journal of Psychology, 5,* 75–87.

Owsley, H., & Scotton, C. M. (1982). *What's my line? Conversational expression of power by TV interviewers*. Unpublished manuscript, Michigan State University.

Putnam, L. L. (1982). Procedural messages and small group work climates: A lag sequential analysis. In M. Burgoon (Ed.), *Communication Yearbook 5* (pp. 331–350). New Brunswick, NJ: Transaction Books.

Putnam, L. L., & Jones, T. S. (1982). The role of communication in bargaining. *Human Communication Research, 8,* 262–280.

Roth, A. E., & Malouf, M. W. K. (1979). Game-theoretic models and the role of information in bargaining. *Psychological Review, 86,* 574–594.

Rubin, J. Z., & Brown, B. R. (1975). *The social psychology of bargaining and negotiation*. New York: Academic Press.

Sacks, H., Schegloff, E. A., & Jefferson, G. (1974). A simplest systematics for the organization of turn-taking for conversation. *Language, 50,* 696–735.

Schelling, T. C. (1960). *The strategy of conflict*. Cambridge: Harvard University Press.

Schutz, A. (1973). *The problem of social reality*. Ed. M. Natanson. The Hague: Nijhoff, 1973.

Scotton, C. M. (1983). The negotiation of identities in conversation: A theory of markedness and code choice. *International Journal of the Sociology of Language, 44,* 115–136.

Spector, B. I. (1977). Negotiation as psychological process. *Journal of Conflict Resolution, 21,* 607–618.

Strauss, A. (1978). *Negotiations: Varieties, contexts, processes, and social order*. San Francisco: Jossey-Bass.

Swingle, P. (1970). *The structure of conflict*. New York: Academic Press.

Tedeschi, J. T., & Rosenfeld, P. (1980). Communication in bargaining and negotiation. In M. E. Roloff & G. R. Miller (Eds.), *Persuasion: New directions in theory and research* (pp. 225–248). Beverly Hills: Sage.

Tedeschi, J. T., Schlenker, B. R., & Bonoma, T. V. (1973). *Conflict, power, and games.* Chicago: Adline.

Theye, L. D., & Seiler, W. J. (1979). Interactional analysis in collective bargaining: An alternative approach to the prediction of negotiated outcomes. In D. Nimmo (Ed.), *Communication Yearbook 3* (pp. 375–392). New Brunswick, NJ: Transaction Books.

Turnbull, A. A., Strickland, L., & Shaver, K. G. (1974). Phrasing of concessions, differences of power, and medium of communication: Negotiating success and attributions of the opponent. *Personality and Social Psychology Bulletin, 1,* 228–230.

Turnbull, A. A., Strickland, L., & Shaver, K. G. (1976). Medium of communication, differential power, and phrasing of concessions: Negotiating success and attributions to the opponent. *Human Communication Research, 2,* 262–270.

Walton, R. E., & McKersie, R. B. (1965). *A behavioral theory of labor negotiations: An analysis of a social interaction system.* New York: McGraw-Hill.

Wiener, M., & Mehrabian, A. (1968). *Language within language: Immediacy, a channel in verbal communication.* New York: Appleton-Century-Crofts.

Wichman, H. (1970). Effects of isolation and communication on cooperation in a two-person game. *Journal of Personality and Social Psychology, 16,* 114–120.

Zartman, I. W. (1977). Negotiation as a joint decision-making process. *Journal of Conflict Resolution, 21,* 620–638.

12 Appositions in Plans and Scripts: An Application to Initial Interactions

Pam Benoit
University of Missouri, Columbia

Vince Follert
Western Illinois University*

Human beings are motivated to action through purpose. Accomplishing everyday activities in a social world frequently requires collaborative action that becomes possible when a speaker is able to express a want that can be understood by another such that a coherent response can be produced to address that want. Communication is possible because the acts of human beings are meaningful through reference to interpretive practices. This chapter introduces the concept of *appositions* as an interpretive practice by which social actors reference conventional relationships between acts and intentions. The term derives from the grammatical concept of appositives and this analogue provides a loose structure for mapping function and structure in grammar onto discourse. Appositives are clauses that supply added meaning to the noun they modify, indicating more clearly the proper or intended interpretation; whereas appositions assign meaning to acts within interactions. Just as there are levels of grammatical organization (i.e., words, clauses, sentences), there are multiple levels of organization in discourse. Thus, appositions function as units within plans and scripts just as words and clauses function as units within sentences and paragraphs. To articulate these claims, this chapter outlines assumptions about communication, describes the function and character of appositions, and details the nature of plans and scripts. This erects a framework for viewing the practical accomplishment of discourse that is applied throughout the chapter to the particular discourse of initial interactions.

---

*deceased

ASSUMPTIONS ABOUT THE NATURE OF
COMMUNICATION

A fundamental ontological premise is that human beings are active agents with symbol-using and meaning-creating capacities. This leads to the claims that the function of communication is the creation of social order and the accomplishment of goals that require the assistance of others in some form; that communication involves acts that are goal oriented; and that interpretive practices are employed by social actors to produce and interpret discourse. The means for conveying acts that are understandable and the means for coordinating interactant's intentions through social interaction become the focal issues.

Communication is the process by which sense making becomes a practical accomplishment and social order becomes possible. Fogarty (1959) elaborates on the role that communication plays in this process:

> Man is not just a rational animal. He is a "symbol-using animal," because his use of symbols is what makes him specifically different from other animals. Also, it is in the use of symbols that a man differentiates himself from other men as he puts his personally projected world in the kind of order he can live with. Further, it is through symbols that he relates himself with others so that, in his organized system of interdependency, he may satisfy his needs. (p. 60)

Interactants engage in social action rather than solitary action because they are dependent on others to accomplish their goals. It is evident from a cursory review of the literature that this is recognized as a fundamental purpose for communication. Bowers and Bradac's (1982) review of the metatheoretical literature in communication indicates that theorists commonly view the intention to perform behaviors that will obtain goals as a necessary condition for communication. Communication from this perspective is "action" rather than "motion" (see Burke, 1978) and explained through "in order to" as well as causal reasons. The position is reflected in the practical syllogism of rules theory (Cushman, Valentinsen, & Dietrich, 1982), the extensive research focusing on strategic choices in communication (see Ayres, 1983; Baxter, 1982; Delia, Kline, & Burleson, 1979; Miller, Boster, Roloff, & Seibold, 1977; Roloff, 1976),[1] and uncertainty theory that describes lines of action for the purpose of reducing uncertainties about others (Berger, 1979; Berger & Calabrese, 1975). Communication theorists emphasize that speakers have goals that generate communicative behaviors, whereas speech-act theorists argue that "when one speaks one means something by what one says" (Austin, 1962; Searle, 1969). The speaker intends to produce an illocutionary effect by obtaining the hearer's recognition of that intention and

---

[1]Strategies implicitly assume that interactants develop plans and select from alternative lines of action those that accomplish their particular goals.

intends that this recognition be accomplished by reference to the rules that conventionally associate utterances with effects (Searle, 1969). Assuming that appropriate goals generate the acts, speech-act accounts offer an explanation of the production and interpretation of the act.

Interpretive practices are taken for granted operations for sense making. Garfinkel (1967) indicates that the conduct of everyday affairs is dependent on individuals assuming that what is said will be interpreted according to schemes that make that saying apparent for its coherent, understandable, or planful character. Cognitive science describes schemes for framing appropriate goals (Clark, 1979; Clark & Lucy, 1975; Miller, Galanter, & Pribram, 1960; Schank & Abelson, 1977) shifting to focus on that which is taken for granted by speech acts. In a constructivist view of communication, Delia, O'Keefe, and O'Keefe (1982) offer a useful distinction between two types of interpretive practices: general interpretive devices are relevant to interaction at all points (e.g., Grice's maxims, 1975) whereas organizing schemes characterize interactional sequences (e.g., scripts, adjacency pairs). The latter exist to classify acts in relation to other acts to "allow one person to produce acts with recognizable implications for another person's behaviors and permit persons to respond coherently and appropriately to acts that have been produced" (Delia, O'Keefe, & O'Keefe, 1982, p. 157). Although theoretically distinct, organizing schemes must function within general interpretive devices. Consistent with this distinction, appositions are a general interpretive practice characterizing all discourse, functioning at the base level of discourse organization; whereas plans and scripts are parallel to organizing schemes that provide the structure for the specific application of appositions and the coherence between acts. These assumptions about the nature of communication are the foundation for this conception of appositions as an interpretive practice.

APPOSITIONS

Interpretive schemes are devices that exist to introduce order, to make it possible to engage in sense making activities. Without such schemes, meaning occurs by chance and communication becomes accidental. Appositions are a fundamental interpretive scheme, the cognitive device that organizes experience into purpose-act units. This device patterns behavior to create order through an explanation of motives that explicitly reject random senselessness. The pervasiveness of this scheme is suggested by Garfinkel's (1967) experiments in which patients asked questions of a therapist and received "yes" or "no" answers randomly. Analyses of the transcripts indicate that despite the actual randomness of the therapists acts, patients construct elaborate explanations of the therapists meaning by searching for probable motives. Social psychological research in attribution (Jones & Davis, 1965) suggests the ubiquity of attempts to assess intentions in order to determine responsibility, and documents the phenomena of blaming the victim to thwart the conclusion that an act could indeed be senseless. Human beings organize a social world that is understandable; appositions are an interpretive scheme for making behaviors "visibly-rational-and-reportable-for-all-practical-purposes" (Garfinkel, 1967, p. vii).

Because human beings engage in communicative behaviors to accomplish some purpose and intentions are made manifest through behaviors, appositions provide the necessary connection between goals and behaviors. Consider for a moment how you could convince someone that you can be trusted, how you could get a sick friend to see a doctor, or how you could get a raise from your boss. For each of these goals, you can generate conceivable lines of action that might achieve the end. Inversely, particular appositions are accessed by the interpreter in an interaction. The hearer witnesses an act and makes judgments about the meaning of that act by determining the motives responsible for its enactment. Thus, a reciprocating self-disclosure may be recognized as an indication of trustworthiness. With the act placed within a context, the most likely explanation of the meaning of the act can be determined. The speaker's ability to generate means to accomplish an end and the hearer's ability to marshall goals that could explain the speaker's acts are possible because appositions package experience into purpose-acts units.

The content of the specific appositions, the lines of action for accomplishing each particular goal, are developed through experience and acculturation. With experience, children learn behavioral repertoires for accomplishing salient goals (see Clark & Delia, 1976, 1977 for an analysis of children's persuasive strategies). Most young children, for example, have an extensive set of behavioral strategies for delaying bedtime. Experience also provides a basis for assessing the effectiveness of various acts, allowing for strategic choice. This suggests that because individuals do have some unique experiences, the content of the appositions stored in memory will exhibit some individual differences. But, also at work, is the powerful process of acculturation, for the social world exists with layers of meaning that must be passed on to each new generation. We are taught conventional means for accomplishing goals. The important purpose-act linkages derived through experience and acculturation are stored in memory and retrievable for future situations with the same or similar goals.

Communication is generally described as being motivated by a goal that is subsequently translated into an action that is made understandable through the shared interpretive practice of appositions. The complexity of the relationship between a goal and an act has only been intimated. A speaker's goal can be obtained through multiple means. A single act may be interpreted by a hearer as the expression of clearly different goals. The complexities of linguistic acts and the presence of equifinality allow for misunderstanding, nuance, and individual style. Even with shared interpretive schemes, human beings preserve their diverse nature in their discourse.[2] Therefore, for any particular goal, a speaker may have multiple lines of action to choose among and the hearer may be forced to choose among various intentions that could account for the action. To compound the complexity, an interactant's act may be grounded in multiple goals. Human beings are quite capable of attending to several goals simultaneously, influencing the choice of acts. In addition, an interest in interaction requires that the scope be expanded to include both interactants' goals and the coordination necessary to orchestrate intentions into a coherent sequence of acts as the discourse unfolds.

In the abstract, appositions are a fundamental cognitive scheme, a way of knowing the social world that is basic to an understanding of communication. A concrete instance of an apposition ties a given goal with specific lines of action. To develop a description of the character of appositions-in-use, initial interactions, a discrete discourse form, are examined for their conventional means for addressing the goals of obtaining information and impression management.[3] Excerpts from transcripts of 12 initial interactions appear in this text to illustrate the generalizations drawn from the entire set.[4]

Previous literature suggests that the predominant goal of initial interactions is to obtain information, and that this can be achieved through passive, active, or interactive strategies (Berger, 1973, 1979; Berger & Bradac, 1982; Berger & Calabrese, 1975). Passive strategies involve observation of the partner; active strategies require the interactant to exert an effort to obtain information but do not involve direct contact with the other person; and interactive strategies involve the use of conversation with the partner as a means for attaining the goal. The latter is of interest here because the focus is on discourse as a means of attaining goals. Verbal interrogation and self-disclosure are interactive strategies designed to reduce uncertainty (Berger, 1979). Representative findings on verbal interrogation suggest that uncertainty leads to high levels of question asking (Berger & Calabrese, 1975; Calabrese, 1975; Frankfurt, 1965; Motl, 1980), initial questions seek demographic information and proceed to attitudinal information (Berger & Calabrese, 1975), excessive questioning is considered inappropriate, and interactants must be willing to answer any question that they pose to a partner. Self-disclosure obtains information because the norm of reciprocity elicits information from the partner. Verbal attenders are also prevalent in the transcripts

---

[2]It is thus possible to reconcile views that perceive human beings as willful and variable and still ascribe to beliefs that human beings are capable of communication and are predictable.

[3]Initial interactions could be defined to include all instances of first encounters (e.g., job interviews, consultations). A more restrictive definition is adopted for this research because my naive intuition suggests that these other forms of interaction are motivated by a different set of goals.

[4]The transcripts were obtained from college students paired in male–female dyads. Interactions lasted between 10–15 minutes and transcripts based on audio recordings were completed for 12 dyads, accounting for 1,546 turns at talk.

analyzed here and are particularly effective when the partner initiates a "pet" topic that provides the opportunity for extensive self-descriptions.

Although each of these are characteristic acts in initial interactions, they are not to be interpreted as an exhaustive catalogue of lines of action for obtaining information. Instead, a consideration of the way in which the shared understandings of appositions-in-use are implicitly reaffirmed through the discourse may be more profitable. In the use of question asking, questions are typically assumed to request information that the speaker does not have. It is clear that this behavior is recognized by the interpreter as an expression of the goal of obtaining information for the hearer responds to that intention by providing elaborated answers to questions:

Example 1
M: I'm—I'm from Crystal Lake.
F: Crystal Lake? Is that up north?
M: Yeah. It's 50 miles northwest of Chicago.
F: Oh. I'm from Carbondale Illinois. That's down south. It's about 50 miles south of Springfield.

Example 2
F: So, do you live in the dorms or?
M: Yeah. Yeah I was—I was in the dorm for a year and a half.
F: Oh.
M: A bunch of us guys—a bunch of us guys and myself got a house already for next fall.

Although a brief response would technically answer the questions, the elaborations indicate that the interactants are aware that this would not respond adequately to the purpose generating the act of questioning. Thus, the hearer's behavior reaffirms the interactant's shared understanding of the specific apposition that connects the goal of obtaining information with the behavior of asking questions. This indicates that Grice's (1975) maxim to "say only what is necessary" is dependent on the goals of the interactants. Contrast this with another interaction that looks on the surface to be quite similar. A clerk records information from a client for a form. The respondent provides minimal information, elaborations are minimized, for the actual goal of the clerk and recognized by the client is to efficiently complete the form. Interactants reaffirm their understandings of the purposes governing the interaction through their discourse.

To accomplish the goal of impression management, the interactant may choose among possible lines of action including positive associations, self-descriptions, and attitude and belief expressions. Schlenker (1980) observes that members of dyads in initial interactions frequently attempt to capitalize upon the advantage of being seen as similar to their partners. Given the goal of creating an impression of similarity, possible lines of action could include imitating the partner's behavior, expression of attitudes known to be held in common, searching for common acquaintances and agreements with the partner's attitudes.

Agreements are selected to illustrate the goal of impression management because they are frequent occurrences in the transcripts and consistent with the relationship development literature that notes that early interactions repress disagreements (Altman & Taylor, 1973). Reciprocal agreements implicitly convey that image claims will be accepted, that impression management is recognized as a goal for explaining the behavior of the interactants. That agreements are recognized as establishing similarity is evident from the course of the discourse. Agreements spawn topic development indicating that the speaker assumes common ground as a basis for the talk. In this example, an initial agreement begins a much lengthier complaint that provides multiple opportunities to establish similarity:

Example 3
M: It's hell out there. I can't live with my parents.
F: I'm sick of it already.
M: Yeah.
F: And it's only been a month and a half.
M: Yeah. I just can't live with my parents. My father does not understand how anyone could drink during a week night.
F: Mom doesn't either.

A speaker's continuation of a topic and further elaboration indicate a clear recognition that the agreement is to be understood as establishing similarity, providing the base for continued topic development. In fact, in those rare instances in which disagreements do occur in initial interactions, they are treated as requiring repair and the interactants collaborate to restore a mutual recognition of the importance of appearing to share similar attitudes and values:

Example 4
C: I was gonna go to Ohio State and I changed—it was just too big.
J: If I had it to do all over again, I think I would go there.
C: Really?
J: Just because of that very reason.
C: I don't know—I just—This place is big man, there's a lot of people here, man.
J: I think that. But Ohio State is—the bigness is what appeals to me most.
C: Oh.

> J: I think because there's so much variety not only in the college but in the town itself. There's a lot more that Columbus offers I think than Bowling Green.
>
> C: Yeah. Actually we just went to Ohio State over the weekend. It's pretty wild down there compared to here.

Although it takes a series of turns to accomplish, the disagreement is rectified and the interactants are eventually able to move to a position that does not threaten their image claims.

Thus, two concrete appositions are demonstrated within the context of initial interactions. The goal of obtaining information is linked to the behavior of asking questions and the goal of impression management is tied to the behavior of agreements. That appositions are available to interactants as they attempt to generate behavior appropriate to the situation is evident in the frequency of their occurrence across dyads. That these behaviors are recognized by interpreters as linked to particular goals becomes apparent as the unfolding discourse reaffirms the interactants' shared understanding of these appositions-in-use.

This should not be taken to suggest that each goal motivates a distinct behavior that is independent of other goals for the discourse. Rather, a more extensive treatment acknowledges that interactants' behaviors are motivated by multiple goals simultaneously and requires coordination of the purposes of both partners. Obtaining information and impression management are simultaneously attended to by the speaker. The attention to multiple goals influences the choice of behaviors produced. Consider why the conventional strategies for obtaining information (e.g., asking questions, self-disclosure, verbal attenders) are adopted when other behaviors, like demanding the information, bribery, or intimidation, could accomplish the same goal. These behaviors are inappropriate because they blatantly fail to attend to the goal of impression management. In contrast, the strategy of question asking can simultaneously elicit information and create the impression of friendly attentiveness. The same is true of impression management, for other possible lines of action can accomplish the goal of creating similarity. Imitating the partner's behaviors is a possible option but this strategy provides no additional information and is risky when knowledge of the other is minimal. The strategy that is used, that of agreements, encourages the partner to continue talk on a common topic, providing more information while simultaneously establishing the image of similarity for the listener.

It is possible to establish that goals are interdependent by considering the differences that would occur in the discourse if it were generated from a single goal. If obtaining information was the only goal (as uncertainty theory suggests), interactants would ask questions that would gather discriminating information. Yet, the questions prevalent in initial interactions request superficial information (e.g., major, hometown, weather) creating minimal risk and insuring that image claims are not challenged. The requests are limited to those that elicit cursory descriptive data and are minimally useful in assessing the partner. Even the structure of the discourse would be altered if this single goal motivated the acts of the interactants. The most efficient means for gathering data would direct the interactant to ask all the questions and the partner to provide answers, resembling an interview format (Gorden, 1980). Yet, Berger (1979) indicates that initial interactions conventionally eschew extensive questioning by one party. An obvious reason is that an interview structure does not allow the interactant to accomplish both the goals of obtaining information and impression management. The interactant occupied by asking all of the questions focuses on the partner and does not have the chance to develop self-descriptions, an important behavioral strategy for creating a positive image. Instead, initial interactions are loosely structured by alternating turns in which each member of the dyad provides data for establishing an impression and seeks information for making a judgment of the partner:

Example 5
W: Are you taking a lot of classes this summer?
B: No. Just two classes right now. Just two classes for this four weeks. I need—I'm gonna work my ass off to get two A's.
W: Mm. That's gonna be tough.
B: Yeah. How many classes you takin?

Example 6
S: So what's your major?
L: I'm a botany major.
S: What's that?
L: Uh. Flowers and plants.
S: Ooh.
L: How about you?

In addition, the structure is suited to the coordination of both interactants' intentions for both need an opportunity to obtain information and build an impression. The loosely structured question–answer chains allow interactants to alternate roles. An interactant asks a question to obtain information and in providing that information, the partner is able to present an image; and in a following sequence, the partner reciprocates and asks a question to gain information while the interactant is given the opportunity to provide a positive self description. Schlenker (1980) describes the same phenomenon, "people usually go out of their way when meeting new acquaintances to ask them about themselves, and they hope that the acquaintances reciprocate. People are usually delighted when an audience requests self-descriptions, since they are then free to introduce pertinent information for identity construction" (p. 169).

Appositions explain how a speaker with a goals or multiple goal is able to enact behaviors that address the goals and how a hearer, in a general sense, is able to connect behaviors back to goals to assign meaning to acts. But, appositions do not explain how a speaker comes to have a goal appropriate to the situation or how a hearer frames the behavior within the context of probable goals. Thus, the discussion moves to a second level of discourse organization and considers plans and scripts as the structures within which appositions are applied.

PLANS AND SCRIPTS

Before an interactant can access appositions and connect a behavior to a goal, the appropriate goals must be selected from the myriad of possible purposes for an interaction. The appropriateness is largely dependent on the nature of the situation. Interactants are confronted with situations that are novel or recurrent. A novel situation demands a plan for identifying possible goals, whereas a recurrent situation calls forth a script, isolating conventional goals for the situation. This section of the chapter describes the nature of plans and scripts, and illustrates the observations concerning scripts through initial interactions.

Plans

A situation is novel when an interactant is unable to call forth appropriate goals from memory. These situations require the interactant to create goals while the interaction is in progress. An interactant might generate a plan for an excursion to an expensive store, an experience at a gay bar, or an interview for an academic job. This is akin to the practices required to execute Schutz's (1964) stranger role. To examine members' taken for granted practices, he suggests that research-ers place themselves in situations in which they accomplish practical activities while lacking all knowledge of the conventions that allow them to do so. The stranger can not rely on the natural attitude, "the general feeling of being in a world known in common with others," (Schwartz & Jacobs, 1979, p. 240) but must improvise and proceed by trial and error. With plans, the situation is unique and the interactants must rely on the context to generate goals to direct the improvisation. The presence of objects, the appearance of the partner, the part-ner's discourse, and the physical surroundings may be searched for appropriate goals. Subjects in one of the conditions for Burke's (this volume) water pump task were placed in a room containing the pieces of the water pump and simply told to make an object that utilized all the pieces. Even without explicit goals to direct their actions, the presence of the pieces in the context suggests the goal of determining a piece-by-piece connection. The context provides the source for goals.

As a speaker constructs a plan, it comes to contain goals for the interaction and a structure for organizing those goals to provide coherence for extended behavior. Interpreters also have access to clues from the context but they do not know which elements have influenced the speaker's goals and must construct their own plans for the discourse. The interpreter witnesses only the behavior of the partner and through appositions is able to infer probable goals accounting for the acts. Speakers and hearers do not share an understanding of the key constituents of the situation and thus conventions concerning goals and behaviors are absent.

It must be noted that this is not the sense in which plans are described in the literature. Plans are viewed as the connection between intentions and action (Burke, this volume; Miller, Galanter, & Pribram, 1960; Schank & Abelson, 1977). This implies that plans are accessible to speakers and interpreters and are distinguishable from scripts by the reliance upon general rather than specific knowledge for connecting the goal to the behavior. This definition leads to the unfortunate confusion between interpretive schemes that connect the situation to intentions (plans/scripts) and those that link goals and behaviors (appositions). Although it is evident that these schemes are intertwined, they operate at different levels of discourse organization. In a plan, the goals that feed into an apposition are created through the context and the interpreter must search a wider array of explanations for the behavior; in a script, the goals are pre-established through convention for the situation and the interpreter accesses a more limited set of appositions to make sense of the behavior. So, although speech acts ignore the appropriateness of the goals, the distinctions offered here explicitly address the origin of the intentions. And, although cognitive science accounts offer noninteractive explanations of discourse, this perspective recognizes that interactants have multiple goals and must coordinate their intentions through their discourse. This perspective is able to offer an account that addresses the origin of intentions and the relationship between acts. It is able to acknowledge both the repetitive rule governed nature of discourse and describe the collaboration between interactants as the discourse unfolds.

Scripts

Scripts are available for recurrent situations. When an interactant has repeated personal experience or has knowledge of the social conventions for a recognizable episode from others, a script for that situation can be called forth from memory.[5] For example, an individual is likely to have a script for bank transactions, classroom interactions, court proceedings, and initial interactions. Goals and behaviors need not be created anew, for the interpretive scheme of scripts organizes experience by episodes that allow individuals to store and recall conventional goals and behaviors by situation. Hence, scripts are available to both speakers

---

[5]Scripts are shared when interactants have social knowledge regarding the convention of the script or when interactants develop their own conventions over repeated experience with a particular interactant.

and interpreters. Speakers identify a recognizable situation, access appropriate goals and design, and call up conventional behaviors for displaying their intentions. Interpreters call forth the appropriate script and access socially shared understandings governing the interaction. The script channelizes the interpreters' inferences, restricting those appositions that must be considered for assigning meaning to the act.

Social episodes are stored in memory with their standard staging requirements for the performance of the script (e.g., number of people, physical surroundings, necessary relationships and roles, appearance, and purpose). For example, a doctor visit script requires the presence of a doctor, nurse, and patient; specifies a subordinate relationship for the patient to the nurse and for the nurse to the doctor; and indicates the physical surroundings for a doctor's office (e.g., a waiting room with outdated magazines, examining rooms with medical apparatus in full display). The script also specifies that the purpose of a doctor visit is for the patient to convey information to the doctor concerning a medical condition and for the doctor to provide a diagnosis and treatment of that condition. The staging requirements of the script distinguish it from other scripts. The speaker comes to a situation, assesses the staging requirements by examining the context, and determines possible goals. These requirements are compared with the repertoire of scripts stored in memory and if a match occurs, that script is selected to guide the performance. To convey to the hearer that a particular script is being called forth, the speaker chooses acts that acknowledge the staging requirements of the script. Having recognized the script, the interpreter selects the means for coordinating their own intentions with those of their partner. This may involve following the script placed into performance by the speaker or negotiating an alternative scheme for punctuating the discourse. If the former is selected, the interactant produces behaviors that the partner will recognize as consistent with the script, whereas the latter option will direct the interactant to enact behaviors belonging to an alternate script or signal the development of a plan uniquely adapted to the situation.

Scripts vary in their degree of elaboration. Some scripts contain detailed goals and specifically delineate acceptable behavior (e.g., wedding rituals) whereas other scripts are more loosely organized (e.g., locker room talk). There are also individual differences in the degree of elaboration for particular scripts. An individual with an elaborated script for classroom interactions may have distinct tracks for seminar and large lecture classroom interactions with a consequent effect on behavior. Or, an individual with an elaborated script may have a more extended behavioral repertoire for accomplishing the goals or instantiate behaviors in more ways than the individual with an unelaborated script. Scripts are initially built up from previous experience and the continual exposure to new experiences introduces individual differences. Meaning is still possible as long as there are essential similarities. Thus, the elaboration of scripts are seen as refinements rather than changes in the essential nature of the script.

In this description, scripts involve conscious attention. This is contrary to recent social scientific theory in general (Langer, 1978; Triandis, 1980) and communication theory (Berger & Douglas, 1982; Berger & Roloff, 1982), which accuse theorists of overattributing conscious thought to the social actor and identify scripts as routine mindless enactments. Evidence for their position is garnered from research that concludes that scripts improve recall (Chiesi, Spillich, & Voss, 1979; Spillich, Vesonder, Chiesi, & Voss, 1979), individuals recall information implied by a script but not stated directly (Bower, Black, & Turner, 1979), out-of-script actions are remembered more than actions consistent with the script (Bower, Black, & Turner, 1979; Graesser, Gordon, & Sawyer, 1979), within script behaviors are responded to in expected ways (Langer, 1978; Langer, Blank, & Chanowitz, 1978), and scripts influence performance in familiar situations (Langer & Wiemann, 1981). Berger and Douglas (1982) argue that "Persons frequently may *not* have clear sets of interaction goals or strategies in mind before, during, or after their encounters with others" (p. 43, emphasis original) and imply that knowing that an interactant has clear goals is evidenced by their ability to recreate them for the researcher. In contrast, Toulmin (1982) indicates that there are degrees of consciousness. At a minimal level, sensibility is a basic sensory responsiveness and awareness of the situation. Attentiveness requires that we act with due attention or readiness to monitor some sequence of events in which we are involved. Articulateness is the ability to give an explicit account of the character of our actions. The degree of consciousness required by Berger and Douglas is at this highest level, having ignored the other senses in which consciousness is possible. An alternative explanation is that individuals are attentive but sometimes unable to articulate their intentions because of the pervasiveness of the natural attitude. Their attentiveness accounts for their ability to recall, fill in implied information, act consistently within the script and so on. These results would not be possible if human beings were mindless.

Consider the points at which consciousness may enter into the production and comprehension of scripts. The speaker must choose between a plan and a script and must select the appropriate script from the repertoire of scripts stored in memory. Cicourel (1974) argues that this selection process involves active processing that evaluates the fit between a schema and available data. To understand the behaviors, the interpreter determines if a plan or a script is appropriate, which script is being enacted, and chooses to follow the script or to advocate an alternative framework for organizing the discourse. Even when a script is enacted by a speaker and recognized by a partner, the coordination of intentions requires conscious monitoring to determine if each behavior is in script or signals a change in script, to detect movement from one goal to another, and to recognize within script behaviors addressing multiple goals. This description rejects a noninteractive explanation of scripted discourse, emphasizing that "the environment, our cognitive scripts, and the goals interact to determine our behavior.

These behaviors change the environment which might change our goals, scripts, and subsequent behaviors" (Schlenker, 1980, p. 41).

Once again, initial interactions provide an extended example to illustrate the conclusions regarding scripts for these interactions are "highly ritualized [and] evidence considerable control by social rules and norms" (Berger, Gardner, Parks, Schulman, & Miller, 1976, p. 161). Consideration of the interpretive schemes for connecting situations to their appropriate intentions brings forth the question: How is it that we recognize situations in which the initial interaction script is appropriate? And, what are the staging requirements that distinguish this script from others? Initially, the script requires individuals with some form of proximity to one another who have minimal knowledge of each other. The script also requires that both parties are willing to converse, because individuals are frequently in contact with strangers where no script is necessary because interactions do not take place. Knapp (1978) notes that interactants in the initiating stage exhibit their openness to discourse through nonverbal indicators such as gaze, openness in body position, and facial expressions (e.g., smiles, the "come hither" look). Although initial interactions can occur in a variety of contexts, basic to each is at least an acceptance of "non-task talk" and in some situations, the encouragement of this form of discourse. This is made apparent early in the discourse as this interaction between a secretary and an incoming student illustrates:

Example 7
Student: Hi! How are you? What's new?
Secretary: What can I help you with?
Student: Uh. Nothing really.
Secretary: Oh. (Resumes typing and student leaves)

The student introduces an act meant to elicit non-task talk while the secretary makes it clear that this form of discourse is not accepted in the office. Elements of the situation may be arranged to actually encourage non-task talk. Recently, I attended the first meeting of the College at a new university. As I entered, I was given a name tag and a colored carnation that signified that I was a new faculty member. I had initially expected this meeting to include a "State of the College" address by the Dean and a formal introduction of new faculty members. But, upon entering the meeting room, I found that all of the chairs had been pushed up against the wall, wine and food tables dominated the center of the room, small groups of individuals mingled, and my colored carnation immediately provided an initial topic of conversation. Elements within this situation clearly signalled that the initial interaction script, with the track for interacting with other faculty members, was the more appropriate script.

Given these elements of the situation, the goals of obtaining information and impression management are particularly relevant. Interactants come together with minimal knowledge of each other and are desirous of, or even expected in some situations, to interact. But, doing sustained conversation requires enough knowledge of the partner to introduce topics that will generate discourse. In the absence of such knowledge, the goal of obtaining information becomes central because each question–answer sequence can reveal possible topics to sustain the conversation. With minimal knowledge, interactants are also unable to assess the utility of these new relationships. The information gathered through the initial interaction is used to form an impression of the other. If the partner can provide assistance in securing future goals, the interactant wants to have created a favorable impression. Interactants attend to impression management to keep the opportunity open for renewing the relationship if they assess the partner favorably. Thus, the goals arise from the character of the situation.

When an interactant recognizes that the staging requirements for a particular script are met within a given situation, their choice must be conveyed to the partner. The selection of a particular script becomes recognizable through the speaker's acts. To communicate the choice of script, interactants acknowledge that the staging requirements for the script are present in this situation. In initial interactions, interactants invariably begin with the exchange of names (e.g., "Maybe we should start by getting to know each other's names"). This beginning makes it obvious that both interactants recognize that they have minimal knowledge of the other. In addition, the mutual use of questions to obtain descriptive information continues to reaffirm an understanding that this staging requirement is met. Acts are also chosen to display the acceptance of non-task talk. Questions directed at eliciting elaborated self-descriptions make it clear that personal rather than task talk is considered appropriate and a willingness to answer such queries with elaborated descriptions indicates a shared understanding of the nature of the situation. In some cases, interactants explicitly negotiate for the acceptance of non-task talk (e.g., "No more shop talk. I want to hear about you") and make reference to those elements of the situation that promote non-task talk (e.g., "This is such a great bar for just talking to people"). Shared knowledge of the social episode directs interactants to look to particular constituents of the situation. When an interactant's acts indicate a mutual recognition of a situation that meets the staging requirements of a script, further acts become understandable through the appositions contained in the script.

Interactants engage in communication to accomplish goals that require the assistance of others. Interaction makes these goals available and interactants coordinate their intentions to accomplish social action. The goals for a particular interaction arise from the character of the situation. In plans, the goals that are plausible are determined by a search of the available cues in the context. Speakers and interpreters do not share an understanding of the key constituents of the situation or the goals appropriate to the context. In scripts, interactants share knowledge of the discriminating features of social episodes and their relevant goals. Speakers and interpreters need only make their selection of scripts apparent through their choice of acts. Although plans and scripts connect situations to goals, appositions function within these units to provide the interpretive device for linking goals to behaviors. A speaker can translate objectives into lines of action whereas an interpreter can utilize the device to give the act meaning by imbuing it with purpose. Of course, the nature of language and the human beings using it, introduce complexity to this basic relationship. Multiple acts can accomplish a single purpose; multiple purposes may be accomplished by the same act and may influence the character of the act; and interactants pursue different goals that must be coordinated to successfully accomplish social action. Interaction is the joint product of this continual jockeying to reaffirm and in some cases, to repudiate understandings between interactants. Initial interactions provide an extended example in this chapter of interactants' recognition and display of a script and their affirmation of appositions-in-use appropriate to this particular script.

REFERENCES

Altman, I., & Taylor, D. A. (1973). *Social penetration: The development of interpersonal relationships.* New York: Holt, Rinehart & Winston.

Austin, J. L. (1962). *How to do things with words.* J. O. Urmson (Ed.). London: Oxford University Press.

Ayres, J. (1983). Strategies to maintain relationships: Their identification and perceived usage. *Communication Quarterly, 31,* 62–67.

Baxter, L. A. (1982). Strategies for ending relationships: Two studies. *Western Journal of Speech Communication, 46,* 223–241.

Berger, C. R. (1973). *The acquaintance process revisited: Explorations in initial interaction.* Paper presented at the meeting of the Speech Communication Association, New York.

Berger, C. R. (1979). Beyond initial interaction: Uncertainty, understanding, and the development of interpersonal relationships. In H. Giles & R. N. St. Clair (Eds.), *Language and social psychology* (pp. 122–144). Oxford: Basil Blackwell.

Berger, C. R., & Bradac, J. J. (1982). *Language and social knowledge: Uncertainty in interpersonal relations.* London: Edward Arnold.

Berger, C. R., & Calabrese, R. J. (1975). Some explorations in initial interaction and beyond: Toward a developmental theory of interpersonal communication. *Human Communication Research, 1,* 99–112.

Berger, C. R., & Douglas, W. (1982). Thought and talk: "Excuse me, but have I been talking to myself?" In F. E. X. Dance (Ed.), *Human communication theory: Comparative essays* (pp. 42–60). New York: Harper & Row.

Berger, C. R., Gardner, R. R., Parks, M. R., Schulman, L., & Miller, G. R. (1976). Interpersonal epistemology and interpersonal communication. In G. R. Miller (Ed.), *Explorations in interpersonal communication* (Vol. V, pp. 149–172). Beverly Hills: Sage.

Berger, C. R., & Roloff, M. E. (1982). Thinking about friends and lovers: Social cognition and relational trajectories. In M. E. Roloff & C. R. Berger (Eds.), *Social cognition and communication* (pp. 151–192). Beverly Hills: Sage.

Bower, G. H., Black, J. B., & Turner, T. J. (1979). Scripts in memory for text. *Cognitive Psychology, 11,* 177–220.

Bowers, J. W., & Bradac, J. J. (1982). Issues in communication theory: A metatheoretical analysis. In M. Burgoon (Ed.), *Communication yearbook 5* (pp. 1–28). New Brunswick, NJ: Transaction/ ICA.

Burke, K. (1978). (Nonsymbolic) motion/(Symbolic) action. *Critical Inquiry, 4,* 809–822.

Calabrese, R. J. (1975). *The effects of privacy and probability of future interaction on interaction patterns.* Unpublished doctoral dissertation, Northwestern University, Evanston, IL.

Chiesi, H. L., Spillich, G. J., & Voss, J. F. (1979). Acquisition of domain-related information in relation to high and low domain knowledge. *Journal of Verbal Learning and Verbal Behavior, 18,* 257–273.

Cicourel, A. V. (1974). *Cognitive sociology: Language and meaning in social interaction.* New York: Free Press.

Clark, H. H. (1979). Responding to indirect speech acts. *Cognitive Psychology, 11,* 430–477.

Clark, H. H., & Lucy, P. (1975). Understanding what is meant from what is said: A study of conversationally conveyed requests. *Journal of Verbal Learning and Verbal Behavior, 14,* 56–72.

Clark, R. A., & Delia, J. G. (1976). The development of functional persuasive skills in childhood and early adolescence. *Child Development, 47,* 1008–1014.

Clark, R. A., & Delia, J. G. (1977). Cognitive complexity, social perspective-taking, and functional persuasive skills in second- to ninth-grade children. *Human Communication Research, 3,* 128–134.

Cushman, D. P., Valentinsen, B., & Dietrich, D. (1982). A rules theory of interpersonal relationships. In F. E. X. Dance (Ed.), *Human communication theory: Comparative essays* (pp. 90–119). New York: Harper & Row.

Delia, J. G., Kline, S. L., & Burleson, B. R. (1979). The development of persuasive communication strategies in kindergarteners through twelfth-graders. *Communication Monographs, 46,* 241–256.

Delia, J. G., O'Keefe, B. J., & O'Keefe, D. J. (1982). The constructivist approach to communication. In F. E. X. Dance (Ed.), *Human communication theory: Comparative essays* (pp. 147–191). New York: Harper & Row.

Fogarty, D. (1959). *Roots for a new rhetoric.* New York: Russell & Russell.

Frankfurt, L. (1965). *The role of some individual and interpersonal factors on the acquaintance process.* Unpublished doctoral dissertation, American University, Washington, DC.

Garfinkel, H. (1967). *Studies in ethnomethodology.* Englewood Cliffs, NJ: Prentice-Hall.

Gorden, R. L. (1980). *Interviewing: Strategy, techniques, and tactics.* Homewood, IL: Dorsey.

Graesser, A. C., Gordon, S. E., & Sawyer, J. D. (1979). Recognition memory for typical and atypical actions in scripted activities: Tests of the script pointer + tag hypothesis. *Journal of Verbal Learning and Verbal Behavior, 18,* 319–332.

Grice, H. P. (1975). Logic and Conversation. In P. Cole & J. L. Morgan (Eds.), *Syntax and Semantics: Speech Acts* (Vol. 3, pp. 41–58). New York: Academic Press.

Jones, E., & Davis, K. (1965). From acts to dispositions: The attribution process in person perception. In L. Berkowitz (Ed.), *Advances in experimental social psychology.* (Vol. 2, pp. 219–266). New York: Academic Press.

Knapp, M. L. (1978). *Nonverbal communication in human interaction* (2nd ed.). New York: Holt, Rinehart, & Winston.

Langer, E. J. (1978). Rethinking the role of thought in social interaction. In J. H. Harvey, W. Ickes, & R. F. Kidd (Eds.), *New directions in attribution research* (Vol. 2, pp. 35–58). Hillsdale, NJ: Lawrence Erlbaum Associates.

Langer, E. J., Blank, A., & Chanowitz, B. (1978). The mindlessness of ostensibly thoughtful action: The role of "placebic" information in interpersonal interaction. *Journal of Personality and Social Psychology, 36,* 635–642.

Langer, E. J., & Wiemann, C. (1981). When thinking disrupts performance: Mindfulness on an overlearned task. *Personality and Social Psychology Bulletin, 7,* 240–243.

Miller, G., Boster, F., Roloff, M. E., & Seibold, D. (1977). Compliance-gaining message strategies: A typology and some findings concerning effects of situational differences. *Communication Monographs, 44,* 37–51.

Miller, G. A., Galanter, E., & Pribram, K. H. (1960). *Plans and the structure of behavior.* New York: Holt, Rinehart, & Winston.

Motl, J. R. (1980). *Attitudes, attraction, and nonverbal indicators of uncertainty in initial interaction.* Unpublished doctoral dissertation, Northwestern University, Evanston, IL.

Roloff, M. E. (1976). Communication strategies, relationships, and relational changes. In G. R. Miller (Ed.), *Explorations in interpersonal communication* (pp. 173–195). Beverly Hills: Sage.

Schank, R. C., & Abelson, R. P. (1977). *Scripts, plans, goals, and understanding: An inquiry into human knowledge structures.* Hillsdale, NJ: Lawrence Erlbaum Associates.

Schlenker, B. R. (1980). *Impression management: The self-concept, social identity, and interpersonal relations.* Monterey, CA: Brooks/Cole.

Schutz, A. (1964). *Collected papers II: Studies in social theory.* Martinus Nijhoff: The Hague.

Schwartz, H., & Jacobs, J. (1979). *Qualitative sociology: A method to the madness.* New York: Free Press.

Searle, J. R. (1969). *Speech acts: An essay in the philosophy of language.* Cambridge: Cambridge University Press.

Spillich, G. J., Vesonder, G. T., Chiesi, H. L., & Voss, J. F. (1979). Text processing of domain-related information for individuals with high and low domain knowledge. *Journal of Verbal Learning and Verbal Behavior, 18,* 275–290,.

Toulmin, S. (1982). The genealogy of "consciousness." In P. F. Secord (Ed.), *Explaining human behavior: Consciousness, human action, and social structure* (pp. 53–70). Beverly Hills: Sage.

Triandis, H. C. (1980). Values, attitudes, and interpersonal behavior. In M. M. Page (Ed.), *Nebraska Symposium on Motivation 1979* (pp. 195–260). Lincoln, NE: University of Nebraska Press.

13 Goals in Discourse

Robert T. Craig
Temple University

The preceding chapters by Burke, Diez, and Benoit and Follert rest heavily on the assumption that discourse is directed toward goals. Each attempts to evidence relationships between features of discourse and certain goals toward which the discourse is supposed to be directed.

The assumption that human behavior is goal-oriented is not, of course, peculiar to these studies. In various forms it pervades several literatures mentioned in the chapters: speech act theory and pragmatics generally, cognitive science, attribution theory, rules theories, and studies of strategic communicative choices in contexts such as negotiation, conflict, compliance-gaining, and interpersonal relationship development. Furthermore, a practical discipline of communication to which the concept of goal would not be central is difficult to imagine; and the pragmatic language of goal, decision, and consequence is in fact the common coin of the discipline of speech communication that has emerged in the United States in this century. Within that discipline it is widely assumed that communicative competence can be improved, that people can become more effective by becoming more aware of their goals, and more practiced in adapting communicative means to achieve them. Such a discipline becomes incoherent unless principled relations can be established between this fundamentally pragmatic orientation and the terms in which theory and research are couched (Craig, 1983, 1984).

But despite the evident importance of the concept and its widespread use, no fully adequate account of goals in discourse has, to my knowledge, yet emerged; nor do I have such an account to propose in this chapter. I can only indicate a few of the problems that research in this area faces and offer some distinctions that might be helpful in approaching those problems. If we take the preceding chapters to represent the present state of thought about goals in discourse, a comparative study of goal-related concepts as they are used in the chapters suggests at least four distinctions that may prove helpful to research in this area: (a) between functional and intentional goals; (b) between positive and dialectical goals; (c) between formal and strategic goals; and (d) among several bases for drawing the inference that a given discourse is directed toward a certain goal. The following sections take up each of these topics in turn.

FUNCTIONAL AND INTENTIONAL GOALS

All of the chapters take a purposive, goal-oriented view of human behavior, but they differ in their specific uses of the terms *goal, purpose* and *intention*. Benoit and Follert appear to use these words interchangeably. Diez refers indifferently to a "sense of goal or purpose," but does not use the term *intention*. Burke, however, finds it necessary to distinguish formally between goals and intentions, for she holds that "communicative intentions are generated by plans and goals." Burke conceives a speaker's communicative intention, following speech act theory (Searle, 1969), to be the action that the speaker performs by making a certain utterance; whereas she understands goal in the fashion of cognitive science (Hobbs & Evans, 1980) to be a cognitive representation of the state of the world that would result from a sequence of actions known as a *plan*. Thus, for Burke, communicative intentions are explained as a consequence of the adoption of goals that can be achieved by following plans that include certain speech acts as components.

What I particularly notice in this formulation is the mixture of two terminologies, the one a teleological, intentionalistic terminology to which concepts like intention and action are central, the other a mechanistic (at best quasi-teleological), functionalistic terminology centered on concepts of cognitive representation and processing. My point is not to deprecate this mixture but to draw attention to the fact that two rather different traditions of thought about the goal-orientation of human behavior are involved. Burke is explicitly critical of both traditions, scoring against speech act theory its failure to account for discourse processing, and against cognitive science its overly mechanistic, computational models. Benoit and Follert mix the two perspectives, but less sytematically than Burke. Diez, in contrast, remains consistently within the action-theoretic tradition (though she does not make use of speech act theory); she is concerned not with cognitive mechanisms by which the mind does things but rather with constitutive rules according to which communicative acts possess significance.

Mixing action-theoretic and cognitive terminologies may not be a bad thing to do, but it requires care to avoid equivocating between two senses in which one might refer to the *goal* of a speaker: an intentional interpretation according to which the speaker consciously intends to bring about a certain state of affairs by means of discourse versus a functional interpretation according to which discourse is best described from the standpoint of an external observer in terms of its functional relation to a certain outcome—the relation mediated, perhaps, by the speaker's "cognitive representation" of the situation. *Cognitive representation* is a functional property of systems such that they incorporate information mapping their environments; the term carries no implication of a conscious mind. The intentional and functional interpretations of goal are not necessarily incompatible with each other. To combine them may be useful or even necessary for some purposes. Nevertheless—indeed, partly for the very reason that one might wish to combine them—it is important to be clear about the distinction and its implications.

For one thing, intentional and functional interpretations are associated with different methodological orientations. Cognitive science tends to embrace a particular species of methodological behaviorism that imposes disciplined limits upon reification. That is, cognitive "things" such as goals legitimately can be said to exist only insofar as they can be shown to play some definite functional role in producing behavior. Cognitive objects are thus defined in terms of their roles in cognitive processes. Schank and Abelson (1977), for example, conceive of goals as cognitive objects that play a certain part in understanding discourse. Goals do not always enter into the process of understanding, and the conditions and ways in which they "must" (in view of what must be accomplished in order to understand discourse) become involved, even though complex, are marked off with some precision. In a functionalist account of discourse production it might similarly be necessary at certain points to call upon a class of cognitive objects (which one might, for heuristic or rhetorical purposes, refer to as goals). When, how, and at how many different levels of analysis one would suppose this class of objects to come into play would depend on one's model of discourse production. The evidence for the model would show that it accomplishes the necessary functions of discourse production.[1]

Does a similarly rigorous methodology exist for dealing with intentional concepts? Searle's (1983) work on intentionality productively combines methods of phenomenological and linguistic analysis. To illustrate how this differs from functionalism, consider one difficulty faced by the study of goals in discourse: that the "same" goal can often be subjected to multiple and quite various descriptions. For example, in a recent colloquium, one of my colleagues presented an experimental study of criticism-giving in which speakers were described as attempting to achieve both "task goals" (conveying the criticism clearly and efficiently) and "social-relational goals" (avoiding damage to the relationship or loss of face by the speaker or the hearer). Another colleague suggested that this

---

[1]Benoit and Follert follow parts of this pattern of reasoning in drawing their distinction between plans and scripts, which involve different processes of arriving at goals. What they fail to consider is how this distinction might be tested, rather than merely illustrated, by reference to data.

characterization is arbitrary and that the situation might as well be described in terms of the single overarching goal of giving effective criticism. Further discussion revealed that still other descriptions of the speakers' goals were possible, for example, in terms of compliance with the experimental instructions. Here the complexity of the speaker's action is revealed, but in a rather confusing way, by the possibility of multiple descriptions. A functionalist might attempt to cohere these descriptions by defining several "functional levels of analysis" such that lower level functions specify in finer detail how higher level functions are accomplished. Descriptions that would not fit into this scheme would not be admitted. Or the situation might be described in terms of a problem-solving process in which the speaker searches for a single course of action that satisfies multiple constraints.[2]

Searle (1983), in contrast, approaches this kind of problem in terms of complex intentions:

> Consider Gavrilo Princip and his murder of the Archduke Franz Ferdinand in Sarajevo. Of Princip we say that he:
>   pulled the trigger
>   fired the gun
>   shot the Archduke
>   killed the Archduke
>   struck a blow against Austria
>   avenged Serbia (p. 98)

Searle's example illustrates "the accordian effect," the expandability of complex intentions. The elements of the list are related to each other in various ways, but they have in common that they are all descriptions of the same intentional act. Quite different, says Searle, are many other descriptions that could be added to the list. For example, adding descriptions "below" the complex intention, one might say of Princip that he:

> produced certain neuron firings in his brain
> contracted certain muscles in his hand and arm

Or, adding descriptions "above" the complex intention, one could say that he:

> ruined Lord Gray's summer season
> convinced the Emporer Franz Josef that God was punishing the family
> angered Wilhelm II
> started the First World War

---

[2]The problem of multiple descriptions is one aspect of the more general problem of goal complexity, which is taken up in the next section.

Although these may be perfectly good descriptions of what Princip did, being functionally related to his act in various ways, they do not (presumably) fall within the scope of his intention. The logic of intentionality reflected here provides a disciplined basis, quite different from the logic of functionalism, for ordering descriptions of an action and considering only some of them to be goals (aspects of the complex intention).[3]

A further implication is that the functional, but not the intentional, interpretation of goals makes it possible to speak coherently of "emergent" or systemic goals distinct from the intentional goals of individuals. Various interactive processes, for example the processes of relational complementarity and symmetry that students of interpersonal communication have found important (Watzlawick, Beavin, & Jackson, 1967), may produce in discourse an apparent order and direction only mediately related to goals consciously pursued by individual speakers. Taking this approach, one would expect to find that the interaction of speakers displays systemic properties such as equifinality, warranting the conclusion that their discourse is directed to emergent goals. The intense information-exchange pattern often found in initial conversations between strangers, might, for example, emerge from systemic processes not unlike the escalation of relational symmetry, the speakers getting caught up in a "logic" leading to outcomes that neither speaker directly intents (compare Pearce & Cronen, 1980, on "logical force").

At another level, the distinction between functional and intentional goals suggests the need to investigate the relation between goal-consciousness and goal-seeking behavior. Even though it may be true, as Searle (1983) claims, that a person can always answer the question, What are you doing now?, the answer to this question may not correspond to the person's goal in a functional sense. Speakers' reports of their goals are often vague and inarticulate. Such reports can be, from a functional point of view, demonstrably wrong (Nisbett & Wilson, 1977). People sometimes even deny having any goals, as I have heard undergraduates in communication classes deny that they pursue goals in informal social conversations, an assertion with which I tend to disagree, as would, I assume, Benoit and Follert. These authors emphasize that certain conditions increase our awareness of goals. One does become aware of having goals in discourse, for example wanting to get a certain piece of information from a certain person. This experience suggests that conscious goals are sometimes very clear and do in fact control discourse. Or one may be quite conscious of having a goal, which, for some reason (perhaps lack of knowing how, or lack of opportunity) one is not actively pursuing. The recent tendency of writers on social cognition and communication is to characterize goal-awareness as being

---

[3]I do not mean to suggest that it is necessarily easy to analyze a given case, such as the criticism-giving study mentioned earlier, in either functionalist or intentionalist terms. My point is just that the two types of analysis differ.

a matter of degree and to caution that the degree is often quite low (Berger & Douglas, 1982; Spitzberg & Cupach, 1984). The development of communication competence may be, from one point of view, a process in which progressively more complex goals are internalized as "tacit knowledge," operating functionally but at low levels of awareness, whereas other, higher level goals become more easily accessible to consciousness. Thus the distinction between intentional and functional goals suggests the importance of investigating what Spitzberg and Cupach (1984) refer to as "the complex relationships between awareness and competence" (p. 83).

POSITIVE AND DIALECTICAL GOALS

A limitation shared by the three studies is that they examine only situations in which goals are considered to be relatively easy to identify, even while admitting that speakers in many natural situations pursue multiple goals in complex ways, or pursue goals that are vague, unstable, or otherwise indeterminate. How should goals be characterized in view of the diffuse, ambiguous states of consciousness in which speakers may often act? From that point of view, how can one make sense of the claim that discourse is goal-directed? What relationship between goals and discourse is implied? Reflection upon puzzles such as these suggests the importance of distinguishing between positive and dialectical conceptions of goal.

In Kenneth Burke's (1969) theory of rhetoric, positive terms refer to empirically observable objects (mouse, house), while dialectical terms refer to abstract principles (positivism, honesty). This distinction implies another which cuts at a bias across that between functional and intentional conceptions of goal. The distinction between positive and dialectical goals addresses not the relation of goals to consciousness but rather that of goals to behavior.

Positive goals are directly involved in a causal process of producing behavior. The computer model that pervades cognitive science would lead us to think of behavior as being directly under the control of goals that determine branching decisions within and among behavioral programs. Computers with their hierarchically organized programs do work this way, and so may people under some description.[4] But opponents of the computer model (e.g., Dreyfus, 1979) have argued that human cognition is open in ways that are radically different from the computer's deterministic "flow of control." Burke (this volume) is critical of the oversimplified accounts of goal-seeking that result from a strict application of the computer model. Openness, ambiguity, and indeterminacy are qualities of goals that seem inconsistent with the computer model of discourse production. It is possible, moreover, that many of the goals of discourse that are of most

---

[4]See Miller, Galanter, and Pribram (1960) for a particularly clear expression of this view.

interest to communication theory would have little or no part in even a very good computer-program model of discourse production, because they are related to behavior in a radically different way. These I propose to call *dialectical goals*.

Conceived dialectically, goals have a looser relation to behavior. The looseness is not just a matter of probability—the difference between positive and dialectical goals is not captured by a distinction between deterministic and probabilistic cognitive control of behavior. Dialectical goals may not be at all directly involved in producing discourse. To put the matter in terms of cognitive theory, dialectical goals may not represent projected outcomes of behavioral plans. High-level goals such as happiness and success are probably best conceived as dialectical goals. Such goals may apply to behavior largely after the fact or as conceptual heuristics that perform functions such as: (a) to interpret and critique behavior; (b) to "discover" goals retrospectively (e.g., to realize upon reflection that one must be more ambitious professionally than one had previously thought); (c) to fantasize about desired objects without reference to means of achieving them; (d) to rationalize behavior; and (e) to explain and justify behavior to others (giving accounts). Thus dialectical goals become involved in verbal–conceptual processes that do not directly "control" the behavior to which they "refer." This is not to say that dialectical goals have no influence on discourse, only that their influence may be indirect and complex in ways that have yet to be clarified.

Like the distinction between functional and intentional goals (to which it is related but not identical[5]), that between positive and dialectical goals does not mark an unbridgeable gap. Both concepts might be found useful, but only if the distinction and its implications are recognized. Consider, for example, implications for the conceptualization of goal indeterminacy, multiple goals, and communicative competence.

The problem of indeterminacy returns us to the questions that opened this section. If goals are often vague, unstable, or otherwise indeterminate, then how can one make sense of the claim that discourse is goal-directed? One obvious hypothesis is that goal-directedness is a matter of degree. From a positive point of view, this would imply that lower level goals (such as to mention a certain item of information at a certain point in a conversation) can emerge in local contexts as a result of free association, emotional response, or some other local

---

[5]The distinction between positive and dialectical goals is different from, though related to, that between functional and intentional goals. According to Searle's (1983) analysis of intentionality, intentions are causally related to actions and would thus count as positive goals in my terms; so positive goals can be interpreted intentionally. Dialectical goals can also be reduced to functional descriptions as, for example, in Schank and Abelson's (1977) theory of discourse understanding in which "themes," which in my terms could be thought of as dialectical goals of a sort, perform certain functions. The two distinctions are correlated, however. In order to speak coherently of intentions as causes, one must translate positive behavior into the language of action, which is essentially dialectical (in Kenneth Burke's sense). And the functional description of a dialectical goal effectively reduces it to positive terms.

contingency, while higher level goals that would structure larger chunks of discourse are either absent or impose only minimal constraints. The positive view assumes that discourse is always goal-directed at some level; degree of goal-directedness means degree of hierarchical organization constraining the selection of lower level goals. From a dialectical point of view, goals may be entirely absent, or they may be present (or potentially present) but only weakly influence behavior. Goals can be vague in the same ways that any verbal concept can be vague. One might, for example, feel that the goal of "motivating" one's subordinates is of utmost importance, yet have little sense of what that means or of what to say that would accomplish the goal in a given context.

Turning to the problem of multiple goals, one aspect of goal multiplicity, the fact that goals can be considered under multiple descriptions, was discussed in the previous section. Quite apart from that, however, people often face the need to do more than one thing at the same time, which considerably complicates the production and interpretation of discourse. Despite their efforts to select relatively structured situations for study, the chapters are not entirely successful in avoiding this problem. Burke ignores self-presentation goals that may influence the behavior of her subjects in important ways. Burke's apprentices may signal their lack of dependence on expert instructions, not only in order to cooperate efficiently in completing the task, but also, or perhaps even mainly, in order display their own intelligence and self-reliance. Sometimes, one would think, these goals must conflict, the apprentices' efforts to display independence of the instructions causing various errors and inefficiencies. Even Benoit and Follert, who provide an interesting analysis of the interdependence of information exchange and impression management goals in initial interactions, fail to consider that interactants in such situations must surely seek still other goals that may interact complexly with those characteristic of initial interactions. And Diez's assumption that the discourse strategies of negotiators represent a balance struck along the continuum between extremes of cooperation and competition is equally reductive. In short, simplified assumptions about the goals that speakers are seeking, even though perhaps necessary for certain research purposes, may obscure important aspects of the discourse. There is, then, the problem of conceptualizing multiple goals in discourse.

The existing literature on the multiple goal problem does not acknowledge a distinction between positive and dialectical goals, but the prevailing conception more closely resembles the positive type. Treatments of the problem by communication researchers (e.g., O'Keefe & Delia, 1982; Tracy & Moran, 1983) exhibit the same basic logic as do cognitive science studies that explicitly follow the computer model (e.g., Bruce & Newman, 1978; Wilensky, 1982).[6] Because

---

[6]McLaughlin (1984) concisely summarizes much of the cognitive science literature on goals in conversation.

goals are conceptualized as projected outcomes of behavioral plans, the basic options when faced with several goals at once are to search for a plan that satisfies all goals, perhaps by subsuming some goals under others, or a plan that strikes an optimal compromise between goals, or one that drops some goals in order to satisfy others.

Strikingly different is the work of Rawlins (1983a, 1983b) on the "dialectics" of friendship. His study of friends' discourse about their relationships reveals dilemmas inherent in the very idea of friendship that prevails in the culture. Friends should express their feelings openly, yet should support and protect each other's feelings; they should respect each other's freedom, yet should be available to give aid when needed. Of primary interest is not the precise way in which these goals are reflected in behavior, but rather the logical relationship among the goals themselves that accounts for their especially problematic character. Ideal friends give of themselves fully and freely and have only the most positive feelings for each other, which they can express openly without hesitation. Actual friends must occasionally experience the needs of their friend as a burden that restricts freedom, and must worry over the expression of ambivalent feelings and other potentially hurtful facts. Pairs of goals within the ideal—freedom and duty, openness and protectiveness—are contradictory, yet essentially interdependent: To fulfill both goals in a pair is impossible; to choose only one is to contradict the idea of friendship; to compromise between them is to suffer the guilty tug of both principles.

Contradiction and paradox are intrinsic to the dialectical mode of discourse, in which principles interact as pure ideas. Human beings as language users cannot, then, hope to avoid entirely dilemmas like those of friendship. From a positive point of view, such dilemmas must be worked out in actual behavior, the tug of principles being reduced to degrees of constraint in the selection of plans. Behavior is positive: It just "is"; it contains no contradictions or paradoxes, though it often displays tentativeness, disorganization, vacillation, and so on, that are the positive consequences of dialectical tensions. The notion of dialectical goals reminds us, however, that goals are ideas that emerge from the interaction of ideas and continue to be involved in psycho-logical processes apart from the production of behavior. Pragmatic paradox, logical force, and relational dialectics are among the concepts with which communication theorists have attempted to capture these dialectical phenomena. The implications of interactions among dialectical goals for the interpretation of goals in discourse are in need of inquiry.

Finally, a brief comment on the implications for communication competence. To find a plan that satisfies all goals is usually considered to indicate optimal communication competence (O'Keefe & Delia, 1982; Tracy & Moran, 1983). This, again, reflects an essentially positive conception of goals. How the competent speaker copes with contradictory or paradoxical dialectical goals is a question that communication theorists have failed to address. One would think that the development of competence involves an increasing ability to engage in discourse without lapsing uncontrollably into disorganizaton, vacillation, withdrawal, and so on, in the face of such difficulties.

FORMAL AND STRATEGIC GOALS

A third distinction that deserves more attention is that between formal and strategic goals. A formal interpretation of goals is implied by the view that conversation is essentially a matter of following conventional patterns or rules. From this perspective, speakers in initial interaction situations of the kind that Benoit and Follert describe follow certain patterns of information-exchange essentially because those patterns are conventionally expected in those situations. A formal goal is equivalent to the official purpose of a patterned event or sequence of acts, as the recitation of vows, bringing about the formal state of matrimony, is the goal of a marriage ceremony. A strategic interpretation, in contrast, assumes:

> that conversationists behave strategically in pursuit of their individual goals, and that whatever structure conversation may have emerges from this process. Rules and standard patterns are not simply followed but are used as resources to accomplish goals. Rules may be broken, transformed, or used in nonobvious ways. Or if rules are followed strictly, as in a sport or game, they may be only a constitutive framework in which non-rule-governed strategic options are played out. (Craig & Tracy, 1983, p. 15)[7]

That both formal and strategic goals exist is obvious to common sense, but the precise relation that should exist between them within a theory of goals in discourse is less obvious. This point occurred to me in connection with a tendency toward equivocation that is noticeable in Diez's theory of negotiation competence.

Diez characterizes the formal differences she observed between different types of negotiation as "constitutive rules" that "function to make an interaction competitive rather than cooperative in the same way that the rules of chess or football define the game by demarcating it from other games." Yet in the body of the chapter those same formal differences are explained by reference to negotiators' strategic use of the discourse to achieve outcomes such as persuasion or power. For example, competitive negotiators are said to make given information explicit

---

[7]Once again, as in the case of positive and dialectical goals, one must resist the temptation to conflate this with the functional-intentional distinction. The concept of strategic goal does not strictly assume intentionality even though it may strongly suggest it; nor does the concept of formal goal preclude intentionality. Computer programs follow problem-solving "strategies" that are defined in purely functional terms. Rules theories, in contract, typically explain intentional behavior by reference to the formal goals that actions pursue.

in order to strengthen their proposals and control equivocation. These explanations are not implausible but they are rather at odds with the view that negotiation competence consists essentially in knowing how to *constitute* interaction as competitive or cooperative by following conventional forms of discourse. The argument equivocates between form and strategy.

Benoit and Follert and Burke avoid this problem: the former by focusing on conventional aspects of initial interaction, the latter by focusing on strategic aspects of planning. What is needed, however, is a more adequate account of the complex, reflexive relations between form and strategy, an account which makes clear the essential interdependency of the two concepts (Craig & Tracy, 1983).

In this regard, Jacobs and Jackson's (1983) "rational model" of conversation as a chess-like game in which players generate coherent sequences of moves by making rational strategic choices within a framework of rules deserves close attention. One can raise questions about the model: whether speech act theory will finally prove too narrow a basis to support a truly general account of form and strategy; whether conversation, even at a level of "deep structure", is really a discrete, well-defined game like chess, whose rules are unaffected by contingencies of play. Nevertheless, the model, in its basic approach to integrating form and strategy, is highly suggestive. It suggests, for one thing, that the differences observed by Diez are not themselves constitutive rules of negotiation, but are instead discourse strategies rationally derived from deeper principles of negotiation, strategies that may indeed have become conventional though repeated use.

At a more general level, the project of integrating formal and strategic conceptions of goal has many other theoretical implications, only some of which can be mentioned briefly in the remainder of this section.

A model that integrated form and strategy would encourage recognition of the interplay between elements of convention and novelty in all situations. Benoit and Follert tend to imply a dichotomy between conventional and novel situations in arguing for the distinction between scripts (conventional forms) and plans (ad hoc strategies) as interpretive practices. Burke clearly expresses the view that discourse always occurs "in the stream of life in concrete situations" that afford speakers and hearers resources of background knowledge, including, presumably, knowledge of conventional forms, for interpreting their actions. This formulation neatly captures the interaction of novelty and convention, though Burke in her analysis does not attend very closely to the influence of conventional forms on the discourse.

A model that integrated form and strategy would similarly encourage recognition of the interplay of cooperative aspects of discourse with competitive and individualistic aspects. Each of the chapters more or less explicitly claims that cooperation is the fundamental purpose of communication, yet to varying degrees they also emphasize that speakers engage in discourse for their own individual purposes, and that the goals of interlocutors can be antagonistic. Burke and Benoit and Follert explicitly claim, as do Jacobs and Jackson (1983) in their rational model, that the basically cooperative structure of communication derives ultimately from individualistic, pragmatic necessity. As Burke puts it: "Individuals communicate with others because they have pragmatic goals requiring coordination and cooperation from them." Diez perhaps does not disagree with this view; and the main business of her study is, after all, to explicate the "competitive-cooperative continuum" of discourse. Yet even so, her claim, following Mehan, Fisher, and Maroules (1976), that the ultimate function of communication, whether "competitive" or "cooperative", is to construct "mutually shared and ratified definitions of situation" has an idealistic ring (it treats individuals as if they had no motives more fundamental than sharing, and takes no interest in the existence of conflicts over the definition of the situation). Is cooperation the ultimate purpose even of competition? Does all cooperation, on the contrary, derive fundamentally from individualistic motives? A model that integrated formal and strategic goals would make clearer that neither cooperative nor individualistic motives are ultimately more basic; that all uses of conventional forms are strategic, while even the most individualistic goals emerge from a social matrix that is constituted of conventions.

The integration of form and strategy would also cast a different light on emergent or systemic goals, suggesting that they arise as speakers seek their individual goals by orienting to conventional forms that imply goals of their own.

Finally, a model that integrated form and strategy would require that the definition of *communication competence* include more than just knowledge of rules. Needed also would be "a level of knowledge representing not rules but rational play within rules" (Jacobs & Jackson, 1983, p. 52), the mastery of strategies by which speakers can achieve goals within the given framework of conventions.[8]

WARRANTING INFERENCES ABOUT GOALS

This last section explores the problem of drawing inferences about goals on the basis of indirect evidence. Because goal, however defined in terms of the distinctions previously discussed, is necessarily an abstract, relational concept, the use of indirect evidence to support claims about the goal-directedness of discourse is unavoidable. On what basis can a researcher warrant the assertion that a speaker is pursuing a specific goal? Hobbs and Evans (1980) offer the very sensible suggestion that:

---

[8]Comparison of this notion with those of "systemic competence" (Cronen, Pearce, & Harris, 1982) and "relational competence" (Spitzberg & Cupach, 1984) might be instructive.

confronted with a fragment of conversation to be analyzed, we make our best guesses, consistent with everything we know, about the participants' goals, the moves that occur in the conversation, the causal knowledge, including conversational strategies, the participants are using, influences on the choices they make, and the planning processes that seem to be taking place. (p. 353)

Burke (this volume) similarly emphasizes the potential relevance of any and all elements of context to the interpretation of a speaker's goals, and that the over-determination of goals by context is a crucial interpretive resource for both participants and observers of discourse. Nevertheless, to isolate and distinguish the various patterns of inference that are involved in these eclectic interpretations of discourse is a useful exercise, one that may facilitate a more rational methodological assessment of interpretive claims. To that end, I propose to distinguish four general bases for warranting inferences about goals in discourse.

Inference Based on the Conventional Appropriateness of the Goal in the Situation. Evident in each of the preceding chapters is some form of the inference that speakers must be pursuing goals that are dictated by the situation. In order to behave appropriately in the situation one must seek certain goals. In Benoit and Follert's terms, whenever a conventional act-intention apposition applies, a speaker who performs the act can be assumed to have related intention (e.g., asking a question in a situation of initial interaction counts as seeking information according to the conventions of that situation). Nofsinger's (1983) study of courtroom conversation, which argues that some peculiar features of such conversation are understandable only in relation to goals appropriate to the courtroom situation, is another example of this inference pattern.

In one variation of this general pattern of inference that is employed in all three of the preceding chapters, the researcher explicitly instructs speakers to seek certain goals (respectively: to assemble a set of parts correctly; to negotiate competitively or cooperatively; to get acquainted), and then assumes, as long as other evidence does not contradict the assumption, that the speakers are obeying the instructions. The experimental studies of conversational relevance reported by Tracy & Moran (1983) also use the technique of instructing subjects to emphasize one or another goal (extend the old topic or introduce a new one).

Inference Based on a Functional Relationship Between the Discourse and the Goal. One can claim that a goal is being pursued if a functional relationship can be established between the putative goal and some formal element of the discourse. One thus assumes, in the absence of evidence to the contrary, that a speaker who says things having a functional relationship to certain outcomes is in fact seeking those outcomes. Even though it might well depend on conventional forms in order to work, a functional relationship is essentially strategic rather than formal. Conventional forms do not dictate the speaker's goal but may function instrumentally to produce a certain outcome, as a speaker might "fish" for a compliment by making use of conventions of reciprocity. Burke follows this pattern of inference in arguing that some apprentices in her study used transformed repeats (repeating the instructions in a more technical vocabulary) as a way of displaying expertise in order get the expert to transmit the instructions without unnecessary details.

A variation of the functional relationship inference is exemplified by work on politeness strategies (Brown & Levinson, 1978). Here one argues that an utterance exemplifies a particular strategy, not on the basis of what the utterance actually meant on a particular occasion of use, but rather on the basis that it *could* have a certain meaning and effect, given certain assumptions about context and intention. In other words, one can imagine a context in which the utterance might function in a particular way. Our recognition as language users that an utterance could have a certain meaning demonstrates that it could indeed have that meaning, but not that it actually did have that meaning (in either an intentional or a functional sense) for the speaker or hearer on the actual occasion of its production. This weaker or more conservative inference (as compared to the more general case of the functional inference) is quite sufficient for many purposes of discourse analysis, though it rules out certain kinds of "coding" (Craig, Tracy, & Spisak, 1984).

Inference Based on the Orientation of the Discourse to an Identifiable Focus of Attention.   If repetition, emphasis, or some other kind of noticeable effort is exerted in producing discourse whose referential content or manner or conditions of utterance can be associated with some focus of attention, then one can infer that the discourse is directed to a goal related in some manner to the focus of attention. Thus Benoit and Follert find that speakers in initial interactions often respond to questions by providing extra information beyond what is strictly required to answer the questions. From this the authors infer that the discourse is oriented to the goal of giving information.

A variation of the focus of attention inference uses evidence of self-correction, repair, adaptation (serial use of more than one means related to the same goal), or other actions consistent with an interpretation of deviation-counteraction or adaptive "tracking" of a certain outcome as evidence of goal-seeking. Ochs (1979), for example, considers repetition and word replacement to indicate planning processes taking place during discourse production. Benoit and Follert and Burke emphasize that speakers' plans are subject to influence during the course of interaction; both chapters criticize the cognitive science literature for under-emphasizing this fact and display examples in which speakers adapt their discourse according to the reactions of other participants. For Benoit and Follert, the effort to repair disagreement indicates that the discourse seeks agreement. For Burke, the apprentices' changing degree of orientation to experts' instructions indicates that they are oriented to the primary goal of constructing the water pump.

Inference Based on Self-Report of the Speaker.   Self-reports should not be overlooked as a source of data. What speakers say about the goals they are pursuing (or not pursuing) can be taken to indicate their goal-orientation, especially with respect to higher level, dialectical goals. None of the preceding chapters makes use of self-reports as evidence of goals, but Rawlins (1983a, 1983b) relied largely upon data from depth interviews in his study of friendship dialectics.

The major sources of error in self-report data are well known. One is *social desirability:* People deny having goals that they actually pursue, because the goals are conventionally frowned upon, or they claim to have goals that they do not actually pursue, because the goals have positive connotations or are conventionally expected in the situation. Clark (1979) found this sort of effect in a comparison of actual message strategies to self-reported goals. A second source of error is *accessibility:* People may simply be unaware of their goals or have inaccurate beliefs about their behavior (Nisbett & Wilson, 1977).

This, however, says only that self-reports, like all sources of information concerning goals, are fallible: They provide only indirect evidence and require interpretation. The fact, for example, that speakers think they should or should not have certain goals does not necessarily mean that they actually behave accordingly, but it still might indicate something interesting about their goal-orientation. For example, speakers sometimes claim that they do not pursue goals at all in informal conversations. This is probably strictly false but it might be taken to indicate a belief that manipulative, ulterior motives are inappropriate to friendly social interactions.

CONCLUSION

This chapter has emphasized the need for a coherent theory of goals in discourse that I am not, unfortunately, in a position to provide. I have only tried to highlight some of the problems that such a theory must address, and have proposed several distinctions that may be found to shed light on those problems. The distinctions between functional and intentional, positive and dialectical, and formal and strategic interpretations of goals may be nothing more than heuristic vehicles for conceptual exploration. The list of bases for warranting inferences about goals can undoubtedly be lengthened and refined. In a more radical mood, one might even consider what a theory of discourse would be like that would do without the concept of goal altogether, though I am not inclined to do so.

Studies such as those by Burke, Diez, and Benoit and Follert, from which we learn about the use of discourse to achieve goals, deserve a central place in the research of a practical discipline of communication. In my view, it would be pointless not to assume that discourse is in some sense and to some degree intentionally directed toward goals. A philosophical anthropology that considers human beings to be proactive and purposive merely accords ordinary speakers the same ethical status that is claimed by researchers themselves. Moreover, an academic emphasis on the goal-directedness of discourse, especially by a discipline that is heavily involved in practical instruction, can influence the cultural evolution of discourse by cultivating awareness of goals. As speakers become more consciously goal-oriented, they become more responsible for the consequences of their acts. It is this sort of pragmatic communicative morality that a discipline of communication can seek to cultivate, and that, given the reflexive implications the practical stance for the cultural responsibilities of the discipline, it *should* seek to cultivate.

REFERENCES

Berger, C. R., & Douglas, W. (1982). Thought and talk: "Excuse me, but have I been talking to myself?". In F. E. X. Dance (Ed.), *Human communication theory: Comparative essays* (pp. 42–60). New York: Harper & Row.

Brown, P., & Levinson, S. (1978). Universals of language usage: Politeness phenomena. In E. N. Goody (Ed.), *Questions and politeness: Strategies in social interaction* (pp. 56–289). Cambridge: Cambridge University Press.

Bruce, B., & Newman, D. (1978). Interacting plans. *Cognitive Science, 2,* 195–233.

Burke, K. (1969). *A grammar of motives.* Berkeley: University of California Press.

Clark, R. A. (1979). The impact of self interest and desire for liking on the selection of communication strategies. *Communication Monographs, 46,* 257–273.

Craig, R. T. (1983). Galilean rhetoric and practical theory. *Communication Monographs, 50,* 395–412.

Craig, R. T. (1984). Practical criticism of the art of conversation: A methodological critique. *Communication Quarterly, 32,* 178–187.

Craig, R. T., & Tracy, K. (1983). Introduction. In R. T. Craig & K. Tracy (Eds.), *Conversational coherence: Form, structure, and strategy* (pp. 10–22). Beverly Hills, CA: Sage.

Craig, R. T., Tracy, K., & Spisak, F. (1984, November). *A critique of Brown and Levinson's politeness theory.* Paper presented to the Speech Communication Association, Chicago, IL.

Cronen, V. E., Pearce, W. B., & Harris, L. M. (1982). The coordinated management of meaning: A theory of communication. In F. E. X. Dance (Ed.), *Human communication theory: Comparative essays* (pp. 61–89). New York: Harper & Row.

Dreyfus, H. L. (1979). *What computers can't do* (2nd ed.). New York: Harper & Row.

Hobbs, J. R., & Evans, D. A. (1980). Conversation as planned behavior. *Cognitive Science, 4,* 317–345.

Jacobs, S., & Jackson, S. (1983). Speech act structure in conversation: Rational aspects of pragmatic coherence. In R. T. Craig & K. Tracy (Eds.), *Conversational coherence: Form, structure, and strategy* (pp. 47–66). Beverly Hills, CA: Sage.

McLaughlin, M. L. (1984). *Conversation: How talk is organized.* Beverly Hills, CA: Sage.

Mehan, H., Fisher, S., & Maroules, N. (1976). *The social organization of classroom lessons.* Technical Report, Ford Foundation.

Miller, G., Galanter, E., & Pribram, K. H. (1960). *Plans and the structure of behavior.* New York: Holt, Rinehart, & Winston.

Nisbett, R., & Wilson, T. (1977). Telling more than we can know: Verbal reports on mental processes. *Psychological Review, 84,* 231–259.

Nofsinger, R. E. (1983). Tactical coherence in courtroom conversation. In R. T. Craig & K. Tracy (Eds.) *Conversational coherence: Form, structure, and strategy* (pp. 243–258). Beverly Hills, CA: Sage.

Ochs, E. (1979). Planned and unplanned discourse. In T. Givon (Ed.), *Syntax and semantics, 12: Discourse and syntax.* New York: Academic Press.

O'Keefe, B. J., & Delia, J. G. (1982). Impression formation and message production. In M. E. Roloff & C. E. Berger (Eds.), *Social cognition and communication* (pp. 33–72). Beverly Hills, CA: Sage.

Pearce, W. B., & Cronen, V. E. (1980). *Communication, action, and meaning: The creation of social realities.* New York: Praeger.

Rawlins, W. K. (1983a). Negotiating close friendships: The dialectic of conjunctive freedoms. *Human Communication Research, 9,* 255–266.

Rawlins, W. K. (1983b). Openness as problematic in ongoing friendships: Two conversational dilemmas. *Communication Monographs, 50,* 1–13.

Schank, R. C., & Abelson, R. P. (1977). *Scripts, plans, goals, and understanding: An inquiry into human knowledge structures.* Hillsdale, NJ: Lawrence Erlbaum Associates.

Searle, J. R. (1969). *Speech acts: An essay in the philosophy of language.* Cambridge: Cambridge University Press.

Searle, J. R. (1983). *Intentionality: An essay in the philosophy of mind.* Cambridge: Cambridge University Press.

Spitzberg, B. H., & Cupach, W. R. (1984). *Interpersonal communication competence.* Beverly Hills, CA: Sage.

Tracy, K., & Moran, J. P. III (1983). Conversational relevance in multiple-goal settings. In R. T. Craig & K. Tracy (Eds.), *Conversational coherence: Form, structure, and strategy* (pp. 116–135). Beverly Hills, CA: Sage.

Watzlawick, P., Beavin, J. H., & Jackson, D. D. (1967). *The pragmatics of human communication.* New York: Norton.

Wilensky, R. (1982). Points: A theory of the structure of stories in memory. In W. G. Lehnert & M. H. Ringle (Eds.), *Strategies for natural language processing* (pp. 345–374). Hillsdale, NJ: Lawrence Erlbaum Associates.

Author Index

13

Subject Index